READY FOR WHAT?

SUNY Series, Early Childhood Education:
Inquiries and Insights

Mary A. Jensen, Editor

READY FOR WHAT?

CONSTRUCTING MEANINGS
OF READINESS
FOR KINDERGARTEN

M. ELIZABETH GRAUE

STATE UNIVERSITY OF NEW YORK PRESS

Published by
State University of New York Press, Albany

For information, address State University of New York
Press, State University Plaza, Albany, N.Y., 12246

Production by Diane Ganeles
Marketing by Bernadette LaManna

Library of Congress Cataloging-in-Publication Data

Graue, M. Elizabeth, 1956-
    Ready for what? : constructing meanings of readiness for kindergarten /
M. Elizabeth Graue.
        p.   cm. — (SUNY series, early childhood education)
    Includes bibliographical references (p.) and index.
    ISBN 0-7914-1203-2 (alk. paper). — ISBN 0-7914-1204-0 (pbk. : alk. paper)
    1. Readiness for school—Case studies.   2. Kindergarten—United States—
Case studies.   3. Child development—United States.
I. Title.   II. Series.
LB1132.G73   1993
372.21'8—dc20   91-38885
                                                                      CIP
10   9   8   7   6   5   4   3   2   1

In memory of Tom Graue

CONTENTS

TABLES

PREFACE

A professional experience that still haunts me occurred in my third year of teaching kindergarten. I learned that a child who had been in my class the previous year was struggling in first grade and his teacher was talking to his parents about retention. Apparently his teacher felt that he just wasn't ready. His parents blamed me for not diagnosing the problem—I had set him up for failure. "How did this happen?" I thought to myself. He was ready in my class. I found myself wallowing in self-doubt, sure that it had been my fault. Every time I saw him in the hall my heart broke a little. Thinking over what Chris (not his real name) had been like the year before I came back again and again to the same thing: he had been ready in my class.

Readiness has been a long-term interest of mine. I remember my confusion over the talk of parents and other teachers discussing youngness in little boys, worrying about whether they might be better off if given the "gift of time." The interest grew as I watched the rhetoric of readiness proliferate in the popular and practitioner press, as lawmakers and academics joined in to produce a contradictory chorus of myth, data, and advice. The work presented in this book attempts to disentangle the jumble of ideas commonly known as readiness. It argues for a new view on an old problem, for examining readiness-in-practice.

The approach taken here is different from the traditional look at readiness. A construct that is usually thought of as a characteristic of a growing child is turned inside out. Discussion of readiness is framed from a social and cultural perspective, as something that is more a matter of adult belief than child behavior. Taking this view has caused me to rethink much of my practice as an early childhood educator, particularly as I work with undergraduates who are preparing to become teachers of young children. I am struck by the depth of their commitment to standard beliefs about readiness and wonder how we can overcome the myth of "older is better." We have a long way to go.

This book is an expansion of my Ph.D. dissertation at the University of Colorado at Boulder. It received funding from the University of Colorado School of Education and the Dean's Small Grant Fund. The Wisconsin Alumni Research Foundation provided support for completion of the project.

So many people helped shape this work. I've often joked that it took two faculty members to get me through the dissertation process; most people only need one advisor. But it was through the unique contributions of Lorrie Shepard and Margaret Eisenhart that this work took its quirky form. They have given support, opportunities, advice, and skiing lessons. Mary Catherine Ellwein and Daniel Walsh have shared insights, encouragement, and suggestions along all points of the project. My colleagues at the University of Wisconsin Department of Curriculum and Instruction have been supportive and challenging as I reshaped the dissertation into a book.

Thanks to my family, who gave me what the people in Fulton would call a good start. As always, my husband, Clark Landis, has been there to take up the slack and to remind me that there is more to the world than this study.

Finally, I owe a special debt to the three teachers who took part in this project. Alice Carlin, Monica Sunden, and Isabel Ramirez made me a part of their classroom life, sharing ideas and fine-tuning my observations. Thanks for your patience, humor, and openness.

CHAPTER 1

𝄐

MANY VIEWS OF READINESS

Browsing through the titles in the popular press, a certain theme seems to come up when people write about kindergarten:

"Delay Kindergarten Until Tot Biologically Ready" (*The Tennessean*, Sunday, March 1984)

"Too Much Too Soon?" (*Principal*, March 1984)

"In Support of Academic Redshirting" (*Young Children*, January 1986)

"Kindergarten: Ready or Not?" (*Rocky Mountain News*, Thursday, May 18, 1989)

"The Redshirt Solution" (*Time*, November 13, 1989)

"Why Kids Flunk Kindergarten" (*Parents*, February 1990)

Why so much press for readiness? It is probably because few topics in the early childhood community have such currency and so many audiences as the topic of readiness for school. Academics study readiness to determine the subdimensions that comprise it as a kind of psychological construct. They correlate the findings of readiness tests with later school outcome measures to determine the instrument's validity and they examine the effects of placement decisions that result from readiness judgments. Policymakers debate legislative actions related to readiness, advocating changes in the entrance age so that children must be older (i.e., more ready) and they mandate testing to determine whether children are ready for promotion between grades. The 1990 set of recommendations for education by the National Governors'

1

Association was headed by the objective that: "By the year 2000, all children in America will start school ready to learn." Teachers talk about readiness as they sort and rank students and make instructional and placement decisions. They weigh factors such as chronological age and sex to make judgments about relative readiness of individual children. Parents anguish over readiness when they make decisions about whether to put their child in kindergarten or wait a year so that their child will have "the gift of time." People with a stake in the education of young children are talking about readiness; it is such a shared idea that everyone assumes they are talking about the same thing.

But is readiness an identifiable characteristic? Is it the same thing in all children, in all classrooms, in all schools? For all the attention and discussion readiness receives, one would think so. A brief look at recent policy related to readiness provides an interesting entrance point to the discussion that is the focus of this book — what is readiness?

Trends in Policy Related to Readiness

Kindergarten policy has undergone dramatic change in recent years. Several policy issues can be traced to readiness concerns that have had profound impact on the nature of the kindergarten program: concern about age at school entrance, the development of readiness screening programs, and availability of extra-year programs in the public schools.

Kindergarten Entrance Age

In response to concerns that the youngest children in a group seem to do less well than their relatively older peers, school districts and states have slowly moved the kindergarten or first grade entrance age back, requiring children to be older to enter school. Moving from dates as late as February 1 thirty years ago, September 1 is now the most common entrance cutoff, with some states choosing dates as early as July 1 (Graue & Shepard, in press). The shift has resulted in the most popular legislated kindergarten entrance age of 5 years, up three months from the mode of 4 years, 9 months in 1958.

Has raising the entrance age resulted in more ready students? For a change in the entrance age to make an absolute difference in readiness for school, the "problem" of being younger would need to be absolute, i.e., there would need to be a readiness threshold that a child would need to achieve to be successful in school and that threshold would have to be related to age. Instead, it appears that the youngness problem is *relative* in that if children are defined in twelve-month age cohorts for school, there will always be a younger group (Shepard & Smith, 1986). Studies comparing the youngest and oldest parts of first grade class age distributions find that there are small, short-term differences favoring the older children (in the range of 7 or 8 percentile points) (Shepard & Smith, 1986). With the shift in entrance date, the children who would have been in the youngest part of an age range under one enrollment date are in the oldest part with a new, earlier cutoff. Have the children changed with this new entrance date? No, only their relative ranking within the group has changed. Judgments of readiness become relative to an arbitrary cutoff rather than an absolute readiness characteristic.

Readiness Screening

Citing work by the Gesell Institute (Ilg, Ames, Haines, & Gillespie, 1978) that has asserted that chronological age was no guarantee of school readiness, some school people were not satisfied that readiness would be assured with earlier entrance cutoffs. Developmental age, assessed by a readiness screening, would provide a better indicator. Screening programs were instituted before kindergarten or between kindergarten and first grade to assess whether children were ready for these experiences. In examining the psychometric properties of the readiness instruments used in these screening programs, it has been found, however, that they are not very good predictors of how children will perform at a later date. Most instruments used for screening or placement decisions have lower than adequate predictive validities, resulting in high rates of misidentification (Meisels, 1985; Shepard & Smith, 1986; Graue & Shepard, 1989; Ellwein, Walsh, Eads, and Miller, 1991). Children are identified as unready when in fact they would have made satisfactory progress.

Extra-Year Programs

Many states, districts, and schools came to the conclusion that to meet the needs of children that were not ready for the regular school experience, they should develop special programs. These programs typically involve providing children with a different kind of curriculum and classroom structure that has a slower pace than the traditional kindergarten or first grade program. With this kind of placement, children would have time to develop more fully, so that they will be more ready for the demands of school. Children generally go through the extra-year program, then on through the traditional school track, requiring them to spend three years to get to second grade when it is usually a two-year sequence.

These extra-year programs can be policy-explicit, such as a developmental kindergarten or transitional first grade, in which the school provides classrooms and staff for children judged to need more time. Research on these extra-year programs finds no benefit for the special placements, with students either not doing as well or performing equal to their promoted peers (Shepard & Smith, 1988). Or extra-year practices can come from what Shepard (1990) has called *backdoor policies* because there are no official programs or criterion for placement. A popular unstated extra-year policy is the practice of academic redshirting or holding out. When children are held out of kindergarten, their enrollment is delayed when they are legally eligible to attend school according to their chronological age. Entrance to kindergarten occurs the following year, when the child is one year older. Decisions about holding children out are based on the idea that readiness only comes with time, so the best way to help children who lack sufficient readiness is to give them more time to develop it. It appears that children are not always enrolled in school when they are legally eligible and that decisions made by teachers and parents are based on individual judgments concerning readiness.

Readiness as a Child Characteristic

Whether academics, policymakers, teachers, or parents are using the concept of readiness, it is almost always conceptualized as a characteristic of an individual child that develops as the child grows. It is usually depicted as some combination of cognitive, psychomotor, and socio-emotional development that should be presented in a balance that is congruent with the child's chronological age. Different theories of readiness depict a variety of mechanisms for readiness development, but all seem to agree that readiness is something *within* a child that is necessary for success in school. It is seen as a stable, measurable capacity that can be assessed by professionals who use results to make educational decisions, including those related to instruction and placement. We should be able to see readiness in children, quantify it, and provide placements that will increase it if there is a deficit.

But in gathering all the information related to readiness issues and policies, a question begins to form. In terms of the perfect school entrance age, readiness appears to be relative to the particular age cutoff chosen. Instruments used to screen for readiness are unable to match readiness judgments at the time of measurement (concurrent validity) or at some future point (predictive validity) and therefore often mis-classify children. When predictive validity is seen as part of construct validity, it becomes necessary to question the very use of the construct of readiness. When these issues are considered in conjunction with the questionable efficacy of extra-year programs, it begins to appear that readiness may not be what everyone thought it was. Perhaps readiness is *not* something within a child that can be measured in a standardized manner and used uniformly by decision-makers. Perhaps it is something else.

The study that is discussed in this book conceptualized readiness from a different perspective. Instead of a child characteristic, readiness was examined as a socially constructed set of ideas or meanings used to shape the first formal school experiences of children and their families. In examining the kindergarten experience in three communities, ideas about readiness were a distinguishing characteristic of the local communities. These ideas emerged from community values and expectations and they were related to individual children in terms of attributes like their age, sex, and preschool experience. Readiness test results also formed the basis of some ideas about readiness, but they represented only a small set of the skills, attributes, and attitudes that were believed necessary to school success. From these ideas representing forces both in and outside the school, children came to be understood in the context of a particular community's meaning of readiness.

This view of readiness clearly departs from the commonly held notions used among teachers and parents, policymakers and academics. It represents a change in view of and response to the child that is framed from a cultural and social perspective. To understand why this shift was necessary, it is helpful to think about the theories that are the foundation for our common use of the term readiness and the practices that come out of those views. The next section reviews psychological theory related to readiness and the research and policy representations of the readiness construct that have shaped much parenting and educational practice.

Readiness

Educational research on readiness has relied on underlying views about child growth and development. Four general schools of thought can be distinguished related to readiness: maturationist, environmentalist, joint consideration of maturation and environment at the individual level, and constructivist. These underlying psychological theories have profound implications for the readiness conceptualization and educational applications that follow.

Those who take a maturationist orientation see readiness as biological. Exemplified best by the writings from the Gesell Institute, readiness is portrayed as a biological unfolding of psychomotor, cognitive, and emotional structures that are the foundation of child behavior. Classification of behaviors, grouped by age, have formed the basis for postulated developmental patterns and sequences. From these guidelines, instructional tasks are presented to children that match their developmental level. Teachers are advised to delay the introduction of activities for which the child is unready (i.e., beyond his/her developmental level). Time for growth is the only mechanism for enhancing readiness. In a journal article titled "Not Ready! Don't Push Me!", Carolyn Hall Hammond exemplified the maturationist approach:

> Why would any parent want to send a child to school who is "Not Ready" and commit that child to an experience that may very well prove to be harmful? Some parents equate intellectual capacity with development. If they do acknowledge that intelligence and development are separate, they feel that intelligence is all one needs to have in order to be a school success. Some believe that development can be taught. Some believe that the child can be "beefed-up"! *Development is something that cannot be rushed!* Time will take its course and the development will happen naturally... "School Readiness" is like a loaf of bread. Flour, water, sugar, shortening, and milk are some of the ingredients needed in a loaf of bread. But if the yeast has been omitted, the bread won't rise. Unconditional love, trust, an average intelligence and a birth date that falls on or before January 2 are some of the ingredients any child needs in order

to experience school success. But when the developmental age of 5 has been omitted, the child may not be able to "rise" to the expectations of parents and teachers (1986, pp. 278-9).

From the environmentalist perspective readiness is understood as skills or experiences that must be comprised in a certain way for school success. The ready child is a puzzle with all the pieces in place. If skills are seen as the pieces of the puzzle, the key to fixing the readiness problem is to (1) identify the missing pieces and then (2) provide instruction to generate their placement. Teachers and caregivers are viewed as having a pivotal role in developing readiness by assessing readiness problems, providing experiences that fill in deficits, and matching abilities with those required by the school. This approach is often used to justify programs for children identified unready due to what has been called at different times in our educational history culturally disadvantaged, environmentally deprived, or at-risk. It is thought that some children come to school unready because they lack the experience to be successful. The school works to fill in those holes by providing extra services for these children: school attendance before the legal entrance age, extended attendance during what is normally a half-day kindergarten program, smaller class sizes, additional staff. The difference between this view of readiness and the maturationist perspective rests in both the mechanism of readiness and remedy for problems: in one case educational intervention is forbidden, in the other it is vital. An example of the environmentalist approach to readiness is the Early Prevention of School Failure program, used in many communities for students thought to be at-risk.

Ausubel (1963) articulated a theory of learning that addressed the issue of readiness as a composite of environmental and biological forces. Ausubel's ideas about readiness were focused on specific tasks but have been broadened to notions of readiness for school:

> By readiness is meant the adequacy of existing cognitive equipment or capacity at a given age level for coping with the demands of a specified cognitive task. It can therefore be considered the developmental aspect of cognitive structure. Empirically, readiness is indicated by ability to profit from practice or learning experience… Readiness is a function of both general cognitive maturity and of particularized learning experience (pp. 29-30).

When readiness is conceived as having both environmental and biological components, remediation of readiness problems is more complex than if the mechanism is based on either one in isolation. In addition, Ausubel introduces a third component: task requirements. Readiness becomes a function of balancing the physical developmental level and the past experience of the learner with the demands of a given task. The question of readiness begins to include "Ready for what?"

The final view of development is very broad and has been called constructivist. From this perspective, the key to development is the interaction between the individual and the environment. Readiness is not an issue for constructivists who focus on the active individual constructing knowledge. The readiness threshold holds no importance. Although very different in their approaches to development, the work of Piaget (incorporated into the Bank Street or High Scope early education models) and Vygotsky (represented by the Kamehameha Early Education Program) could be seen as examples of constructivist perspectives. This developmental view is mentioned here because it has had such a powerful impact on academic curriculum work and it represents some of the most promising theory in the field.

From the description of developmental theory, it can be seen that views of child development are related to conceptions of readiness, including its developmental mechanism and proper intervention strategies. While there has been much work done on readiness in educational research, the focus of almost all of it has been from either the maturational or environmental perspectives. From either view, readiness is treated as if it were a child characteristic. There is a sense that children are ready (or not), that the level of readiness can be assessed, and that some kind of intervention program can be developed and used to increase readiness.

Research on Practices Related to Readiness

Examining the literature on readiness is of interest for more than the traditional review purpose. The image of readiness presented in the literature indicates not only how the academic community has conceptualized the construct but can also be seen as shaping readiness ideas in other communities as well. Examining research on readiness over time helps us track the changes in ideas about readiness and provides the foundation for its treatment in this work.

The literature on readiness can be divided in a number of different ways. In terms of this study, readiness was conceptualized as a global category; a multidimensional construct that is implicitly analogous to competence or maturity.[1] The implicit definition of readiness is interesting in this research because authors very rarely *define* readiness. It appeared that most authors assumed that readiness was accepted as an idea to such an extent that its meaning was universally known. Readiness for school was often operationalized as performance on a kindergarten-administered test or by comparing younger and older children on performance (grades, teacher ratings, test scores).

Prior to 1985, the literature on readiness tended to be limited to individual studies speaking to single readiness-related policies. In general, these studies fell into four categories: the impact of age on performance or youngness research, studies based on youngness work that examined the kindergarten entrance age, studies of kindergarten readiness testing and the examination of extra-year programs.

Youngness

Following the idea that younger children in a group are at a disadvantage relative to their older peers, much research has compared the performance of the youngest and oldest children at various points in their school careers. In these studies, readiness is the ability to perform at some later date (usually first grade) and there is an assumed relationship between readiness and age (Shepard & Smith, 1986). For these comparisons, the youngest children in a group almost always fare less well than their older classmates (Bigelow, 1934; King, 1955; Green & Simmons, 1962; Carroll, 1963; Hall, 1963; Halliwell & Stein, 1964; Beattie, 1970; Davis et al., 1980; Kalk, Langer, & Searls, 1981). The differences between younger and older students were never as large as the talk in the early childhood community would imply (in the range of seven or eight percentile points) and the gap usually disappeared as the children got older (Miller & Norris, 1967; Langer, Kalk & Searls, 1984). An interesting factor in these studies was noted by Weinstein (1968-69) and Gredler (1980). They suggested that the use of outcomes like retention and referral to special education could very well be biased because they were influenced by teacher expectation and belief about the relationship of child age and performance. Teacher willingness to deal with various ability ranges becomes the key issue. Therefore, in studies that find that the youngest children were more likely to be retained (Langer et al., 1984; Uphoff, 1985), referred to special education (DiPasquale, Moule, & Flewelling, 1980) or labelled learning disabled (Maddux, 1980; Diamond, 1983), the outcomes are very likely the result of teacher ideology.

Kindergarten Entrance Age

In response to the youngness research, many states and districts enacted policies that resulted in an older kindergarten population. Policymakers reasoned that children would be more ready for school if their kindergarten enrollment were delayed. In response there has been a steady trend to require children to be older before starting school. A 1958 survey found that most districts had either December or January 1 cutoffs, allowing children to enter school at about the age of four years eight months (Educational Research Service, 1958). By 1985, state-level data showed a substantial shift in entrance polices, with a September 1 cutoff the most popular and two-thirds of the states having an entrance date on or before October 1 (Education Commission of the States, 1985). This results in a modal kindergarten entrance age of four years eleven months. The students in the window between the two entrance dates move from being in the youngest part of the kindergarten age cohort to being in the oldest part of the age cohort. Because of the belief about the relationship between age and readiness, children that would have, in general, been seen as the least ready would now be judged to be the most ready. In addition, this move in the entrance cutoff requires a delay in entrance for approximately 25% of the kindergarten population who falls between the old and new cutoff.

Gredler (1975) responded to these trends by pointing out that the issue of the "optimal" kindergarten entrance age has been overblown by the educational establishment as it is a relative rather than an absolute problem. He noted that no matter what entrance cutoff is set, there will always be a youngest group who will do a little less well than the oldest children in the class.

Heightening awareness of the relative nature of readiness judgments, Gredler broadened the scope of entrance age studies by looking to policies in other countries. Citing a study by Jinks (1964) Gredler noted that British educators categorized younger and older children in the same way that American educators would, i.e., the older students were seen to be more competent than their younger peers. Noting that in Britain, with its entrance age of 4½, "the *older* group which is found to do so well in Jinks' investigation is the *younger* group in American studies! This obviously points up the relativity of the judgments being made" (p. 209).

Readiness screening

With a persistent concern about fixing readiness problems, policymakers turned with increasing frequency to the adoption of screening programs to identify at-risk children. Broadening their focus beyond early intervention models that were developed for the handicapped (for placements under PL 94-142) or the disadvantaged (for placements in Head Start programs), screening began to focus on issues of readiness or developmental immaturity (Meisels, 1987). Readiness screening focused on removing unready using something more precise than chronological age; they chose a readiness indicator embodied in a test.

A key question raised about these tests is whether they are valid enough to use for individual placement decisions. Meisels made an important distinction between developmental screening tests and readiness tests that focuses on their use: developmental screening tests "provide a brief assessment of a child's developmental abilities" while readiness tests "are concerned with those curriculum-related skills a child has already acquired" (Meisels, 1987, p. 4). The former are useful for identification of children in need of some kind of intervention program (should Jack be placed in developmental kindergarten?) while the latter are helpful in curriculum planning (should these children be introduced to the alphabet at this time?). Unfortunately, the two types of tests have been used interchangeably, which is not appropriate. Developmental screening tests are not valid for readiness testing and vice versa. Not every test with the word readiness in its name is appropriate for placement decisions.

A recent predictive validity study of the *Brigance Kindergarten and First Grade Screen,* the *Developmental Indicators for the Assessment of Learning-Revised,* the *Daberon Screening for School Readiness,* and the *Missouri Kindergarten Inventory of Developmental Skills* conducted in Virginia examined these tests' predictive validity. Ellwein, Walsh, Eads, & Miller (1991) found that males, children of color, low SES and relatively younger examinees were much more likely to be identified as unready or at-risk. None of the screening tests had impressive predictive validities, with classification errors a necessary danger.

12   *Ready for What?*

Extra-Year Programs

To deal with children found to be unready by test results or professional judgment, schools have frequently developed programs to give students what is often called "the gift of time." These alternative programs include holding children out of school for a year, in-school prekindergarten programs, retention in kindergarten, or transitional programs between kindergarten and grade one. In making the case for extra time, Donofrio (1977) suggested that it is better to allow unready children to "mark time" until they are able to meet the demands of a classroom with children who are like them in terms of their developmental age, a euphemism for a concept that describes a child's level of maturation rather than chronological age.

In contrast to the beliefs of most parents and educators (Byrnes & Yamamoto, 1984), the results of research about extra-year programs have been primarily negative. When compared to children of the same ability who were promoted, retained students do not perform as well on measures of academic or social-emotional level (Rose, Medway, Cantrell, & Marus, 1983; Holmes & Matthews, 1984). Nor does retention reduce the variability of student ability in classrooms (Bossing & Brien, 1979; Haddad, 1979).

An interesting problem with these studies is that they confound the validity of the readiness construct and the validity of the treatment. In many cases, it is impossible to disentangle the utility of the assessment instrument used to determine readiness and the extra-year program that follows the identification. The extra-year programs may look ineffective either because children are misidentified or the treatment does not work.

There is argument among those in the developmental placement community about whether all extra-year programs are equal. Is it the same to retain a child in kindergarten as to place her in a transitional program? Separate analysis of transitional programs was completed by Gredler in 1984. Of the five studies he reported, four found no difference between the children placed in extra-year programs and those who had been recommended for the transition program but had been placed in first grade. The one positive study (Raygor, 1972) had differences in favor of the transition program students that disappeared by grade three. A study by Leinhardt (1980) compared the performance of (1) transition room children who participated in an individualized instruction program with (2) at-risk children who were promoted with no special instruction and (3) children recommended for transition room placement who were promoted and received individualized instruction. There were no differences between the first two groups and the group that had the best performance was the promoted group with special instruction. Lower self-esteem and self-confidence were found in transition room children than was reported for at-risk children who were promoted (Bell, 1972). Finally, May and Welch (1984) studied a developmental placement program in which children who were identified as unready by the *Gesell School Readiness Test* were recommended to "Buy-a-Year" and spend an additional year before entering second grade. Children who refused this special placement were called "Over-placed." On both the state achievement test at the end of third grade and the *Stanford Achievement Test* given in second, fourth, and sixth grades, there were no differences between the two groups who had both been defined as at-risk. In addition, on the Stanford there were no differences between these initiallyhese results, May and Welch called into question both the predictive validity of the Gesell School Readiness Tests and the treatment validity of the extra-year placement program.

   Studies that examine the unstated policy of holding out are more recent. Only three studies were found in a review of literature during the period of 1970 to 1990. In an evaluation of a district kindergarten program, Katz, Raths, and Torres (1987) found a pervasive concern about holding out voiced by teachers, parents, and district administrators. Longitudinal data from within the district indicated that the average age of kindergartners in the district was rising, which could be seen as evidence of delayed entry of significant numbers of students. Recommendations of the evaluation team included enrollment of age eligible children into unscreened kindergarten programs, using age as the sole criterion for entrance.

   Cameron and Wilson (1990) focused on the effects of chronological age at school entrance and gender on academic achievement and retention. Students who entered kindergarten a year after they were legally eligible were compared with students who entered in their first year of eligibility and who were classified by birthdate. Results on the *Cognitive Abilities Test* in first grade were used as a covariate. There were significant differences in second grade performance on the *Iowa Test of Basic Skills* reading and composite scores for those students who were oldest in their kindergarten cohort (had a birthdate between September 15 and December 15, with a September 15 entrance cutoff) and the rest

of the kindergartners (including redshirted students). These
differences held up in measures of performance in grade four,
although they diminished in size. For children retained in grade,
there were no differences in frequency of retention by gender or
age group. The authors noted that:

> those students we described as redshirts did not appear to gain
> competitive advantage as a result of delaying entry to school.
> We concluded that delay of school entry is not advisable in this
> district and should not be encouraged by administrators or
> teachers as a means of insuring better academic performance
> (pp. 262-263).

In a study of kindergarten age distributions, Shepard, Graue,
and Catto (1989) surveyed 19 Colorado school districts, representing approximately two-thirds of the state kindergarten
population. Estimates of holding out, calculated from the proportion of children missing from the youngest six months of the
kindergarten age range, were developed and compared to the
proportion of students overage for their grade placement. Patterns
of holding out were more prevalent for boys than for girls and
appeared to be more pronounced for districts with September
entrance cutoffs than those with either summer or late fall dates.
In the one district that contributed individual student SES data,
there was no relationship between SES and being overage for
girls, while for boys the correlation was .18. When only those
schools with holding out effects greater than 10% were included,
the correlation rose to .37. This follows the common perception
of early childhood specialists that more advantaged parents are
more likely to hold their sons out of kindergarten.

A Change in the Representation of Readiness Issues

In 1985, the Boulder Valley Kindergarten Study addressed
the issues of readiness and retention from a more integrated
perspective of policy analysis, rather than the previously splin-
tered, single issue approach (Shepard & Smith, 1985). In response
to a request from the local school district to examine the process
by which children are retained in kindergarten and measure the
effects of extra-year kindergarten programs, Shepard and Smith
designed a study that took a holistic approach to the main aspects
of readiness that had been represented in the literature: youngness

(the relationship between child age and retention decisions as well as school performance), entrance age (the search for a good entrance age), readiness testing (validity and reliability of the *Gesell School Readiness Test*), and extra-year programs (cognitive and emotional benefits of retention, child characteristics that lead to a retention decision, and characteristics of developmental and transition classrooms). The authors went beyond the normal cause and effect examination of a single problem in a local setting and assessed the assumptions surrounding the main questions and their attendant sub-questions.

The existing literature did not support academic or social-emotional benefit from retention of "immature" children. These results held up in the local study, with the only positive result coming in a one month gain in reading when children who had been retained were compared with like children in low retaining schools. From parent survey data, no benefit was found for either kindergarten retention or extra-year kindergarten programs on first grade performance, school attitude, peer interaction, or readiness for second grade.

In addition, a new dimension was added to the study of readiness. The nature of teacher philosophies about child development, the characteristics of unready children, descriptions of their kindergarten program, and their views of kindergarten retention were joined to develop a picture of readiness as a belief held by teachers. Teacher belief about readiness as related to retention varied along a dimension of nativism.[2] Teachers ranged from those who saw child growth and development as solely a biological process, to those who viewed it as a product of the environment. Teachers tended to utilize their beliefs about readiness in practices like retention, with teachers holding the biological view having higher retention rates. At a school level, teachers in the same building tended to share readiness beliefs.

From this point, readiness was more frequently addressed in terms of the related policy issues, especially in the practitioner-oriented press. With increasing public attention focused on early education, a parade of review articles appeared pulling together research on readiness, examining the policies (like setting an entrance age or implementing a screening program) that come out of assumptions and beliefs about readiness (Shepard & Smith, 1986; Connell, 1987; Meisels, 1987; Peck, McCaig, & Sapp, 1988; Charlesworth, 1989; Bredekamp & Shepard, 1989; Freeman, 1990).

These reviews consistently found that the previous patterns of results held in the more recent studies.

In terms of the youngness research, several studies have found that the youngest in a class do not do as well as their older classmates in academic achievement and adjustment (Uphoff & Gilmore, 1986; Karweit, 1988), but Kinard & Reinherz (1986) noted that initial differences at school entry disappeared by grade three. In a review of twenty-one studies on children admitted to school prior to the mandated entrance age, Proctor, Black, and Feldhusen (1986) found no apparent harmful effects. In a review of entrance age policies, Graue and Shepard (in press) showed that trends to require children to be older before starting kindergarten continue. For example, one state (Missouri) moved to a July 1 entrance cutoff, requiring children to be five years two months old before entering school.

National professional associations (NAEYC, 1988; National Association of Elementary School Principals, 1990) have issued strong criticisms of the use of standardized testing with kindergartners, including the readiness tests that have become so popular. Meisels (1987) outlined the appropriate testing practices with young children and warned against the use of tests for purposes other than what they were designed and proven to be useful.

In a review of research on kindergarten extra-year programs, Shepard (1989) extended the number of studies examined by Gredler in 1984 and did separate analyses of retention and transition programs. The overall finding agreed with Gredler's that retention and transition rooms are not effective interventions. There was no difference between the performance of children who had been placed in transition classes and those who had been recommended but had refused placement. In measures of academic performance, differences between transition room and control students disappeared in follow-ups that examined their work in third or fourth grade. On social-emotional measures (which were rarely included in these studies), extra-year students were the same or showed negative effects when compared to controls.

In an international comparison of readiness policies and issues, Engel (1989) reviewed five areas of interest in Australia, Britain, Japan, New Zealand, the Soviet Union, Sweden, Switzerland, and West Germany. In terms of school entrance age, children started school as early as four years old in Great Britain and Australia and as old as seven in Sweden. Age-related differences in performance within groups were found with British,

U.S., and Swedish children, who entered school at age 5, 6, and 7 respectively, indicating that the advantage of being relatively older existed regardless of entrance age. Adoption of an entrance age comes as the result of historical, political, and climate forces rather than for educational reasons. Readiness testing was not required at the national level in any of the countries included in the study. However, at the state and local level, there were a number of assessments of readiness used that ranged from checklists to standardized tests. Examining the use of ability grouping in kindergarten, Engel found that New Zealand and Britain had some kind of ability grouping in place, while Sweden and Japan explicitly did not participate in that practice. Although Japan and the Soviet Union did not retain students in grade, West Germany, Switzerland, and New Zealand retained children (with rates as low as 5% and as high as 33%). The content of the kindergarten curriculum was debated in England, Japan, and the Soviet Union as it was in the United States. It appears that readiness is an international topic, not just an issue in the U.S.

In an ERIC document on Readiness for Kindergarten, Nurss (1987) echoing Ausubel, defined readiness as

> a term to describe preparation for what comes next: readiness for kindergarten involves both the child and the instructional situation. Any consideration of the preparation a child needs to be successful in kindergarten must take into account the kindergarten program and the teacher's expectations of the child (p. 1).

After exploring social and behavioral, sensory-motor, cognitive and language expectations as well as chronological age and the kindergarten curriculum, Nurss concluded:

> Readiness for kindergarten depends on a child's development of social, perceptual, motor, and language skills expected by the teacher. It also depends on the curriculum's degree of structure, the behavior required by the instructional program, and expectations of what is to be achieved by the end of the program (p. 2).

This definition, in a document often disseminated to practitioners, stressed the contextual nature of readiness. Nurss identified both the child and the instructional situation (including teacher expectations) as salient in a determination of readiness, not just an inherent child characteristic.

In a NAEYC Public Policy Report, Willer and Bredekamp (1990) called for a redefinition of readiness as an "Essential Requisite of Education Reform" (p. 22). Citing the fact that recent reform efforts have tied readiness assessments to school accountability measures, the authors noted that this promoted the idea of readiness as a gatekeeping mechanism which is antithetical to the goals of the National Association for the Education of Young Children. They focused on how faulty assumptions about readiness lead to this gatekeeping mentality and asserted that the focus should move from determining whether children are ready for school, to ensuring that children are ready to succeed. Again this piece was an attempt to address the issue of readiness through the policies that come from assumptions about how children learn. It was followed closely by a position statement by NAEYC (1990) on the topic of school readiness issues that addressed practices in schools related to readiness and emphasized the importance of the school being ready for all children.

Readiness has often been conceptualized in the literature and policy arena as a characteristic of a child which must be assessed to determine whether that child can benefit from certain school experiences. Changes in the late 1980s shifted the way that readiness is represented in the literature. With increasing frequency, it was discussed in terms of the policy implications of the child characteristic model and finally in terms of a teacher belief system that influences instructional and policy decision making. It is this view of readiness that makes the concept of social construction in the conceptualization of readiness particularly compelling.

The next chapter provides an overview of social construction theory, with a discussion of its application in contemporary research. In addition, a theoretical framework is proposed that is compatible with the social constructionist perspective, as well as a description of how readiness might be studied from a social and cultural orientation. Chapter 3 describes methods used in this study to examine readiness meanings. Chapter 4 analyzes the stated curriculum in the Thomas School District, the site of this study. Chapters 5, 6, and 7 are case descriptions of the construction of the meaning of readiness in the communities of Fulton, Norwood, and Rochester, respectively. The final chapter compares these meanings across settings and posits implications for this new view of readiness.

CHAPTER 2

ès

THEORETICAL FRAMEWORK

A pivotal point in framing a study that examined the social construction of readiness was the idea that ideas get used in social contexts and they are socially constituted. This follows the work of Erickson (1982), who talked about the way in which context "mediates" learning by individuals as different from "constitution," where the context actually provides the pieces that form what is learned.

> In these studies [of teaching and learning in classrooms], social organization and social life are considered as a residual category that "mediates" the engagement of an isolated learner with an abstract curriculum. In contrast to this essentially asocial view of learning tasks and of time on task, a socially and culturally realistic view of actual learning events sees the social participation structure as an essential and constitutive aspect of the learning task environment—a *medium* of instruction that is fundamentally and powerfully entailed in the message of instruction (p. 170).

From this perspective, ideas can be seen as socially constituted because they come out of the contextual arrangements that emerge from a setting.

In addition, these contexts are built by people in interaction — people construct meanings as they interact, becoming a part of the meaning themselves (Mehan, 1980).

> Contexts are not to be equated with the physical surrounding of settings like classrooms, kitchens, and churches; they are constructed by the people present in varying combinations of

19

participants and audience (Erickson and Shultz, 1977; McDermott and Roth, 1979). As McDermott and Roth have put it,
contexts are constituted by what people are doing, as well as
when and where they are doing it. That is, people in interaction
serve as environments for each other. And, ultimately, social
contexts consist of mutually ratified and constructed environments (p. 136).

Taken together, meanings are seen as socially constituted (formed
from the context) and socially constructed (built in interaction).
    How have others utilized the concept of social construction?
From what disciplines have they come and what kinds of topics
did they address? The next section explores the assumptions that
form the foundation for this general category of scholarly
approach. The next section reviews some of the recent work in
the field, particularly that related to educational practice, contrasting the approaches used to make the case. Finally, a theoretical
framework is proposed that can be used in social construction
research that not only describes construction but explains the
mechanism in a coherent manner.

Social Construction

    Work relying on a social constructionist framework calls into
question many of the taken-for-granteds of human experience.
Instead of assuming that the nature of objects and categories
exist in physical reality, the social constructionist focuses
attention on the meanings constructed in interactions of people
in a setting. Category definition is seen to exist in social relations
rather than as an inherent feature of a given thing.
    The nature of social constructionist thought can be best
understood by contrasting it with traditional empiricist models.
Often the knowledge we use in everyday life is conceived as
objectively derived and accumulated from observation. This is
most clearly represented in the way that most people think of
science, seen frequently as the most rational of knowledge seeking
enterprises. From the commonly held scientific perspective,
human understandings of categories and relationships are
developed inductively by individuals and groups over time,
representing a growing comprehension of the law-like nature of
physical reality. Our knowledge is seen as coming out of observations of characteristics that exist in the things around us.

Rather than assuming that what we know is tied to observations of nature, the focus for the social constructionist is on
the social construction of reality. According to Bruffee (1986):

> A social constructionist position in any discipline assumes that
> entities we normally call reality, knowledge, thought, facts, texts,
> selves, and so on are constructs generated by communities of
> like-minded peers. Social construction understands reality,
> knowledge, thought, facts, texts, selves, and so on as community-
> generated and community-maintained linguistic entities — or,
> more broadly speaking symbolic entities — that define or
> "constitute" the communities that generate them (p. 774).

From this perspective, our knowledge is generated from social
practice.

Scholars taking a social constructionist view come from
diverse fields and they often use the term without explicit definition
of their theoretical framework. Recent literature is rife with studies
framed within this general orientation but it is difficult to discern
their shared attributes beyond the social construction label. In
much the same way that people use the idea of readiness, various
groups are using the idea of social construction assuming that
they are speaking about the same thing.

Work from the social constructionist perspective proposes a
different way to think about how it is that we come to know things.
Ideas about knowledge generation and accumulation are at its
foundation; therefore the assumptions that this work tends to
share relate to knowledge. The first assumption is that the
accumulation of knowledge, rather than emerging objectively from
unbiased observation, is in fact culturally and historically bound.
Culture, in terms of the meanings we hold for our experiences,
provides a focusing mechanism as we construct knowledge of the
world. Our interpretations of what we see and how it relates to
other aspects of our experience are framed in terms of the tools
we have available, the institutional supports, and the political
context in which we act. What it means to know something, what
counts as data, and how those data are communicated change
over time and from group to group. This proposition is extended
to the systematic knowledge generating practices such as science:
knowledge changes as the tools and ideas we have to probe it
evolve over time and across settings. What we know is inextricably
bound to when and where we know it: "the objective criteria for
identifying such 'behaviors,' 'events,' or 'entities' are shown to

be either highly circumscribed by culture, history, or social context or altogether nonexistent" (Gergen, 1985, p. 267).

Second, knowledge, rather than being generated by individuals as they build cognitive models, is seen as a social activity. Knowledge is something that people do together (Gergen, 1985). Geertz (1973) describes the social nature of thought in this way: "Human thought is consummately social: social in its origins, social in its functions, social in its forms, social in its applications. At base, thinking is a public activity — its natural habitat is the houseyard, the marketplace, and the town square" (p. 360). From this perspective knowledge is characterized more as a matter of consensus than verifiability; we agree upon what we know rather than uncover a universal reality. Due to its social nature, knowledge maintains communities by providing a shared lexicon that forms the basis of communication and action (Bruffee, 1986). Our conceptions of "what is" holds us together and provides us the currency we need to interact, to make decisions and to judge the adequacy of our actions and those of others.

The terms we use to depict our understandings of the world are inseparable: knowledge and language are identical from a social constructionist framework. This is a shift from an empiricist notion in which language comes out of knowledge and physical reality. In its place, the social constructionist proposes that language and knowledge constitute each other, neither can stand alone. This represents an interpretive approach to the generation of knowledge (Gergen, 1985). The structure of language is tied to what is rendered as knowledge.

The literature on social construction is varied and reflects the foundations of the disciplines in which the work locates itself. While there is an assumption that social construction means a single thing, it is an amusing example of the construct itself. Social construction is itself socially constructed (Turiel, 1989). The conceptualization is framed by the disciplinary tradition, the language community, and the historical context in which it is used. For the anthropologist, social construction is part and parcel of the academic discipline — it is assumed that meanings vary across cultures because cultures vary. For the psychologist, social construction is a radical turn away from the individualism and empiricism of psychological thought — moving categories to the group level of consideration requires rethinking of individual characteristic model. For the educator, who works from a hodge-podge of disciplinary traditions, social construction moves attention from individual students to the context in which the student is situated. Unfortunately, no model is provided within education to support that shift.

The thrust of social constructionist thought is to provide broader understandings of commonly used categories or labels by showing discrepancies in their enactment in everyday life. These discrepancies are uncovered through comparison of various kinds: across time, across cases, across settings. In illustrating the differences in conceptualization, the social constructionist pulls attention away from the object/category and focuses on the social processes and resources that provide the foundation for its emerging meaning. Through careful analysis of the underlying assumptions, linguistic markings and pragmatic implications, common categories are unravelled to illustrate their social nature.

Social constructionist literature can be broadly categorized into two types: theoretical and empirical. The theoretical work deals with the sociology of knowledge in general and the social constructionist perspective in particular. Examination of knowledge generation and use has focused on scientific knowledge as social product (Kuhn, 1970), knowledge as social justification of belief (Rorty, 1979), and the social construction of reality as exemplified in the relationship between sociology of knowledge and the sociology of language (Berger & Luckmann, 1966). This work was the basis of later reviews of social constructionist thought within psychology (Gergen, 1985) and across disciplines (Bruffee, 1986).

The empirical work attempts to deconstruct specific categories used in everyday life, arguing that they are social products rather than inherent characteristics. Psychological constructs ranging from gender, sexual identity, special education labels, and policy categories are among the topics addressed in the social constructionist tradition. The typical approach is a comparative analysis of differences in constructs presented as evidence of the lack of internal coherence in the label. Varied contrasts are chosen to highlight the differences in definition.

Some authors compare application of a construct across time. This is the strategy of choice in studies of the definition of the child (Kessen, 1979), development (Polakow, 1989) learning disabilities (Sleeter, 1986), mental retardation (Ferguson, 1987), and at-risk status (Lubeck & Garrett, 1990). When comparisons are made across time, attention is focused on how the labels change in a specified period given the historical context. For example in Sleeter's study of learning disabilities, the emergence of the label is tied to the increases in standards during the post-Sputnik educational reform era. According to Sleeter, the educational category of learning disabilities was created to allow white middle-class children to escape the stigma of failure imposed by higher standards of reading achievement. Political and historical forces often play an important part in this kind of analysis.

Differences in definition across settings provides a second contrast in social constructionist work. Settings are defined either in terms of identifiable cultures, as in the case of anthropological work, or in terms of local settings within a single culture. In the case of cross-cultural work differences are tied to the cultural meaning systems in which practices exist. For example, Gergen, Gloger-Tippelt, & Berkowitz (1990), compared conceptions of the child in the United States and Germany and found that they were more related to the experiences adults had with children (whether or not the respondent was a mother) and with the gender of the child in question than with some inate characteristic of children themselves. Differences in application and implication of the label at-risk in two different school districts were explored by Richardson, Cassanova, Placier & Guilfoyle (1989). In intra-cultural work, there is an assumption that the cultural expectations and meanings are more shared than disparate and that the divergence in application of a label arises from local context and institutional forces.

Contrasts can be set up across cases in a local context to examine the issue of social construction. It is assumed that when a label is applied differentially across cases in a setting, that the characteristic is the product of social forces within the milieu rather than existing within an individual person. This approach has been used in attitudes about lesbianism (Kitzinger, 1987), administrator views of policies and programs for at-risk pre-schoolers (Lubeck & Garrett, 1990), application of learning disabilities as a functional label (Smith, 1982), and the process of identification and service provision for special education (Mehan, Hertwick & Meils, 1986). This approach highlights the social negotiations inherent in differential application of various labels to individuals within a single cultural setting.

A final group of studies present the social construction of activities rather than characteristics, focusing on the social enactment of a procedure, normally thought to exist rationally and individually. Unlike the earlier studies discussed, these examinations are not explicitly comparative. Instead they address the construction of the activity at the social level of participation, advocating a turn away from an individualist perspective. Examples of this type of work include literacy (Cook-Gumperz, 1986), grading practices (Pestello, 1987), scientific writing (Meyers, 1985), writing (Bruffee, 1986), and the development of order in a classroom (Davies, 1983). Differences in social organization of these practices result in differences in products, which are usually thought to be objectively generated.

Mehan (1981) has contrasted social constructivist thought in psychology and sociology. Through the work of Husserl and later work in the early ethnomethodological tradition, Mehan tracks study of the social construction of social practice. An increased emphasis on the construction of meaning among people through their face-to-face interactions has shifted the attention from individual to group practices. Mehan follows a similar trend in psychology in attention to the social construction of cognitive structures. Comparing the constructivist, but still individually oriented perspective of Piaget with the socio-historical approach of Vygotsky has focused on the importance of context in understanding competence.

The authors utilizing this framework come from diverse fields: psychologists, anthropologists, sociologists, literary theorists, and educationists have all used the social constructionist view to examine commonly held ideas and have taken the characteristics apart to uncover the social nature of their definition. This turn of view is usually proposed in the context of changing practice. For example, when a label used to sort individuals is defined socially rather than individually, the implications of the label are quite different. If the label of at-risk is a function of the setting rather than the child, responsibility falls more heavily on contextual factors than on the individual. Change in our work is a fundamental aspect of the social constructionist approach.

The social constructionist prompts us to think of the objects of the world as social accomplishments. "When perceiver and object come together, what is perceived is a function of the interaction between culturally provided categories that the perceiver brings to the interaction and new information about the object that occurs in the interaction" (Mehan, et al., 1986, p. 86). This is frequently done without an explicit discussion of the underlying theoretical assumptions that frame their application of the term. The next section proposes a theoretical orientation that is appropriate for exploring socially constructed phenomena, work based on a Vygotskian perspective.

Vygotskian Theory

One of the main points that guided the development of the theoretical framework for this study was that meaning is socially constructed and constituted. It happens among people in interaction in a context that they create. This orientation has been highlighted in the research community of late with the recent English translations of the work of Vygotsky. At the most general level, Vygotsky's work could be described as an examination of human mental functioning within its social context. More specifically, Wertsch and Toma (1990) have described it as "sociocultural approach to mediated action," which proposes that mental life cannot be abstracted from the cultural, historical, and institutional contexts in which it occurs. Using this perspective, the normal focus on individual mental functioning is turned on its head. Instead of examining single individuals trying to make sense of the world on their own, attention is given to the sociocultural context in which individuals act. In the study of the construction of the meaning of readiness, the focus becomes the ways in which communities work to develop an understanding of readiness, examining the cultural, historical, and institutional forces that shape it. Of secondary interest is the way that individuals internalize that meaning and use it in their lives.

Wertsch (1985) outlined three themes that work to structure Vygotsky's work. The first theme is Vygotsky's use of "genetic" or developmental method. According to this idea, it is not possible to understand human mental functioning if it is examined in terms of the static products or development, for example, the results of a readiness test. Instead, Vygotsky asserted that understanding only comes by considering how and where it comes in development:

> We need to concentrate not on the *product* of development but on the very *process* by which higher forms are established...
> To encompass in research the process of a given thing's development in all it phases and changes — from birth to death — fundamentally means to discover its nature, its essence, for "it is only in movement that a body shows what it is." Thus the historical [that is, in the broadest sense of "history"] study of

behavior is not an auxiliary aspect of theoretical study, but rather forms its very base (Vygotsky, 1978, pp. 64-65).

In the development of mental processes, such as the development of meaning, no one factor and set of explanatory principles can provide a complete account. To understand how meaning is constructed, it is vital to examine all forces that shape it in all phases of its development.

The second theme that Wertsch sees in Vygotsky's work is the assertion that higher mental functions, those that make us uniquely human, have origins that are social. Working from a traditional Marxist viewpoint, Vygotsky's work was based on the idea that the social relations in which individuals exist must be understood first before one can understand the actions of the individual. This is illustrated in two quotations that have been used extensively as Vygotsky's writings have been incorporated into recent educational research. The first is Vygotsky's belief that "the social dimension of consciousness is primary in time and fact. The individual dimension of consciousness is derivative and secondary" (Vygotsky, 1979, p. 30, in Wertsch, 1985). This view is reflected in his *general genetic law of cultural development*, probably the most widely quoted Vygotskian text:

> Any function in the child's cultural development appears twice, or on two planes. First it appears on the social plane, and then on the psychological plane. First it appears between people as an interpsychological category, and then within the child as an intrapsychological category. This is equally true with regard to voluntary attention, logical memory, the formation of concepts, and the development of volition. We may consider this position as a law in the full sense of the word, but it goes without saying that internalization transforms the process itself and changes its structure and functions (Vygotsky, 1981, in Wertsch, 1985).

Using this model for the construction of meaning, Vygotsky would assert that the meaning of readiness is negotiated in the inter-psychological plane first, among participants in a setting. This socially constructed meaning would then be internalized by individuals like parents and teachers. He further explained this view when he defined the idea of external as social:

> It is necessary that everything internal in higher forms was external, that is, for others it was what is now is for oneself.

Any high mental function necessarily goes through an external stage in its development because it is initially a social function. This is the center of the whole problem of internal and external behavior... when we speak of a process, "external" means "social." Any higher mental function was external because it was social at some point before becoming an internal, truly mental function (Vygotsky, 1981, in Wertsch, 1985, p. 62).

According to Wertsch, Vygotsky is doing more than just asserting that individual mental functions come out of social participation. His theory requires a fundamental redefinition of the idea of mental function reoriented to occur on the linked social and the psychological planes.

The final theme that comes out of Vygotsky's work is that human mental functioning is mediated by tools and signs. These mediational tools, such as language or symbols, transform the actions of individuals. More than just simplifying what people do, using mediational tools fundamentally changes the action itself. This occurs because the tool determines the structure of the act, just as the use of a hammer changes the act of building. The action, the individual who carries it out, and the context in which it occurs are melded to form a whole that must be investigated together for complete understanding. In the study of readiness, an analysis of language used by participants in local settings would be vital to understand how the meaning of readiness was constructed and utilized.

The use of a Vygotskian perspective implies an effort to build a single approach to understanding the social interaction, speech, and cognition in their actual connections with concrete social practices (Minick, 1989). It aims at building a "cohesive theory of human psychological development which takes the social, the cultural, and the historical as fundamental" (Minick, p. 183). Mehan (1981) has described how Vygotsky's socio-historical approach

proposes a strong relationship between culture and cognition, the social interactional processes that constitute activity in culture and the psychological processes of its members. The connection is achieved because an individual's psychological functioning develops through the internalization of culturally organized interactional processes (p. 75).

Educational applications of Vygotskian theory have been explored in the last quarter of the twentieth century in the United States by groups of scholars representing different disciplines and academic traditions. Their focus has been the exploration of the social origins of human cognitive functioning in varied contexts. Although examining a broad array of activities, settings, and participants, this work shares an emphasis on the mutual constituency of the social and the psychological. In contrast to the individually oriented work that comes from the American psychological tradition, Vygotskian-inspired studies highlight the process of learning through interaction, of the formation of individuals through their cultural context. People and their actions are situated in a particular social, cultural, historical, and political context that provide certain tools and support.

Basic is the idea that individuals learn through their interactions with more competent others. Vygotsky hints at this when he says that:

> From the very first days of the child's development his activities acquire a meaning of their own in a system of social behavior and, being directed towards a definite purpose, are refracted through the prism of the child's environment. The path from object to child and from child to object passes through another person. This complex human structure is the product of a developmental process deeply rooted in the links between individual and social history (1978, p. 30).

In applying the notion of social origins of individual development, Vygotsky proposed the *zone of proximal development* as the foundation for relationship between social and psychological functioning. The zone of proximal development (ZPD) is "the distance between the actual developmental level as determined by independent problem solving and the level of potential development as determined through problem solving under adult guidance or in collaboration with a more capable peer" (Vygotsky, 1978, p. 86). It is within the zone of proximal development that individuals negotiate their understandings of everyday problems with the help of more experienced members of the group. Through this help, the novice is able to develop a shared understanding of the task and social tools used to accomplish it.

Much of the work applying Vygotskian theory has relied on the idea of ZPD, particularly focusing on learning specific concepts or particular cultural activities when the learning situation consisted of an expert and a novice. Rogoff and Wertsch (1984) suggested the following themes that have come out of work about the ZPD:

1) "The zone of proximal development involves the joint consciousness of the participants, where two or more minds are collaborating on solving a problem.

2) Both participants play an important role in using the zone of proximal development even in situations that are not directly conceived of as instructional by participants.

3) Interaction in the zone of proximal development is organized into a dynamic functional system oriented toward the child's future skills and knowledge" (p. 5).

Using the concept of ZPD, studies have explored the idea of scaffolding (Wood, Bruner, & Ross, 1976), assisted performance (Tharp & Gallimore, 1988), cognitive apprenticeship and guided performance (Rogoff, 1990), cognitive change (Newman, Griffin, & Cole, 1989), and instructional conversation (Rueda & Goldenberg, 1991). All of these are variations on the idea that learning is a social activity that occurs within interaction.

What differentiates work within this framework is the definition of the context and social interactions that occur. How much context is incorporated into analysis of the social plane? At the most basic level is work that relies on the physical and intellectual interaction between more and less expert participants on a given task. This usually involves an analysis of adult-child or teacher-student interaction based on a reciprocal teaching method. This type of study includes mothers teaching their children about numbers (Saxe, Gearhart, & Guberman, 1984), adult-infant interaction (Rogoff, Malkin & Gilbride, 1984), socialization at mealtime (Valsiner, 1984), grocery shopping (Lave, Murtaugh, & de la Roche, 1984), training of tailors (Lave, 1988) and weavers (Greenfield, 1984), and reading instruction (Applebee & Langer, 1983; Brown & Campione, 1984; Moll & Diaz, 1983; Au & Kawakami, 1984). An excellent review of work examining the process of guided participation among caregivers and children across many age levels is provided by Rogoff (1990). Although the effects of culture and social forces are implicit in these studies, they can be seen as in the background to person-to-person interactions.

Specific applications of these ideas have been proposed to change the nature of instruction, advocating a move from the recitation script to a more interactive mode of teaching and learning. This has been the focus of books by Tharp & Gallimore (1989) and Newman, Griffin, & Cole (1989). Changes in teacher education have been advocated to facilitate this type of interactive teaching (Gallimore, Dalton, & Tharp, 1986; Dalton, 1989) and assessment applications have also been explored, particularly as they relate to understanding both independent and assisted performance (Campione, Brown, Ferrera, and Bryant, 1984).

A second use of Vygotskian theory has addressed the interaction in which people learn nested within a broader social and historical context. Although the other research frequently takes an implicit cultural context perspective, this work explicitly focuses on the constraints and affordances in a particular social and historical setting. A branch of Soviet psychology called activity theory has provided the basis for an emerging body of research that integrates the social origins of psychological functioning within particular contexts and also broadens the focus beyond learning cognitive tasks to the development of meaning.

Activity Theory

The concept of activity was exclusively a Soviet construct until the rebirth of interest in Vygotsky in the 1970s. A simple definition of activity is that it is "a unit of analysis that includes both the individual and his/her culturally defined environment." (Wertsch, 1979, p. viii). A theme that recurs in the work of Vygotsky, Rubinshtein, and Leontiev and that forms the foundation of activity theory is the interdependence of the human and the setting.

Definitions of activity settings have been developed that range from the theoretical and abstract to the lyrical and concrete. For example, Wertsch (1985) saw activity settings as

> social institutionally defined setting... grounded in a set of assumptions about appropriate roles, goals, and means used by the participants in that setting... one could say that an activity setting guides the selection of actions and the operational composition of actions, and it determines the functional significance of these actions (p. 212).

In contrast, Tharp and Gallimore (1988), used more common language to describe the same concept. They concentrated on the everyday nature of activity settings:

> they are as homely and familiar as old shoes and the front porch. They are the social furniture of our family, community, and work lives. They are the events and people of our work and relations to one another. They are the who, what, when, where, and why, the small recurrent dramas of everyday life, played on the stages of home, school, community, and workplace... We can plot our lives as traces of the things we do, in dissolving and recombining social groups and energy knots. Those are activity settings... The name "activity settings" incorporates cognitive and motoric action itself (activity), as well as the external, environmental, and objective features of the occasion (settings) (p. 72).

The work that has utilized the idea of activity and activity settings has varied from problem solving (Wertsch, Minick, & Arns, 1984), understanding sibling care arrangements and applying them to school interaction contexts (Weisner, Gallimore & Jordan, 1988), home literacy activities with low income, Hispanic kindergartners (Gallimore & Goldenberg, in press), the social construction of lives of families with mentally retarded children (Gallimore, Weisner, Kaufman, & Bernheimer, 1989), and the relationship of parental literacy experiences and literacy acquisition (Reese et al., 1989). The key idea in these studies is the analysis of cultural resources and constraints available in a setting that influence activity. Tharp and Gallimore have adapted the biological idea of ecocultural niche to describe the manner in which activity settings are deterministic of action by providing pressures and resources to participants. What people do is related to the tools available in a setting.

Various researchers have constructed different analytical frameworks for analyzing activity based on their interpretation of the theory. Wertsch, Minick, & Arns (1984) use the framework specified by Leontiev in his classic work on activity. They specify that activity is analyzed on three levels. The first level is that of activity and can be discerned by their motives. The second level is that of actions, which are distinguished according to their goals. The third is operations, which are differentiated by the conditions under which they are carried out. Wertsch (et al.) used these levels to analyze how mothers and teachers interacted differently with children as they worked to reproduce a model of a farm scene with toys. Their understanding of the differences between mothers and teachers in their interactions were enriched by their activity analysis because they focused on the goals that these groups had for the activity. Teachers took the goal to be that of teaching, while mothers took on the more difficult parts of the task so that it would be carried out more efficiently.

In work that focused more heavily on culture as something that shapes activity settings, Weisner, Gallimore & Jordan (1988) proposed the following as constituent elements: personnel, motivations, cultural scripts for conduct, daily tasks and activities, and cultural goals and beliefs. These proposed elements have been tied to Soviet activity theory, the behavior setting concept, and the work of a number of neo-Vygotskians (Gallimore & Goldenberg, in press). This framework has been used in a number of settings to "unpack" cultural effects that are often misunderstood when they examined on a surface level only. Activity settings have been the basis of work that compared home and school activity settings, suggesting incorporation by the school of home interaction patterns to facilitate learning (Weisner, Gallimore & Jordan, 1988). It has been used to examine literacy learning in low-income, Hispanic homes, finding that the amount and type of literacy activity is much greater than might be expected given the SES or ethnicity labels that could be used to describe families. The father's use of literacy in his job appeared to influence the types of literacy activities that occurred at home (Reese, Goldenberg, Loucky, & Gallimore, 1989). Gallimore and Goldenberg (in press) compared the child-parent interactions in two types of homework for low-income Hispanic kindergartners and found that by changing the task demands, they could change the nature of the interactions that occurred. Meaningful text, in terms of small books, provided more elaborated, language rich interactions than the typical reading readiness homework activity. Gallimore, Weisner, Kaufman, & Bernheimer (1989) studied families of developmentally delayed children, finding that they construct a daily routine to manage the stresses that this situation puts on a family. In each of these studies, there was a concerted effort to disentangle the elements in the immediate environment while considering the cultural context in which activity occurred.

In the framework developed for this study, Eisenhart and I (1990) modified the elements suggested by Weisner, Gallimore & Jordan so that we could explicitly examine both the social and psychological aspects of meaning making. We felt that this was important given Vygotsky's explicit definition of social and psychological plane of human functioning. In addition it would allow us to explore the process by which communities define ideas and actions and individuals internalize them in their daily lives. We saw the activity setting for this study as the emerging arrangements of the meaning of readiness in chosen contexts and its representation in educational policies and practices such as enrollment, curriculum, instruction, and standard setting.

For the activity setting, elements were defined that had both social and psychological dimensions. The elements we developed were: *actors, interpretations, task structure,* and *motives.* In each case we proposed a social and psychological aspect to this element, recognizing that individuals act within a given social context. What follows is a brief summary of how each of the elements was defined in the context of this study.

Actors are the people involved in the construction of the meaning of readiness in a particular setting. An actor plays a role given by society, but also takes an active part in that role. Defined in this way, the concept of actor includes both the socially defined aspect of each person's role and the individually chosen manner in which the role is played. On the social plane, individuals are given roles to play. The roles related to readiness might be the teacher, parent, or child; the roles of the lawyer or waitress probably are not. On the psychological plane, individuals create a style in which they play out their socially defined role. For example, the role of a mother is generally defined by society. The way that an individual carries out those duties is developed through her role identity. One mother may choose to protect her child from stress and undo challenge by choosing a pre-school that fosters social and emotional development through play. Another mother might see herself as her child's promoter, and choose activities that will allow the child to excel in areas such as sports or academics.

The meanings attached to institutions, actions, images, utterances, events, and customs of a group are called *interpretations* (from Geertz, 1987). On the social plane, collective interpretations of readiness would be models developed by a family, school, or community about what indicates or counterindicates readiness. These are more or less shared ideas about factors like how children grow and appropriate instructional methods. On the psychological plane, individual actors respond to the collective interpretations by developing individual interpretations. Because they are seen as a response to the collective interpretations, the interpretations held by individuals are both distinct and related to social interpretations. In a community that expects children to attend pre-school before entering kindergarten, the parent who chooses to keep her child at home because she does not feel that he could handle a group environment has used both knowledge of the institutional models of the community and her personal knowledge of her child to make that decision.

The organization of resources, such as materials or time, and interpersonal relations, are described as *task structure*. Task structure frames the interactions and academic activities in classrooms, it differentiates the environments of various schools and communities, and it affects the content of educational activities at home and school. We used task structure broadly to include both social participation structure and academic task structure. Social participation structure describes the patterns of interaction in a setting, including the rules for interactional etiquette. In the study of readiness, the rules for interaction are expected to differ among groups of actors and they are dependent on the context. On the social plane, institutional patterns of interaction develop in a given setting, constraining or enabling participants to gain access to information and experience. On the psychological plane, individuals respond to the institutional social participation structure in particular ways. In a particular setting a child's ability to function within a given structure will become part of the information that a teacher uses to determine child readiness. With different rules for behavior or with different classmates a child may be seen ready in one place and unready in another.

Academic task structure comprises the cognitive and motor skills required and the materials and activities used to carry out an instructional program. At the social level, academic task structure is connected to both the stated and enacted curriculum. It is the activities and ideology constructed in the classroom work. On the psychological plane, it describes the responses made to the demands and structure of instruction in a given classroom. Individual children interpret task structure differently given their ideas and experience. Ideas of readiness are represented in the way that activities are organized, the grouping of children, pace of instruction, and the standards set for performance. Part of the tag of ready or unready depends on what the child is asked to do.

Motives include the goals and objectives for activities related to meanings of readiness. This is one of the most important aspects of activity theory, as it is assumed that action is oriented by the motives for action. On the social level, schools, families, and communities develop goals and objectives for the educational process. The school personnel have goals for kindergarten, which depend on their ideas about what purpose it serves in the scope of the elementary school program. Kindergarten screening has different implications if the results are used to place children in special programs than if they are used by individual teachers to plan instruction. One type of screening program has a goal of sorting the ready from the unready, while the other is focused on potential educational activities in the classroom. On the psychological plane, individuals have their own goals and objectives. Each individual's motive for involvement is related to the way she carries out her job (her role identity). Parents will act differently if they see readiness as a prerequisite to kindergarten than if they see kindergarten as the place to develop readiness.

From past policy, research, and practice, it appears that viewing readiness as a child characteristic has not proven to be profitable. A more constructivist view is proposed; in particular, taking a Vygotskian perspective, attending to both the social and psychological dimensions of the developing meaning of readiness is recommended. This view of readiness required a different kind of approach to its study, one that focused on how the meanings of readiness were constructed by participants working with young children. The next section describes one way to tackle the problem.

CHAPTER 3

❧

STUDYING READINESS

Most research on readiness focuses on untangling the complexity of child characteristics that comprise the ready child. This work utilizes tests and teacher judgments of readiness, analysis of performance by age, and comparisons of the effects of special programs for children who are identified as unready. None of these models seemed appropriate when considering readiness from a social and cultural perspective. Here the focus was the construction of the meaning of readiness among participants in the kindergarten experience. My interest was the social negotiations and practices that come out of a local meaning of readiness, the resources and constraints that shape actions, and the practical educational implications for children.

This section provides a general overview of the approach and methods used to study readiness. The theme here is descriptive, attempting to portray the characteristics of communities and their practices as well as my role as a researcher in the study. A more complete discussion of the study's methodology, including description of sampling, data collection and analysis, can be found in Appendix One.

Focusing questions

This work examined the construction of the meaning of readiness in three kindergarten settings. I proposed that readiness had a specific local meaning that emerged as participants interacted in a kindergarten experience. These interactions and constituent meanings were framed in the context of local demo-

37

graphic characteristics, local history, community values and
power structures. Nested community settings were the source of
these constructed meanings and included the home, the neighborhood, the school, and the classroom. The following questions
guided the research process:

> How was the meaning of readiness constructed in a given
> community?
>
> How was the meaning of readiness described by participants
> in the setting?
>
> Who were the participants in its development?
>
> What power did participants have in the definition of the meaning
> and its subsequent instantiation in the school?
>
> How did the local meaning of readiness shape the instructional
> practices and interactions between home and school in a given
> classroom?

The Study

Schools within a single district were chosen that represented
different orientations to readiness in terms of the enrollment and
promotion practices in the early grades. This was based on the
assumption that decisions about whether to enroll, redshirt, or
retain a child are rooted in beliefs about how children develop
readiness. In addition, site selection was made with an eye to
varying levels of socioeconomic status. Especially when considering readiness for school experiences, differences among
children may be related to previous socialization to school-like
activities in addition to factors such as age or ability (Heath,
1983). This exposure is often related to socioeconomic status.

The process of choosing a district and schools was an interesting example of the negotiations that must occur in fieldwork.
In the initial planning for the study, four schools were sought to
exemplify varying beliefs about readiness and economic resources.
From demographic information and informant suggestions, four
schools were identified and the principals of each school contacted.

The Thomas School district represented a variety of settings
in a large geographic area in the West. The majority of the district's
schools were in located in Broadview, a town of approximately
85,000 working-class people. In outlying areas, the district also
encompassed a suburban area of white-collar professionals and

rural towns with a mixture of agricultural workers and laborers. Schools were relatively autonomous in decision-making, although they shared common curriculum objectives and school entrance age. There had been recent talk of discouraging practices like retention district wide, but no official policy had been passed by the school board.

Berkeley was the first school that I visited to gain volunteers for my study. A meeting was scheduled before school on a late spring morning with the principal, Bill Morrison, and one of his kindergarten teachers, Evelyn Winston. We sat at a round table in his office and I gave them a brief outline of my study: I was interested in how kindergarten teachers use the concept of readiness to make decisions in their teaching. I described my time frame and what kind of role I saw myself playing in the classroom. When I finished with my description, Mr. Morrison leaned closer to the table with his arms crossed. He looked straight at me and said, "I want to tell you that I don't want to be part of work done by [the University]. I think their stuff sucks. Their research has done a real disservice to our profession and I don't want to be a part of them doing any more damage." He took a breath; his face was turning purplish and he pounded on the table, "I don't want you coming in here being judgmental about what we do... You know, we are part of public education. It's our duty to take all children wherever they are. If we can't retain kids, we can't help them." Slightly taken aback, I tried to explain that I was hoping to describe what was happening in different schools and that I felt very strongly that this would be a process in which the teachers would be working with me every step of the way, giving me feedback on my observations and checking my understanding of their setting. While I certainly came into this study with particular beliefs about educating young children, this was not meant to be an evaluation of their school or the kindergarten program. I felt it was really important for their voices to be heard. At this point Mrs. Winston quietly added, "I don't understand how some people think that kids need to have certain skills before they come to kindergarten. I mean, I think we need to take kids where they are and work with them from there..." We spent about fifteen more minutes talking about how much time I would spend in their school, what benefits I saw for the teachers, and what kind of demands I would be making on their time. I left, finally understanding why all books on qualitative methods have a section on the difficulty of gaining access to field sites.

Ultimately, Mr. Morrison told me that they did not want to participate in my study. I regret that I did not have a chance to find out more about Berkeley Elementary because I think that including it would have enriched my work. My failure to persuade them to participate taught me a valuable lesson however; research definitely is not some dry characterless enterprise. It involves people; people who have very strong emotions about their interpretations of research. I began to develop a thick skin.

Gaining access to the other sites was not nearly as difficult as my first experience seemed to foretell. The three other schools identified initially were those included in the study. Fulton was a rural school with a working-class population. It had a number of special programs for children including bilingual classes and Chapter One services. Norwood was a middle-class suburban school that was described by almost everyone as "yuppie" in its population and orientation. Rochester was located in the town of Broadview and had a very mixed population, with students from a wealthy neighborhood and children of migrant workers. Tables 1 through 3 provide information about the communities in which the schools were located, the schools themselves, and finally the classrooms that were the focus of the study.

The negotiations with teachers at Fulton, Norwood, and Rochester in many ways foretold how my role would be constructed in each setting. At both Fulton and Norwood I was awarded to the teacher with the most seniority, almost as if I were a prize. Ms. Carlin, from Fulton, had been teaching for sixteen years and Mrs. Sunden was in her fifth year at Norwood. No one volunteered initially at Rochester but with some prodding by the Director of Research and Evaluation, Mrs. Ramirez came forward, telling me later that having just finished a Masters' she knew how important research was and that she felt sorry for me. She was in her eighth year as a teacher.

Originally I had restricted my sampling to half-day classrooms, as the extended-day programs were designed to meet the needs of children at-risk due to their incoming skills levels. Keeping type of program constant seemed appropriate. When only Mrs. Ramirez, who taught a bilingual extended day kindergarten class volunteered, I began to rethink my strategy. It seemed that the reason that her students were placed in the extended day program was that they did not meet some criterion set by the district for readiness. Because they were identified as unready, they were put in a program that was given more resources than the standard

Table 1
Demographic Characteristics of Study Communities
1990

Community	% Anglo	Median Household Income	% Population in Poverty	% Spanish Origin	Median Home Value	Median Rent	Median Years of Education	% Un-employed	% White Collar
Delano (Fulton)	88.7	29444	9.1	17.0	59000	275	12.3	5.0	33.3
Norwood	96.6	52917	3.6	3.1	93333	342	15.3	0.9	70.6
Broadview (Rochester)	93.1	37121	6.0	7.6	69857	298	12.8	4.1	55.8

Table 2
School Characteristics

School	% Eligible federal Free & Reduced lunch program	Socio-economic Status	Ethnicity	Academic Redshirting (males)	Kindergarten retention	Number of kindergarten sections	Number of extended-day kindergarten sections	Number of bilingual kindergarten sections
Fulton	42%	Working-class	Mixed	Unpopular (7%)	Unpopular (3%)	5	3	1
Norwood	8%	Middle-class	Primarily Anglo	Popular (14%)	Infrequent in kindergarten but popular at grade one (12%)	3	0	0
Rochester	50%	Mixed	Mixed	Popular (25%)	Unpopular (0%)	6	2	1

Table 3
Classroom Characteristics

School	Teacher	Years experience	Program Type	% boys overage	Ethnicity
Fulton	Alice Carlin	16	1/2 day	9%	Anglo
Norwood	Monica Sunden	5	1/2 day	41%	Anglo
Rochester	Isabel Ramirez	8	Extended day bilingual	0%	Hispanic

kindergarten program. I thought a comparison of the way that the meaning of readiness was constructed in that kind of setting and in the two half-day situations might be interesting. For some reason, at that point the fact that I did not speak Spanish was not seen as a drawback. I decided to enroll in a beginning Spanish class and learn about bilingual kindergarten.

Fieldwork

These schools were sites for a participant observation study about the construction of meanings of readiness. Multiple data sources were used to weave together an understanding of how community members thought about and enacted meanings of readiness as they participated in the kindergarten experience. Once per week during the fall and once in January and May, I worked as a teacher aide in the kindergarten classrooms chosen for the study. Taking the role of teacher aide, I became a part of the school community and was included in the day-to-day lives of these teachers. Fieldnotes of my visits were provided to the teachers and their comments on the notes were included as data. Monthly interviews outside of classtime focused on the emerging themes in the construction of readiness concepts. Documents like lesson plans, curriculum guides, and home-school communication were collected throughout the year.

To gain the parental view of readiness, a group of parents from each school was interviewed in the month prior to the opening of school and a different group of parents from the study classroom was interviewed at the end of the first quarter of school. These interviews examined parents' expectations and concerns about their child's kindergarten experience. Children from each classroom were interviewed about how they viewed the things they did in kindergarten and whether they had ideas about the relative ranking of the other students' abilities in the classroom.

Analysis of these data (interviews, fieldnotes, and documents) was an ongoing process throughout the project and included themes suggested by the theoretical framework and emerging themes within local settings. This process was iterative in that the teachers provided feedback about the representativeness of both the data and inferences that came out of it.

Constructing the Researcher's Role

One of my primary interests in this study was to develop an understanding of how readiness was constructed in a setting, from the perspective of both teachers and students. As a former kindergarten teacher, I knew that I would not be comfortable in a purely observational role, sitting in the back of the classroom taking notes. I was aware that I have skills that could be used in a classroom and I knew that I wanted access to the kind of information that is available only through instructional interaction with students. I wanted to be a participant observer, but I knew that I was too old to be a child, that I was coming into someone else's classroom, and I was not a parent. I took the role of teacher aide (Hart, 1982) which seemed somewhere between a teacher and other adult. From this orientation, I could examine the ways that the teachers were constructing their classroom environments, as I took direction from them related to instructional activities. The teachers involved in the study would have trained help in their classrooms, which is rare in these days of lean budgets (and I think that this is one of the reasons that the teachers at Fulton and Norwood were so enthusiastic to participate). I would have a school-affiliated status with parents, who would see me not only as an outsider from the university but also as someone who worked with their child. And finally, I would have many opportunities to interact with children in their kindergarten environments.

The role of teacher aide was invaluable to me in helping to understand both the teacher's and child's point of view. Children did not question my constant notetaking until I came back after a long absence in May. In fact, on the first day that I visited Norwood, one of the kindergartners, Mitch, stopped me as I was taking notes about their discussion of their tour of the school to say, "That's not really the way it happened. They forgot…" He proceeded to fill me in about what he thought about the course of events. By May I think that they had learned that adults with notepads were not the ordinary fare in kindergarten.

As a data collection technique, working as an aide had some pitfalls. I was often engaged in an activity so that my hands and mind were not available to make notes. I found that I had more detailed notes of times that I typically was not with students, during group time, for example. Two of the three classrooms operated on a center rotation model, with groups of children moving about the classroom to various activities. I often worked one of the centers, so I could not observe what was going on at the others. I tried to get around this problem by tape recording the action at another center or by asking children about what they did when they were not with me. Also, I found myself thinking as a teacher, not as a researcher many times. By using my professional knowledge in my interactions with children while standing back to examine why I was making those choices within the particular classroom framework, I found that I could develop a more grounded understanding of the setting.

My Role in Each Setting

One of the most important characteristics of a good teacher aide is the ability to adapt to the teacher's professional style, working in the classroom often without her prompting. In addition, I wanted my presence in the classroom as a researcher to be unobtrusive so that interactions would be relatively typical. I know that the teachers chose to do certain things with their students when I was there because they had an extra pair of hands available. However, they were never so unusual that I felt my presence made any of the observations I made invalid. Each of the teachers I worked with had a very distinct style, which shaped my role in her classroom. In turn, this shaped our interactions and the data gathering process.

FULTON

The community served by Fulton Elementary was tightly knit with a traditional rural feeling. People have known each other for a long time and they know what to expect in interactions. In some ways, I think that I was seen as an urban outsider; someone who would not necessarily understand or belong. My relationship with Ms. Carlin had a cautious air to it initially; she mainly interacted with me in a teacher-to-aide manner. Because she had no paraprofessional help assigned to her and she rarely could get parent helpers in the classroom, Ms. Carlin enthusiastically took advantage of my visits to get things done around the room. She generally had all the time before class planned so that I could get a number of projects ready for her students and I was often busy far into the kindergarten session. In interviews, I think that she was a little uncomfortable in her role, not being used to having her words recorded or to responding to specific questions about her teaching practices and beliefs.

As time passed, Ms. Carlin spent more and more time showing me things in the classroom that she thought would be interesting in the light of my study and she pulled in her colleague, Mrs. French, to get her point of view when we talked before school. I found that I made many comments in the fieldnotes for her class and she tirelessly responded to these comments in an assertively thoughtful manner. I did not get much feedback from her on how she felt about this process but I found that as the year passed her comments often wove elements from earlier questions I had posed, indicating that at least her interactions with me were framed in large part by the research context.

NORWOOD

Mrs. Sunden enthusiastically involved me in the development of her students' kindergarten experience, incorporating me into the planning and material development process as a peer. My input was sought as she worked with the other teachers to plan and get things ready for her students and all of them asked at one time or another if I had seen any really neat ideas in the other schools that I had visited. At times I felt that I was in a semi-expert role; seen as someone from the University who could provide them with insight that they did not have themselves. I was often given choices among activities to choose from and Mrs. Sunden never gave me the impression that I was doing things incorrectly according to her model of educational practice.

In terms of feedback on fieldnotes or transcripts, Mrs. Sunden rarely made comments. Part of that could be due to the fact that her style of teaching and the students she had were very close to my previous professional experiences and I found myself not questioning the reasoning behind it. I had to force myself to examine the ways that she did things in her classroom from the perspective of an outsider, making the assumptions explicit rather than implicit. Most of this came out in the interviews, I think, which were very helpful in clarifying the themes that I saw operating in that setting.

ROCHESTER

I had an outsider status at Rochester for a number of reasons. On the one hand I was an outsider at the school level because the teachers at Rochester kept close tabs on visitors at the school.

The first day that I worked with Mrs. Ramirez I helped with kindergarten screening. Much of my time was spent entertaining children as they waited to be tested. At least five staff members stopped and asked who I was and what I was doing in their school, all in a friendly but pointed way. As the year progressed they greeted me in the halls but rarely engaged me in conversation.

In the classroom, I had a different status than I did at the other schools because Mrs. Ramirez had an aide working with her half-time. I was not providing services that she sorely needed so my skills had a different kind of value to her. In addition, my ignorance about bilingual education definitely reduced my role as expert in her classroom. I think that she saw me more as a researcher looking for information.

Finally, my monolingualism separated me in a very concrete way from the students in a manner that I did not experience in the other settings. As I attempted to learn what little Spanish I could, the students tried to help me out, with the ones with some facility in both English and Spanish smoothing the way for me. We often spoke in a muddled "Spanglish" mess that left us all laughing. I was unable to talk to their parents on my own so I brought an interpreter for both parent teacher conferences/interviews and again when I did the student interviews in January. I was dependent on what translation could be given to me as we talked, which impeded our communication.

At times, however, I think that my outsider status provided me with a unique vantage point to understand the setting. Many things that I might have taken for granted seemed so new to me (the difference between Spanish and English beginning reading, for example). Because I did not always understand the words that were being said, I found myself attentively focused on aspects like participation structure to provide contextual cues. Mrs. Ramirez explained many things to me that I presume the other teachers left unsaid. Even for the children, I did not quite have adult status because I could not speak Spanish. In this in-between role, they often reinterpreted situations for me, pointing out things that they thought were important.

While data generation was necessarily different at Rochester than at Fulton or Norwood, I do not think that difference compromises its validity. In fact, in some ways, it may heighten the value of my observations. I was truly an outsider so I paid close attention to the ways that the kindergarten experience was developed in that classroom.

What follows in the next chapters are cases that describe how the meaning of readiness was constructed at Fulton, Norwood, and Rochester. I begin by describing the stated kindergarten curriculum in the Thomas School District, then move onto the local site descriptions. In the final chapter, I make comparisons among the three schools.

CHAPTER 4

ें

THOMAS KINDERGARTEN CURRICULUM

Formal school documents like curriculum guides, textbooks, and report cards are developed to shape practice by serving as guideposts for appropriate educational activities and standards. The form that they take, whether they are behavioral objectives or global goal statements, points actors in certain ways, encouraging them to perceive the educational process as the document is written. The focus the documents take, whether they are teacher or student oriented, helps to distribute responsibility for action in the classroom. They represent philosophies about learning and teaching and value judgments of many kinds. Because they are concrete manifestations of an institutional (local, state, or national) conception of education, my discussion of the construction of the meaning of readiness begins by examining formal documents that are used to direct kindergarten programs in the Thomas School District.

Schools in this district shared a central administration and funding base, educational policies, curriculum documents, and report cards. While kindergarten was not mandatory in the state, districts received funding for half-day programs on an attendance basis. The district had developed both a half-day program for the general population and an extended-day program for children perceived to be at risk for academic failure. The two programs shared a common set of "Core Conceptual Objectives," which outlined curricular expectations in the form of outcomes-based statements organized by academic content area. In addition, the extended-day program used the Early Prevention of School Failure curriculum (EPSF) which was structured to enhance skills in the areas of auditory, visual, language, fine and gross motor development. No textbook series had been adopted at the district level for kindergarten.

Most of the discussion here will focus on the Core Conceptual Objectives and the common report card because they were designed to guide all kindergarten activities. The EPSF curriculum will be briefly examined as well in the section about Rochester, where I observed its implementation.

The Kindergarten Curriculum Objectives

The best source or organization of the kindergarten curriculum has been a subject of debate for a number of years. Spodek (1973), who defines curriculum as "the organized experiences provided for children in a school setting" (p. 82), has outlined various organizational themes that early childhood educators have used to develop curriculum models. These themes include the activities and characteristics of children themselves, developmental theory, learning theory, standardized test items, and school content. When the curriculum comes from children themselves, professionals use the "natural" activity of children to determine what should go on in a classroom. Froebelian and Montessori programs exemplify the child-oriented approach.

Developmental theory supports the choice and sequencing of activities in a particular way, depending on the theory being employed. Gesellian theory considers child development to be a function of biological maturation and advocates waiting until children are "developmentally ready" for any experience chosen for them. Gesellians assert that pushing children beyond their developmental abilities is one of the greatest causes of failure. They argue that inappropriate activities should be excluded from the curriculum, "protecting the right of the child to be five." Activities are chosen from a normative understanding of what five year olds are like and children who do not fit those normative expectations are placed in other programs, such as developmental kindergarten or transitional programs between kindergarten and first grade. Theoretically, Gesellians would not advocate the inclusion of what had previously been defined as first grade reading activities in a kindergarten program because they have traditionally been seen as used with six year olds. Piagetian-based developmental programs conceptualize knowledge as more than accumulation of information, experience, and maturation. They are based on the idea that individuals actively construct their knowledge and use their experience as a data base and source of validation. Piagetian curricula, such as the High Scope program, work to engage children actively in the learning process by having them do things like use language to reflect on and structure their experiences. In mathematics programs based on Piagetian theory, children are given practice in the use of such concepts as one-to-one correspondence, classification, and seriation to develop intellectual schema (Spodek, 1986). Behaviorist learning theory is oriented to short-term change of behavior through simple cause and effect relationships and can be seen in the strict use of behavioral objectives. Behaviorist learning theory is the basis of programs like the DISTAR program, which breaks learning up into very small, discrete units which are taught-tested-retaught-retested until mastery is achieved. The use of test items to determine classroom activities has been cited not only in early childhood classrooms, but with all age levels when tests have high stakes attached to student performance (Shepard, 1990). When test performance is perceived as a measure of instructional effectiveness or student proficiency, instruction is often oriented to the test items themselves rather than the broader curricular goals. The final source that Spodek discusses is the content of later schooling, based on the traditional subject matters studied in schools. When curriculum comes from school content, it is thought of in terms of reading, math, science, etc.

The Core Conceptual Objectives used in the Thomas School District were organized according to subject matter content: Art, Computers, Health, Language Arts/Reading Readiness, Map/ Globe Skills, Math, Science, and Social Studies. These objectives were reviewed and revised on a regular, rotating basis by committees of teachers and administrators. The most recently revised sets of objectives were in the following format: subject area, conceptual objective, enabling processes, primary trait, application level assessment activity, and rating criteria. Appendix 2 lists the kindergarten Conceptual Objectives for each subject matter area. Appendix 3 is an example of the complete format for one conceptual objective in math.

Examining the configuration of the Conceptual Objectives, it is clear that they were organized by subject matter. What does this say about the place that the kindergarten has in the elementary program? One implication of this arrangement is that it indicates that kindergarten is thought of as a downward extension of the later grades. Spodek notes that when school content is the source of the early childhood curriculum, it is assumed that kindergarten is preparation for later school work in the content areas. This is a departure from earlier conceptualizations of kindergarten, which over time have been based on education as experience (Owen, Dewey), the unity of the world in the child, God, and nature (Froebel), sensory training (Montessori), and active construction of educational experience (Piaget). In other words, earlier kindergarten programs have been based on beliefs about how children gain knowledge; on *engaging in activities* rather than *producing some outcome*. When kindergarten curriculum takes on an academic content structure, programs for five year olds lose the special status that kindergarten was often given, as something with a nature distinct from the rest of the early grades. The model for the education of five year olds that emerges from a subject matter organization is oriented to the disciplinary structure, which may be different for each content area. The traditionally defined, unique needs of the kindergartner (which stress active learning based on social interaction) may or may not be addressed within this curricular framework, as they are not an organizing principle.

In the Thomas District, the objectives for a given content area combined items derived from discipline-oriented skills (e.g., for Math, Measures time) with processes derived from a view that young children should actively, concretely, and socially engage materials in the kindergarten environment. The processes incorporated in these objectives include manipulation of real world objects, the expression through language of the child's everyday experiences, the development of cognitive concepts, and socialization to school behaviors. Table 4 provides examples of the core objectives and their categorization.

Table 4
Core Conceptual Objectives by Categorization

Subject Area	Objective	Category
Art	The student will select the appropriate elements of art in order to express him/herself	Manipulation
Health	The student will compare the body parts and the associated five senses	Conceptual

Table 4 *continued*
Core Conceptual Objectives by Categorization

Subject Area	Objective	Category
Language Arts/ Reading Readiness	The student will use speaking & listening skills to interact with others in classroom situations	Language
Math	The student will verbalize, compare, and extend patterns with concrete objects	Manipulation/ Language
Social Studies	The student will demonstrate acceptable ways of acting in various situations	Behavior

To explore the priority placed on the knowledge developed in the kindergarten program, objectives were grouped by process focus and the relative proportions calculated:

Content Area	Number of Objectives
Manipulation of objects:	5 (10%)

    Typical terms used: form, assemble, select, use materials

Language/vocabulary	15 (29%)

    Typical terms used: describe, identify by name, use terms, talk
        about

Manipulation & language	2 (3%)

    Typical terms used: verbalize & extend, combine & describe

Concepts	21 (41%)

    Typical terms used: understand, solve, compare, investigate,
        practice, demonstrate awareness

Behavior	9 (17%)

    Typical terms used: demonstrate ways of sharing, acceptable
        behavior, responsibility

One of the current debates in the early childhood field centers on what most people would describe as the increasingly academic content of the kindergarten curriculum. There has been a steady movement away from a focus on the social-emotional development of five year olds, to an emphasis on the acquisition of cognitive "readiness" skills such as learning initial consonant sounds and counting sets of objects (Spodek, 1986). The Thomas objectives clearly emphasize academics (found in the categories of manipulation, language, and concepts); however, they also give some attention to knowledge of self and development of relationships (found in the behavior group). These affective objectives speak primarily to rule-oriented behavior or showing evidence of being socialized to the school experience. The district objectives concerning acceptable behavior, coping with experiences and change in an appropriate way, demonstrating responsibility of self, developing and adopting classroom rules constitute less than 1/5 of the total number of objectives, compared to the academically-oriented objectives that represent more than 80% of the total.

The language used to communicate these Conceptual Objectives was formal and jargon laden, often presented in a more complex form than was necessary (note especially the one objective for computer education). They were obviously written for the educational establishment, in the format of performance statements against which individual behaviors can be measured. In the objectives most recently revised, rating criteria were developed that focused attention on attainment of a certain standard of performance. For example, in math, each objective listed an Application Level Assessment Activity. Rating criteria had four levels of performance: Proficiency, Minimally Attained, Unattained, and No Response. For Language Arts/Reading Readiness, the rating criteria were classified as Applying the Concept, Making Progress Toward the Concept, and Introduced to the Concept. The objectives communicated a standard against which child performance was compared. By providing criteria or indicators of inadequate performance there was an implication that children who did not meet that standard were in some way deficient. Among the documents, no procedure was outlined for the remediation of deficiencies or for the consequences of deficiencies that remained at the end of a school year.

In summary, the Core Conceptual Objectives for the Thomas School district were organized primarily by academic subject matter categories, rather than child skill areas. This implies a downward extension of the elementary program structure into the kindergarten and focused attention on the development of academic skills that would prepare students for academic work in later grades. Objectives related to social and emotional development in kindergartners comprised only 17% of the total and were stated primarily in the form of rule-oriented behaviors.

There was little integration between the strong press of the academic skills focus of the Core Conceptual Objectives and the rule oriented behavioral skills, with a resulting feeling of fragmentation. There did not seem to be a coherent model for the kindergarten program, instead the structure of each discipline had been translated to the kindergarten level and some elements of earlier kindergarten programs retained.

When objectives are academically oriented and written in skill format, they focus attention on the accumulation of disciplinary knowledge. With explicitly defined standards for their rating, it is implied that failure, or at least inadequate performance, is possible. This anticipates the expectation that readiness assessment (both formal and informal) can and should be undertaken at two points, before and during the kindergarten year. The first would be a prekindergarten assessment of readiness to determine whether students have the necessary skills to achieve the curriculum objectives during the year and the second is assessment during the year to determine whether the objectives have in fact been attained. Depending on the local interpretation of the meaning of readiness, unready children could be held out or put in special programs to increase their readiness.

The District Report Card

One way of understanding the kindergarten curriculum is to examine the expectations that define performance. Freeman and Hatch (1989) used report cards as representations of expectations for kindergarten performance represented by report cards. Using a stratified sample of kindergarten report cards from Ohio school districts, the authors addressed the following questions: (1) What are kindergarten children expected to be able to know and do? (2) What assumptions about child learning and development do the report cards represent? (3) What aspects of development are most valued? (4) What is the organization of these report cards and what kinds of marking procedures are used? These questions are used to examine the report cards used in the Thomas district. A list of the objectives listed on the Thomas kindergarten report card can be found in Appendix 4.

Organization

Freeman and Hatch found three types of organizational patterns in the report cards they examined: chronological lists (with sets of skills grouped by reporting period), skills lists (with a place to mark mastery for each marking period), and strands (organized into categories of skills, attributes, or attitudes which represent the emphasis in the curriculum). The Thomas report card had a strand organization with the following categories: Personal Information, Integrated Activities, Behavioral Skills, Motor Development, Math Readiness, Language Arts/Reading Readiness, Recognizes Letters & Sounds, Recognizes Colors & Shapes, and Recognizes Numerals.

One aspect of organization not discussed by Freeman and Hatch was the timing of evaluation on the report card. Thomas kindergartners did not receive a report card at the end of the first quarter. This policy is based on the belief that the teachers do not know the kindergartner well enough at that point in the year to make a valid evaluation of his/her performance.

The report card also had space to record parent conference attendance, attendance by quarter, and judgment as to whether work was affected by absences or tardiness. Two blank spaces were included for addition of skills that were not listed on the report card. No space was allocated for notes to parents or for narrative comments on the child's progress.

Marking Patterns

Three types of marks were used to represent evaluations on the Thomas kindergarten report card. In the categories of Personal Information (can give) and Integrated Activities (participates in), checks were given if performance was satisfactory. For Behavioral Skills, part of Motor Development, Math Readiness, and Language Arts/Reading Readiness, the skills were rated O (Child is doing very well), S (Child is making satisfactory progress), N (Child needs time and help to develop, and I (Not graded at this time). Items attained were circled for some Motor Skills, Recognizes Letters & Sounds, Recognizes Colors & Shapes, and Recognizes Numerals. These marks reported progress relative to an assumed, normative standard. Except for the items which were circled when attained, a child's performance was being compared "relative to an absolute external standard or a group norm rather than relative to the child's own previous performance or potential for growth and improvement" (p. 599). In this evaluation model, children were assessed relative to a normative distribution of characteristics or behaviors. A positive-negative continuum of performance was portrayed by these marking patterns bounded by "Child is doing very well" and "Child needs time and help to develop."

Expectations

The skills listed on the report card can be used as evidence of what kindergarten students are expected to know and do. Comparing the items on the Thomas report card with those examined by Freeman and Hatch, there was considerable overlap between the two sources. Items that appeared on more than 50% of the Freeman and Hatch's sample of report cards matched the Thomas card in every case except "Dresses self," "Follows rules," and "Completes work" (from the Freeman & Hatch sample). Conversely, a number of the Thomas items did not appear on the most frequently occurring study cards: "Can give birthday"; "Draws basic shapes"; "Controls large muscles"; "Controls small muscles"; "Recognizes and completes patterns"; "Combines and separates sets of objects"; "Speaks in complete sentences"; and "Uses drawings and written symbols to record thoughts." It appears that the Thomas report card represents a broader curriculum than the Freeman and Hatch sample. The first four report card objectives listed here (from Can give birthday through Controls small muscles), are also not included in the Core Conceptual Objectives; indicating that they are in addition to the standard district curriculum.

Theoretical Orientations

Freeman and Hatch used a categorization scheme developed by Schickedanz et al. (1982) to examine the philosophical orientations underlying their report cards. Report cards with a maturationist orientation assumed that immaturity was the cause of a child's inability to meet expectations. "Needs more time to develop" was used in this type of report card. Behaviorist assumptions were represented by lists of skills in behavioral objective format and organized from simple to most complex. Interactionist philosophy could be seen in report card elements that considered both the individual and environmental aspects of learning. In their study, over half of the report cards had combinations of orientations. The Thomas report card was a combination card, having components of all three theoretical orientations. Maturationist ideas were shown in the performance evaluation "Needs more time and help to develop," behaviorist theory was evident in statements such as "Recognizes letters & sounds," and interactionist ideas in items like "Uses drawing and written symbols to express thoughts." In some ways, a maturationist perspective predominated in a report card that clearly used a time premise to explain deficit and remediation. When a maturationist perspective is used in kindergarten education, the key to remediation is time, allowing the child to mature more to meet the demands in the setting. The evaluation statement did include the idea of providing more help in addition to time for attainment of these objectives, which softens the pointedness of time as a remediation technique. From the combined use of both time and help, it would appear that the district was spanning both the maturational and interventionist perspectives.

The analysis of the Thomas report card revealed that the focus of the kindergarten appeared to be on the mastery of specific skills, particularly in work habits, reading, and math readiness. From this, it is fair to say that Thomas report cards represented an academic focus to the kindergarten program. The evaluative statements on the cards included both positive and negative comments, which implied that children can fail in their expected performance.

The lack of focus on play, which was the cornerstone of kindergarten curriculum until the late 1970s, was also indicative of the press to achieve discrete academic skills in preparation for later school experience. This emphasis represented an investment in activities that would increase the probability of success in later academic settings and a devaluing of activities and experiences that were oriented to the enrichment of the child's present life. In light of present understanding of developmental theory, which underscores the importance of play as a mode for the child's construction of knowledge (Saracho, 1986), the value statement underlying the Thomas district's deemphasis of play departs sharply from consensus within the academic community.

Freeman and Hatch question the very process of grading kindergarten performance, agreeing with Napier (1976) that especially when scoring systems compare children to some standard, the onus of failure is placed squarely on the child's shoulders. When marking systems are anchored on a "Satisfactory" evaluation, it suggests that performance unlike that described by the objective is unsatisfactory and therefore unacceptable. This reflects a normative approach which sorts children into ready and not ready groups for instruction and promotion. It implicitly puts the curriculum in the foreground of concern and implies that the child must fit performance expectations. This is in direct opposition to the National Association for the

Education of Young Children's statement of Developmentally Appropriate Practice (1987), which makes a distinction between the following appropriate and inappropriate practice:

> Each child is viewed as a unique person with an individual pattern and timing of growth and development. The curriculum and adults' interaction are responsive to individual differences in ability and interest. Different levels of ability, development, and learning styles are expected, accepted, and used to design appropriate activities (p. 54).

versus

> Children are evaluated only against a predetermined measure, such as a standardized group norm or adult standard of behavior. All are expected to perform the same tasks and achieve the same narrowly defined, easily measured skills (p. 54).

Comparing the Core Conceptual Objectives and the Kindergarten Report Card

It could be assumed that the report card is a performance evaluation of student proficiency in mastering the kindergarten curriculum. The report card and curriculum should be connected to a large degree in terms of the content and behaviors they represent. However, when an attempt was made to map the district objectives to the report card performance standards, I found places where the match was incomplete. Some report card items could be interpreted in the context of several objectives; for example "Distinguishes likenesses and differences in objects" could map onto both Science or Math objectives. Some objectives were not covered on the report card, which in fact is reasonable if the report card is seen to be a sample of the skills taught in kindergarten. More surprising were the report card items that were not included in the Conceptual Objectives list (see Appendix 5 for a referenced list of item matches). If skills are not listed in the objectives, what rationale is there for including them on the report card? This discrepancy results in variable interpretations of the appropriate document to use as the final authority for kindergarten curriculum decisions. In fact, this came up as an issue several times during the study and will be discussed later.

In summary, the Thomas School District Kindergarten curriculum was guided by the Core Conceptual Objectives and the common Kindergarten Report Card. The Core Conceptual Objectives were organized by subject matter area, which indicated a downward extension of the elementary curriculum structure into the kindergarten. The primary focus was on the mastery of academic skills, with only 17% of the objectives related to social-emotional development focused primarily on rule-oriented behaviors. As written the objectives contain rating criteria which imply a pass-fail mentality. Although it is implicitly noted that children can fail the kindergarten objectives, no mechanism was provided for remediation or placement consequences when children fail. Little integration existed among the objectives or between the academic focus and the behavior oriented types of skills listed.

The Thomas Report Card had a focus on skill mastery, again with an academic focus with standards that have a positive-negative performance continuum. There was little focus on play as a worthwhile part of the kindergarten program; the omission of play, combined with the academic focus seems to indicate that kindergarten was seen as an investment in skills for later academic payoff. There was a mismatch between the skills listed on the Report Card and the objectives covered by the Core Conceptual Objectives, with a number of report cards items unreferenced in the objectives for curriculum.

To understand how the kindergarten curriculum was personalized in each local school setting and to explore the construction of the local meaning of readiness, I now turn to a description of those processes, starting with the case of Fulton Elementary.

CHAPTER 5

಄

FULTON ELEMENTARY

Approaching Fulton Elementary from the west, you pass through a wide expanse of flat farm land dotted with fields of pumpkins, broccoli, corn, and grazing sheep, cattle, and horses. The area has a decidedly rural feeling, with many more pickup trucks than are seen in Boulder. Occasionally you might pass a truck carrying migrant workers on their way to the fields; sitting together on the back of a flat-bed truck. Past the grain elevators and over the railroad tracks, you head to the town of Fulton, which pops up out of the fields with little warning. At the edge of town there is a group of trailers with children and puppies playing outside. A public health clinic is housed nearby. At the center of Fulton is the downtown area, with small commercial buildings housing bars, restaurants and the local paper. Around a truck in front of the Pasttime Tavern, a group of men are gathered talking. As you drive down the street you see people out on their porches sitting in porch swings. Most of the townspeople know each other well and are catching up on the news.

Fulton was one of three small towns within about five miles of each other that share a school on the Colorado plains. Fulton, Delano, and Goodyear were close enough that families move back and forth among them as if they were different parts of the same town. The people who lived here were primarily working class; they were truck drivers, factory workers, manual laborers, semi-skilled laborers, migrant workers. There had been a slow trickle of new rural professionals moving in during the last few years; they were in the minority. The recent recession had left this area hard hit; many jobs were lost in the oil industry and the factories. In most families, both parents worked out of necessity, not by choice. There had been an increase in "moving away from the rent," which a Fulton resident described as follows: "A lot of them move in and out of the district; moving away from the rent. You know, they live there for three months and they're going to be evicted so they move on somewhere else for three months before they get evicted and move on. So there's a lot of economic hardship right now." Because of the upheaval caused by hard times, the area had an interesting mixture of long and short term roots. Some had families who have lived in the Fulton area for generations, others had been there since they got a job at the turkey plant when they left high school. Some came for a few months at a time, up from Texas or Mexico to work the fields. Most of the important information in the area, like signs at the health clinic, was in both Spanish and English.

Fulton Elementary was at the edge of the town of Fulton, a single level modern building that stood out against the bright blue sky. Larger than it looked from the front, it had one of the biggest student populations in the Thomas School District housing over 700 students in grades kindergarten through six. It was surrounded on three sides by fields and backed to Fulton High School on the fourth. Portable classrooms sat between the new building and old Fulton Elementary, which was used by the Community School program. A large playground with new, wooden play structures was almost always busy, during the day with students and after school with neighborhood children. The school was arranged in pods around the Instructional Materials Center and its interior was bright and airy. Hallway windows allow those moving through the school to catch a glimpse of classroom action. Built during the open classroom movement in the 1970s, the classrooms were originally large open spaces shared by groups of teachers. They had been divided over the years into single classroom units.

Fulton Elementary worked with many special needs students and had a number of special instructional programs. Out of five sections of kindergarten, three were extended-day classrooms. Fulton had a strong bilingual education program and was designated as a Chapter One school by the federal government. More than 40% of Fulton students were eligible for the federal Free and Reduced lunch program. With so many working parents, there were not many parent volunteers available to work in the school. Aide time was allocated primarily to special programs. Teachers with regular education classes found it necessary to work out ways to get all of their preparation work done, with little planning time or help.

The school worked hard to forge strong ties with its families. Many activities that provided entertainment and education for the residents were held at the school. The Community School program had activities planned almost every night of the week at school. Because parents could not come into school frequently to talk with teachers and staff, communication between home and school was a key issue. Taking into account the language level of many of the parents, the rule of thumb at Fulton was that anything sent home should be at a third grade reading level.

Many children travelled quite a distance by bus to and from school. In the past, this resulted in important school papers getting lost. Parents had a hard time keeping track of their children's work, exacerbating the disconnection between home and school. The school had developed a policy, known as "The Folders," to try to alleviate the problem. Most notes and student work done during the week were saved in an individual folder for each child and sent home every Friday. On Monday morning, parents were to send the folder back to school, signed, with any incomplete work finished as requested. The school expected that parents were more likely to see school papers when they were gathered together this way and because "Folders" was a school policy, almost all students consistently brought them back to school.

The staff at Fulton was very large and since Carole Brock-Carlino became the principal four years earlier, they had been trying to work together as a team. They had made a concerted effort to get away from the "closing the door and working alone" model of teaching and move to staff relationships that help them see each other as resources. Teachers tried to share ideas and materials so that children could get what they need. Ms. Carlin, one of the kindergarten teachers at Fulton described it this way:

> We have a pretty good staff relationship and we can talk to each other and pass our ideas on. It takes a few years for people to feel comfortable about changing things; in the past, there were a lot of teachers who thought this was their classroom and this was their job to do alone. Now things are much more open and people work together and share. Like I had these Spanish speaking kids who were ready to start working on a little bit of reading so I went to the first grade teacher and asked her what she had because I couldn't find anything. She gave me lots of names of books and then I did find some. So there's a freedom to be able to do that kind of thing. We have the first

grades come down and read to us and if we have something
going on we might invite them down or even bigger kids. The
older kids come and help sometimes.

Kindergarten at Fulton

Going to kindergarten was their first school experience for
many children around Fulton. A number went to pre-school but
many stayed at home or with a babysitter during the day. The
kindergarten experience started when parents registered their
children in the spring for entrance in the fall. In the spring, parents
filled out forms and gave information that was pertinent to their
child's school enrollment: birthdate, health history, etc. The school
contacted them by mail in July and August about the kindergarten
screening program, which identified children for the extended-
day kindergarten program. Fulton was a busy place during the
screening period, with parents bringing their children in to take
the one hour battery of tests. Parents were notified the week before
school started whether their child qualified for extended-day
placement. If children did not qualify or their parents refused
to allow them to participate, they were placed in one of the two
sections of half-day kindergarten at Fulton.

Alice Carlin taught one of the half-day classes. She was a
veteran teacher, with twelve years with kindergartners in her
sixteen years of teaching. Much of that time had been spent at
Fulton. Ms. Carlin was an athletic looking woman with a shock
of prematurely gray hair who did everything with authority and
conviction. Living in Fulton for the last seventeen years, Ms.
Carlin had two roles in the community; she was both a teacher
in the local school and a neighbor. She saw the parents of present,
former, and future students at the grocery store, the post office,
at church. Alice took being a community member very seriously
and incorporated it into her job:

> Well, part of my job is to get these kids started at school and
> I'm real involved in the community around here too. Working
> with parents, that's real important to me, too. Living in this
> community, I do get a lot of comments and questions from parents
> so it's a pretty touchy situation. Other times it's a pretty nice
> one cause you can really help people you know. Whenever they're
> frustrated and they see my own kids as being less than perfect
> too... Some teachers don't want to be in the community where
> they work, but to me that's kind of a brush off. Especially in

> this area because it's a really small, close-knit area... Working
> with the parents in the community is pretty important to this
> job and working with the kids.

With a four year old still at home, Ms. Carlin taught the afternoon
kindergarten section, sharing a classroom with Joan French who
taught the morning session. They had worked together for a long
time and divided up the responsibility for developing activities
and materials for the classroom.

In August of 1989, when my study began, Alice and Joan
met at school the week before classes started to get the room in
shape, to put up bulletin boards, and to talk about the themes
they would focus on for the year. They decided which toys to
put out on the shelves, and when to open the easel area or the
water table. As they worked, they could hear the children going
through the screening program next door. Infrequently they heard
sobs and someone hollering, "Mommy! Don't leave me here!"
Everyone was anticipating the coming year with high hopes.

At this point, I turn from a general description of the setting
at Fulton to a more specific description and analysis of the process of constructing a meaning of readiness there. To explore
this process, the focus will be the themes about readiness that
emerged in my interactions with Fulton's parents, teachers, and
children and consequent analysis of the actors, interpretations,
task structures and motives. I begin this section with a vignette
about Ellen, the mother of a soon-to-be Fulton kindergartner
named Hilary.

"Getting a Good Start"

From the kitchen window, Ellen can see Hilary swinging in
the back yard. The way that she kicks her feet makes Ellen catch
her breath; she's sure that Hilary will come flying out of the swing
and land with a horrible thud by the garden. She hasn't done
it yet though and neither has her little brother. Maybe the thing
is safe.

"Seems like that girl swings for hours," Ellen thinks shaking
her head. Turning away from the window, she spies the Kindergarten Screening notice on the refrigerator door. Tomorrow is the
big day. Can't believe her baby is going to school! Asking about
getting school supplies and new clothes and wondering what she'll

do and who she'll see, Hilary's never asked so many questions. Sometimes Ellen wonders who is more excited about this—Hilary or herself. Living in a small town and staying home with her, Ellen worries that Hilary really doesn't have many friends her own age. Kindergarten should give her all kinds of opportunities to make friends. Finally, a social life.

It was hard to tell Hilary about the test tomorrow, because she didn't really have a good idea of what it would involve. "They just want to ask you some questions to find out what you know," was all that she could come up with. Wished she knew more than that herself. Maybe they'll fill her in when she goes in for the test with Hilary. She's not even sure what to ask.

Maybe she's a little prejudiced, but school seems like it should be wonderful for Hilary. She knows her colors and her shapes; she can even write her name. That test should be a breeze. Just hope that she'll be able to do things like following directions when her teacher wants her to do something... and behaving herself... Can she remember to be quiet? She'll be learning her ABC's and her numbers; maybe even learn to read a little! Getting a good start in school is so important. If she likes it, everything else will be easier. Hope she gets a good teacher—

With a whack, the door slams and Hilary bounds into the kitchen. "Is it time for lunch yet?"

What Does Getting a Good Start Mean for People at Fulton?

Kindergarten is a big step, not only for the children going to school but for their parents. It is the first step away from home for many children, whether they had stayed at home with mom or had gone to the babysitter's house. It is symbolic of independence, of education, of growing up. In interviews with different groups of parents from Fulton in the month before their children entered kindergarten (n=6) and at parent-teacher conferences in November (n=6), one theme that emerged was that the purpose of kindergarten was to get a good start. They saw it as a beginning.

When Fulton parents talked about kindergarten, theme of a good start was defined with four dimensions. For some parents (n=5), a good start meant that their child would get a grasp of the fundamental concepts like learning the alphabet and numbers. Mark's mother talked about what she hoped kindergarten would be like for her son: "Basically, to get him started on the basic fundamentals. Writing, the alphabet, learning it, counting, becoming group oriented, able to handle different situations that he'll experience in kindergarten." In her vision of kindergarten, Mark's mother wanted him to get the skills he needed to build a foundation for school. She wanted him to learn his ABC's and numbers and to begin to write. In addition, she mentioned some social-emotional skills that would help him in the classroom, dealing with many children and learning to cope with new situations.

This social component is the second part of a good start. Some parents (n=3) hoped that their children would develop people oriented skills so that they could get well along with others:

> I'm hoping that they have a good quality of teacher there that can teach them the things they need to learn. Justin is very bright, extremely smart—has a good vocabulary and I think if he can start out now learning how to deal with the public and everything, he'll have a good chance of turning out to be somebody when he grows up.

This social aspect of getting a good start is the traditional heart of the kindergarten curriculum and involves that shift away from having a large proportion of an adult's attention at home to being one of a group of more than twenty at school.

Another dimension of getting a good start focused on the need to develop good school attitudes. Several (n=4) parents viewed kindergarten as the place where their children would learn to love school and learning. They were convinced that if those foundational attitudes were formed at the beginning of their children's formal education, they would find life easier as they went through school. Mark's mother was a high school dropout who did not have much support from her family as she went through school. She wanted to make sure that things were different for her son:

> That he would enjoy it and that he would have the want to try. I never had backing as far as parents and stuff. I believe that's a very important issue for young kids. If they can enjoy it in elementary and in the first couple of years, they can make it the rest of the time.

The fourth dimension of getting a good start portrayed kindergarten as preparation for later schooling or life. The parents who shared this theme (n=4) did not think of kindergarten as having an intrinsic value of its own; instead they focused on its role in getting children ready for later experiences. Hilary's mother was concerned that her daughter would spend the kindergarten

year playing and then find herself in over her head when she
went to first grade the following year:

> Well, I want her to learn how to write her name and her
> ABC's and to really learn what's going to happen when she
> gets into first grade. More times than not, kids in kindergarten
> just kind of play all day and they don't learn anything and
> then when they get in first grade, it's harder for them. I just
> want them to be prepared for what happens when they do get
> into the higher grades.

For these parents, the connection between kindergarten and the
rest of their child's life is clear: the kindergarten sets things up
for later learning. To do this successfully, the curriculum must
take into account the skills that are necessary for each successive
level, emphasizing a linear approach to education and knowledge.

Finally, Karl's mother turned the idea of getting a good start
on its head by defining it in terms of what would make a bad
start. She was worried about the fact that he had a birthdate
very close to the enrollment cutoff and was concerned that he
might be too young to benefit from kindergarten this year. She
was playing with the idea of holding him out and sending him
when he was six and more mature, "I don't know. I say some
of these kids... they just look so tiny. They're in there and it's
just push, push, push. Well, they're going to be in school for twelve
years. If they get a bad start... It just makes me wonder sometimes
about going in that early." Her concern about youngness (which
will be elaborated later) provides a context for her interpretation
of how the kindergarten provides a good start.

In sum, the Fulton parents talked about four dimensions that
they felt were important to providing their children with a good
start. For them a good start included learning the fundamentals
(ABC's and numbers), developing social skills, developing a good
attitude about school and learning, and getting prepared for later
experiences.

The idea of getting a good start in kindergarten was echoed
by Ms. Carlin when I interviewed her for the first time before
the school year started in August. She had broad-ranging goals
for her program that covered three of the four dimensions of
parental ideas about children getting a good start, but she defined
them in a slightly different way. Ms. Carlin talked about developing the academic skills (such as learning the alphabet and
numbers) and getting her students prepared for first grade. In

addition she thought that the kindergarten program worked on meeting the social needs of her students, which included getting them socialized to the school environment. Although the parents saw developing social proficiency as generally becoming a member of a group and learning to deal with new situations, Ms. Carlin included specific school behaviors that characterize good students. These comments focused on behaviors that were idiosyncratic to the school environment and contributed, in her mind, to an orderly, group setting:

> Well I've got a pretty good beginning program that keeps going on in the school. You know, I'm trying to meet their social needs, and get them so they can walk quietly in the halls and so they'll sit still and listen and work independently both in large group and small group kinds of activities and trying to get them where they're academically prepared to go on to first grade.

When I asked her how she thought the principal would define her job as a kindergarten teacher at Fulton, Ms. Carlin again talked about giving her students a good start and broadened the scope of the program to include the parents of her students:

> What's my job description? Well, I think just trying to get the kids—my job is being the first teacher for a lot of these kids and giving them positive feelings about themselves and giving them a good base to start school socially, emotionally, academically, and everything else. And also being with parents, working with them.

Like the parents, Ms. Carlin talked about kindergarten as providing a good start, discussing describing her program and how she thought the principal might interpret her job. She broadened the parents' conception of social development to include school management behaviors. She indicated her concern for classroom management, to which the parents may not be attuned and which provided a dimension for the assessment of readiness which was not initially shared by the parents. She also included working with the parents as part of her job, which the parents did not mention. This indicated that she Ms. Carlin anticipated the parents' role in the kindergarten experience; and that the parents felt that kindergarten would be their child's experience, not their own.

Tables 5 through 7 show how various parents and Ms. Carlin talked about the ways that kindergarten provides a good start for children:

Table 5
Kindergarten as Getting a Good Start

Parents interviewed before kindergarten started (by student name)	Fundamental skills	Social interaction	Attitudes for learning	Preparation for later
Mark	Get started on basic fundamentals, writing, the alphabet, counting	Become group oriented, able to handle different situations	Set up in a good pattern, to enjoy it & want to try	
Justin		*If start now learning how to deal with the public, he will have a good chance to be somebody when he grows up*		If start now learning how to deal with the public, he will have a good chance to *be somebody when he grows up*
Miranda	Just the basic ABC's and the numbers and maybe a little bit of reading	Learn to tone down a little bit		
Katie		Learn some patience		
Hilary	Learn to write her name and her ABC's			Really learn what's going to happen when she gets into 1st grade
Karl		Defined in terms of a bad start		

Table 6

Kindergarten as Getting a Good Start

Parents interviewed at conferences in November	Fundamental skills	Social interaction	Attitudes for learning	Preparation for later
Andrew	Starting to write a little bit. Some math & stuff like that.		Starting with those little minor things to get him going.... in the right direction	
Matt				
Dennis				
Sally			To build self-confidence & enjoy going to school	
Andi	Know the alphabet & numbers. Maybe adding & subtracting		Settle in & concentrate & pay attention. Her ability to want to learn & pay attention	
Annie	A thorough understanding of what Ms. Carlin is teaching	A positive self-image and being able to relate comfortably to a teacher & not be afraid to speak in a group		

Table 7
Kindergarten as Getting a Good Start

	Fundamental skills	Social interaction	Attitudes for learning	Preparation for later
Ms. Carlin	Trying to get them where they're academically prepared	Social needs & getting them so they can walk quietly in the halls & so they'll sit still & listen & work independently in both large group & small group kind of activities		Prepared to go to first grade
How Ms. Carlin thought the principal would view her job	Good base to start school academically	Good base to start school socially	Good base to start school emotionally	

How Does the Model of a Good Start Get Developed?

One way that the meaning of kindergarten as a good start could be examined is to look at the way that parents approached their child's kindergarten year. How did they think about the experience? What were their perceptions of their child's skills and what did they know about the program's structure and demands? Answering these questions provides a context to understand how they came to think about kindergarten and provides the mechanism they might use for attending to standards and making judgments about things like readiness.

Talking to the Fulton parents was a really upbeat experience. These were clearly parents who were excited for their children to start school, especially because they thought that their children were above average. Parents talked about their children as being bright, smart, quick to catch onto things. Some were even worried that they might be bored by the material that was presented in kindergarten:

> Of course, we may be being prejudiced like a lot of other parents, but we think that she's pretty smart for her age. We are looking forward to it because we think she'll do real good. She can already write her alphabet, her capital letters. She can't read. She's real willing to learn and we're just real enthusiastic about it... She loves books, she *loves* reading. So that's going to be a real asset when she learns to read.

> We were just pretty much excited because in general, she seems to have above average intelligence. That by itself was something that we were looking forward to see how she would handle things. She's really quick to pick things up... Her memory is fantastic.

> I wouldn't want him to get real bored already but I do feel like if he doesn't go now he's going to get bored. I think he pretty much knows what they're going to teach him. He knows his ABC's, he knows how to count to 1000... I just hope that he doesn't get bored, knowing all this already.... He would probably get ornery or mean or just not do very good, I guess.

When I finished with these interviews, I felt like I had talked to parents from Lake Wobegon (the mythical town where all the children are above average). Of the twelve parents interviewed, six described their children as smart or bright, three felt that they were quick to catch onto things, and four worried about what might happen if their child got bored by the kindergarten activities.

There was a solid pattern to the way that these parents rated
their child's ability vis-à-vis kindergarten, but the frequency of
these responses does not tell the whole story. In comparing how
one group of the parents talked about their children before school
started and another group talked at the time of the first parent-
teacher conference in November, there seemed to have been an
adjustment in how a child's performance was perceived and
ranked by her parents. In the interviews with parents before the
school year started, each of the parents used one of the descriptors
that indicated that they felt their child had superior ability. When
a different group of parents was interviewed after they had spent
the first quarter in school, the tone of discourse had changed.
They were happy with their child's kindergarten experience so
far, but this group was much less likely to describe their son or
daughter in such glowing terms. Table 8 shows how the pre-
kindergarten parents frequently spoke of their child's ability when
asked about their thoughts about their child's school enrollment.
Note the relatively small number of x's in the lower half of the
table, which depicts how the interviews at parent-teacher conferences rarely elicited reports of ability.

Table 8
Parental Descriptions of Their Kindergarten Children

Parents interviewed in August (by student name)	Bright	Catches on fast	Parent worried about boredom
Mark		x	x
Justin	x	x	x
Miranda			x
Hilary	x		x
Katie	x		
Karl	x		
Parents interviewed during November conferences (by student name)			
Andrew			
Matt			
Dennis			
Sally	x		
Andi	x	x	
Annie	described as well-prepared		

Why did Fulton parents so confidently voice their perceptions of their child's abilities before they started kindergarten? How did that voice become muted as the year proceeded? One way of looking at these questions is to examine what parents knew and expected about kindergarten at these two points of the year.

Anticipating the Kindergarten Experience

In talking to parents before their children entered school in August, it was apparent that they did not know much about what this thing called kindergarten was all about, beyond what they might remember from going to kindergarten, if in fact they went. Their expectations were relatively global and the message that came through in their talk was that they were excited about this experience for their child. They were looking forward to their child learning the alphabet and numbers and getting a good start. Their talk focused on their child, rather than the program, as evidenced by their glowing descriptions of how their child would do in kindergarten. Hilary's mother's response was typical when she answered the question "What are you expecting her kindergarten year will be like?"

> We have real good feelings about it so far. As far as exactly what it involves and what they'll be doing, I don't know yet. I have a lot of questions for them when I take her in for her screening. At this point, and I guess they won't know what to tell me until she takes this screening test... I don't know exactly what we're in for yet. We have really good feelings about it. We have an idea about what the basics are for any kindergartner. As far as exactly what they're going to be doing, we really don't know yet.

Three parents, including Hilary's mother, even went so far as to mention that they had not talked to anyone about their child's upcoming kindergarten entrance. There did not appear to be a network to provide parents information about the kindergarten program before their child was enrolled, beyond knowing that they had to take a test. Two of these parents were putting their first child in school in the fall.

Three of the six parents discussed the extended-day program briefly. Mark's mother explained that it was structured to be more extensive than the shorter, half-day program:

> The extended day is more extensive. They give the kids the
> structure, they have more time. They help them with their motor
> skills and stuff like that. Whereas the morning class doesn't really
> have that much time. They just get them going with the basics
> that they need for kindergarten.

The other two focused on the types of children to which the
program was geared. One said that it was for less skilled children:
"Well they have a full-time, all-day class for the less skilled
students, it'll be only a half-day for the most skilled students.
I don't want to say smarter or brighter, you know." The other
understood that it was for younger children and those who were
having problems:

> Out here they have an all-day kindergarten for the younger kids
> and for the ones that are having problems in special areas...
> it goes an hour less than the regular school, but it's there to
> help the younger kids, to help the special-ed kids get through
> the problems that they can't get through on a half a day schedule.

These parents had developed an idea about what the extended-
day program was like and not surprisingly from the way that
they portrayed it, only the first mother was interested in having
her child placed there. Her son had gone through Head Start and
had moderate speech and language problems. She saw the
extended day program as a way that he could have more time
in the structured school setting. Two of these three parents already
had children in Fulton Elementary and probably got much of
their information through their interactions with the school.

When the parents talked about the kindergarten program at
Fulton, they did not seem to know much about the curriculum
or its focus. Some of them indicated that they had not talked
to anyone about the program and some only made the distinction
between the extended-day and half-day programs. Their understanding of Fulton kindergarten was limited to programmatic
alternatives and general understandings from their experience
in kindergarten. Imagine comparing these parents, who had
almost no information about school with parents who knew things
about a school's kindergarten which would allow them to make
a comparison among the the school's curriculum, their hopes for
their child's kindergarten experience, and an assessment of how
their child's abilities matched the first two. Given their information base, the Fulton parents were not in a position to make

judgments of the adequacy of the kindergarten program before their child started school or of how their child would fit into that program. Because they did not have this information, they talked about readiness for school in a different way than they would have if they had knowledge of the program.

Reflecting on the First Quarter of Kindergarten

After parents had some experience with the kindergarten program, they possessed more information to allow them to begin making judgments about how their child was progressing. When the parents I talked to at conferences reflected back on what they had been thinking about their child's upcoming enrollment in August, they sounded very much like the parents I interviewed at that time. They talked about being excited about their child going to kindergarten (n=2) and did not express many concerns (n=4). They probably felt much like the group that spoke so glowingly about their children before they started, feeling that their child should have no problems with the kindergarten program.

The parents varied greatly in terms of the kinds of things they were thinking about after their child had completed the first quarter of school. Only one of them had a specific concern: Dennis' mother was upset that his handwriting was so messy compared to his older sister's. Andi's parents were more generally wondering what Ms. Carlin was teaching because Andi just talked about the fun things she did in school, not hard work. They also wanted to make sure that she was behaving. Five of the parents felt that they had an understanding of what was going on in the classroom from the papers that came home weekly.

Matt's mom had an interesting perspective on his first quarter in kindergarten. She was also the mother of a fifteen-year-old daughter and she could compare the experience her daughter had ten years ago with what Matt had been doing the last few months. She was one of two mother helpers in Ms. Carlin's classroom, so she had more exposure than other parents to what her child did in school every day. She was amazed by how much more they were doing in Matt's class this year:

> I don't think that I really had any apprehensions because he had gone to preschool so I think that I was really prepared for kindergarten. Then I have an older daughter. But it just really amazes me the difference—she's 15—between the kindergarten

program when she was in and when he is in now... Like when she was in, they didn't start writing their sentences and sounding out words and all that. That really amazed me. It's just wonderful. And getting into their numbers and all this. I was shocked.

Changes in the kindergarten curriculum were mentioned by Ms. Carlin as well and will be discussed later.

With a quarter of kindergarten behind them, the parents were no longer focusing their talk on their child alone. They now considered their children in the context of what they understood about the kindergarten program, and they appeared to feel comfortable with its demands and their child's ability to perform. Some of the excitement had probably faded, so they were not quite so expressive about their child's abilities.

When I asked Ms. Carlin what she thought Fulton parents expected for their child's kindergarten experience, she talked about academic expectations that were too high and about developing a good attitude toward school:

Ms. Carlin: Sometimes I think it's too much. Too much academic kinds of expectations.

Int: Where do you think they get that?

Ms. Carlin: Oh, from the community. From their neighbors. Especially if they spend the day, the parents [want to know] do their kids need more readiness kind of activities... Some parents expect them to be reading in kindergarten and some kids are. And that's really pushing it as far as I'm concerned... It's really hard because some of them don't expect anything,... but the other ones push their kids too much... But I think that most of them have a pretty good attitude towards school and just expect their kids to learn how to get along. A lot of the social behaviors and stuff and learning how to work in the classroom. And then learning their numbers and I think most parents are really satisfied with what their kids are learning in kindergarten... So I feel like whatever their expectations are, whether they're academic, social or behavioral or whatever, for the most part we meet them. And it depends on the family. They're hard too, each one has totally different expectations. In kindergarten, a lot of them will come and think, "Oh, we didn't

do all this stuff in kindergarten," and then the
others are saying, "Well, why didn't you do this
and this?" And then if they come from a real
traditional kind of background, it's "Well, why
aren't you having all these worksheets and papers?" And I say, "Well look at all this stuff the
kids do without worksheets, papers, and stuff like
that." So some of them do expect a lot of worksheets... but we don't do a lot of worksheets.

Ms. Carlin said that she had had some frustrating experiences
with parents demanding more academic experiences for their
children. She had to work hard to get them to understand the
value of what they were doing in the classroom. In my observations
and conversations with parents, however, none of them expressed
a concern that the level of curriculum was pitched at too low a
level. In fact, with the parents I interviewed before school started,
fear that their child would be bored with the activities in kindergarten was a predominant theme. No one mentioned boredom in
the conference interviews.

*Other Differences Between Parents & Teacher in the
Meaning of Getting a Good Start*

Several of the parents were looking forward to the social
opportunities that would be available to their children in the school
environment. Parents could anticipate a whole new dimension
added to their child's existence when they could interact with
peers. Almost every parent (n=5) I interviewed before the school
year started indicated that they were excited about their child
meeting others. As Hilary's mother said in the vignette, living
in a small town and staying home with your child, it is hard
for her to make many friends her own age. Miranda's mother
said that she was looking forward to "a lot of extracurricular
activities and meeting and interacting with other kids." Mark's
mother felt that he had been isolated due to his hearing loss and
that she was "looking forward to the fact that he'll get to meet
a mixture of people, different situations."

The parents I talked with during conferences echoed this
sentiment as well. Four of these parents said that they had looked
forward to the social growth that their child would have during
her kindergarten year. Annie's mother talked about how she
needed to make some friends:

In our neighborhood, her best friend moved in August. So I knew that was coming. And most of the neighborhood kids are boys and because she is the age she is, she hasn't yet been allowed to expand so I was looking forward to her being in an environment where she had the opportunity to make friends. Cause she needed that.

Of those four parents, Dennis' mom and Sally's parents were a little bit concerned about how their child would handle being with a large group of children. Dennis was isolated because he lived out in the country: "We live out in the country and that was one of my concerns, how he would adjust to being with a group of children, since we don't have that. Cause he's kind of quiet." Sally's parents had made a decision to keep her at home until kindergarten and they worried about how she would make the transition into a large group of children.

The Fulton parents valued the social opportunities that kindergarten provided, both before their child started kindergarten and as the year progressed. None of them talked about the educational or academic value that these opportunities provided, indicating that these social experiences had value in themselves and that they felt that kindergarten served more than just an academic purpose. To these parents, getting a good start involved an ever widening social world. Interestingly, Ms. Carlin never mentioned social opportunities available to children when she discussed her program. Even though she was a member of the Fulton community and could understand the isolation many of these parents felt, her talk about the social aspect of kindergarten was keyed primarily to school behavior (like learning to be a member of a group or raising a hand to talk) rather than the development of friendships or extracurricular activities.

Ideas About Age and Readiness: A Final Aspect of
Getting a Good Start

The final aspect of getting a good start according to the Fulton parents involved whether they felt their child was ready for kindergarten. When parents were asked to describe the things they were thinking about as their child approached kindergarten enrollment and their concerns, the issues of age and readiness frequently were discussed.

Because age is the legislative marker used to determine whether children may enter school, it is necessarily of interest to parents. In addition, there is an abundance of educational and parental lore associated with (1) the influence that age has on child ability to perform and adapt in the kindergarten classroom and (2) the definition and characterization of readiness for school in individual children. In this section, I will discuss the ways that Fulton parents talked about age and readiness in terms of their child's kindergarten enrollment and experience. Consideration of Ms. Carlin's beliefs and actions related to readiness will be delayed until discussion of the way that work was structured for children in her classroom.

Parents interviewed before school started ranged from not mentioning age and its effects at all (n=2), to a couple of parents who mentioned it in passing, to two parents who had strong concerns about their child's age at school entrance. Katie's mother talked about how her older sons had birthdays close to the enrollment cutoff and had been held back in first grade. She was not really worried about how relative age would affect Katie:

> Both of my boys were at the young end and both of them were held back in first grade which I think made them stronger; that they had to repeat. They knew they weren't stupid... The teachers explained to them that they just need to learn more before they could go on to the next grade. So really as far as being on the young side of age, it doesn't really bother me at all... Even though they are early birthdates they can do just as well as the kids that are older than them.

Miranda's mother thought about how close her birthday was to the age cutoff: "She'll be five in September so she'll be in school a month before she turns five. So we were a little leery about putting her in, being so young." Miranda's preschool teacher told them that she thought Miranda would do fine in kindergarten, so they decided to go ahead and send her.

Both Mark's and Karl's mothers were concerned about the age issue and developed ideas about how it should be handled in relation to school entrance. Mark's mother told me how glad she was that he was going to be six when he got into kindergarten because that would make him stronger:

> I'm happy with him entering kindergarten. He's 5½ now and I'll be glad that he'll be 6 because then he'll be a little bit more mature. He'll feel stronger about himself... I don't think they should put those just 5 year olds in kindergarten. They've still

got a lot of their tendencies to be close to mom and the immaturity. It shows up with the shyness, the awkwardness. I think they need to be a little older.

Karl's mother had recently come to the realization that he was going to be one of the youngest in his kindergarten class and that worried her. Her mother was a kindergarten teacher in another school district and she had heard about the dangers of placing children in school when they were close to the entrance cutoff. At this point, she was seriously considering holding Karl out of school and entering him the following year when he would be six:

> I hadn't really thought about it much until about three months ago. I just thought that he's going to kindergarten. Then I began to think he just had his birthday today (8/12) and it's so close. Maybe if it were three or four months earlier, I'd probably go ahead and put him in. I think three or four months at this age makes a big difference... I just have my reservations and I'm not trying to baby him or anything... My other one, his birthday is November and that's almost a year older... I just thought, his birthday is so late. I began to watch him and I began to think about some things and I've even thought about going to the library and looking at books at what kindergartners should be able to do.

Among the children whose parents were interviewed before school started, five of the six had birthdates that put them in the youngest part of the age distribution for their kindergarten placement. Each of these five had birthdays in August or September in a district that had an October enrollment deadline.

Of the parents I talked to at conferences, only Andrew's mother mentioned age. Considering that Andrew had been retained in kindergarten the previous year and that his teacher had used the ideas of immaturity and Andrew's birthdate as reasons to support the retention, her comments made much sense:

> This is Andrew's second year in kindergarten... When he started last year, he was just kind of young. Because his birthday lands in August. So he just turned five when we stuck him in kindergarten. His teacher last year told me that he was just a little too young for it. He didn't have the patience for it.

There were patterns in the ways that parents interviewed in the month before school started discussed the topic of readiness. Those who had not talked about age either did not mention it or merely said that they had checked the district entrance age and were glad that their children (Justin, Hilary) had met entrance guidelines because they seemed quite ready. The parents who seemed to show some awareness of, but little concern about, the age issue both said that it appeared that their daughters, Miranda and Katie, seemed ready to go to school. Both Mark's and Karl's moms had solid ideas about readiness, one in relation to the general school population and the other in reference to her son. Mark's mother talked about the need for a test for all kindergarten children to make sure that they were ready for the school experience:

> I would make sure that kids are ready for kindergarten... by testing them. Just because they're five years old doesn't mean that they are mentally ready to start... [The test should have] academics to prove that they can do that. Check their motor skills. Interview the kids to see how they are with other kids, to see how they are emotionally... They can be academically smart but emotionally they can be very immature.

After coming to the realization that he was going to be younger than many of his classmates, Karl's mom thought and thought about whether she should put him in kindergarten or wait a year. Much of her confusion came when she compared Karl with his older brother who had a November birthday, making him almost six when he entered kindergarten:

> I don't want to hold him back if he is ready but I just kept watching him... Emotionally I don't think he is ready. He's kind of babyish in some ways still. A little immature in some ways. My other one, his birthday is November and that's almost a year older and he was ready. This one, if I have any reservation, I just feel that you're not going to hurt him by holding him back. And he's just begun to get interested in the alphabet in the last month and the other one... I worked on all his phonics sounds and he knew all that before he came in. But this one wasn't even interested in learning phonics until about a month ago.

In comparing the way that parents talked about age and readiness, it became obvious that they were related. The more concern parents voiced about the impact that age might have on kindergarten success, the more likely they were to have strong feelings about readiness. In Table 9 quotes from parents have been arranged from least concern about age to most concern about age. Note the concomitant pattern for readiness.

Table 9
The Relationship Between Views About
Child Age and Readiness
Pre-kindergarten Interview

Name	*Age*	*Readiness*
Justin		
Hilary		Checked district entrance date... felt she was ready... didn't want to hold her back if we didn't have to
Miranda	She'll be 5 in September so she'll be in school a month before she turns 5. So we were a little leery about putting her in, being so young.	Her preschool teacher seemed to think she was plenty ready to go.
Katie	Both of my boys were at the young end and both of them were held back in 1st grade which I think made them stronger... So really as far as being on the young side of age, it doesn't really bother me at all... Even though they are early birthdates, they can do just as well as the kids that are older than them.	She's ready to go out on her own.
Mark	He's 5½ now & I'll be glad that he'll be 6 because then he'll be a little bit more mature. He'll feel stronger about himself... I don't think they should put those just 5 year olds in kindergarten. They've still got a lot of their tendencies to be close to mom and the immaturity. It shows up with the shyness, the awkwardness.	Would make sure kids are ready... would give test... with academics to prove they can do it... check their motor skills... check emotional development.

Table 9 *continued*
The Relationship Between Views About
Child Age and Readiness
Pre-kindergarten Interview

Name	Age	Readiness
Karl	Then I began to think he just had his birthday today and it's so close. Maybe if it were 3 or 4 months earlier, I'd probably go ahead & put him in. I think 3 or 4 months at this age makes a big difference... I just have my reservations & I'm not trying to baby him or anything... I just thought, his birthday is so late. I began to watch him... & I've even thought about going to the library and looking at books at what kindergartners should be able to do.	I don't want to hold him back if he's ready... Emotionally I don't think he is ready. He's kind of babyish in some ways still. A little immature in some ways... [If] I have any reservation I just feel that you're not going to hurt him by holding him back. And he's just begun to get interested in the alphabet in the last month & the other one... I worked on all his phonics sounds & he knew all that before he came in. But this one wasn't even interested in learning phonics until about a month ago.

For the parents interviewed in November, there was little said about readiness that indicated that they were very concerned at the time of their children's school enrollment. Dennis' mother felt that he should have been in extended day kindergarten rather than half-day because she thought he was slower than his sister and needed the extra help. Andrew's mother felt confident about his readiness this second time around in kindergarten: "I think that extra year between five years old and six years old is the difference" [Andrew, line 197]. Three parents felt very comfortable with their child's readiness as they approached the start of school:

His preschool teacher said that he was more than ready to start kindergarten.

I thought she was ready to come to school. I thought she knew her letters and her colors.

She was so well-prepared. For only a couple months into the school year, she was just so prepared before she got here that I just see repetition of things that she already knew. She knew her shapes and her colors.

Because only one of these parents talked about age in their interviews, no pattern could be found in their accounts of concern about age and readiness.

Issues of age and readiness were quietly salient concerns for some of the Fulton parents as their children approached kindergarten entrance. A few of the interviews indicated that the two topics were connected in the minds of some parents, with a relationship shown in which parents with high concern about age also indicating a concern about readiness. As the year progressed, the frequency of parents mentioning age and readiness shifted from moderate to virtually none, except for a child that had been retained the previous year. This shift can be attributed to the way that Ms. Carlin interpreted readiness for these parents, which is the focus of later discussion.

Kindergarten Tasks at Fulton Elementary

Under the umbrella of giving children a good start, we can look at the kinds of activities that are used to set up that beginning. The ways that the children in Ms. Carlin's classroom were introduced to the concepts of the kindergarten curriculum; the messages that they took away from those activities about learning and school; and the interpretations that informed the development of the Fulton program were all aspects of the construction of the meaning of readiness that will be explored in this next section. To start off this discussion, vignettes will be presented that describe the two general types of tasks that occured in Ms. Carlin's classroom. The first tells about the class and Alex, doing a worksheet on triangles, in which the emphasis is on "doing it right." The second describes how Ms. Carlin's class, and particularly Annie, work on learning to write stories.

"Doing It Right"

"Alex, go sit down at your table. You're being rude." "OK," Alex replies brightly, smiling at Matthew to whom he has been talking for the last five minutes. The main attraction in the classroom was supposed to be the story that Ms. Carlin was reading. Alex heads for his chair at the diamond table and places his face flat on the table, his hands dangling at his sides.

"Alright. We have a lot of work to do today." The children sense that the gears have shifted and they tune in closely. "Today we are going to start on a new shape. What shape did we do the first week?" [She turns and draw a circle on the board]

"Circle."

"And the next week, we did what shape?" Ms. Carlin draws a square on the board.

"Square."

"How many sides does a square have?"

"Four."

"And what's special about those four sides?"

"Same size."

"That's right... This week we're going to work on a shape that has 3 sides. Know what it is?"

The group mumbles, but distinctly you can hear Alex reply, "Triangles."

"Boy, I can hardly hear anybody."

"Triangles," they respond in unison.

"That's right, triangles. Do you know what tri means?"

"Three, three, three, three, three," Alex chants into the table top.

"Three sides. We have a couple of things to do today that have to do with triangles. I noticed that when I was having you draw shapes, that it was kind of hard for some of you to draw triangles, so we're going to have a paper today that has boxes and inside the boxes, you have 3 dots and what you are going to do..."

Penny whispers to Hannah. Ms. Carlin has turned and is drawing 3 dots on the chalkboard and puts a box around them. "Shhhh, we have some people who are talking and not listening... When you draw a triangle, you are going to start at the top and you're going to make one line from the top to this dot at the bottom, then go back up and draw a line to the other dot. Then connect the two dots at the bottom. So you're going to draw your lines: one, two, three. The best place to start is at the top and go down to your sides and make your legs first. Then come across and make the bottom. I want your name to go at the top, on top of this triangle, you see the triangle that is already made? Then in each box, you'll draw what?"

"Triangles."

"And where do you start?"

"The top!"

"Great." Josh, Jack, and Andi hop up and move toward Ms. Carlin to get a paper. "Oh, wait. I have more I need to tell you. Now we also have some funny little animals on our follow-the-directions sheet and you all know the directions to these now. What's the first thing we do?"

"Color it."

"Color it! Do we color these spaces that have the dotted lines?"

"No."

"Which triangles do we color?"

"The bottom ones."

"The bottom, right. We color the ones on the bottom. So you're going to color these, then you are going to cut them out and then you're going to glue this great big one right here on this little guy."

"No."

"No?"

"The big triangle goes with the big bear." Matthew says, correcting her.

"Oh, it goes over here to the *big* one. The little one goes up *here*. Goodness, so I don't need to tell you what to do. You have to remember, see where the scissors are here. You need to cut that all the way off. Last week I think I got some papers where a couple of people forgot to cut that off before they cut out their squares. Remember to try to keep your scissors on those lines very carefully so they stay the same size and same shape that they are right here. And super nice colored and cut papers are gonna get stickers! When you are finished with the drawing paper, come and put it in the Finished Basket and come get the coloring paper. OK, let's get started."

The children swarm around Ms. Carlin to get their papers and then head off to their tables. Ms. Carlin asks her parent helper to circulate around the room and check the children as they work and help them write their name at the top of the paper. Pulling their pencil bags from the baskets at each table, the children settle down to writing their names and drawing the triangles. Ms. Carlin goes from table to table, watching as the students work. At one point she stops to watch Alex, who is doing his triangles in a smooth motion, drawing it counterclockwise from the top. The lines are smooth and fluid. Ms. Carlin stops him and reminds him that he should do the two legs from the top and then connect them from the bottom. As he is almost finished, Ms. Carlin erases a couple of the triangles he has done at the bottom of the page and asks him to do them according to the directions: legs first, then connect across the bottom.

As the children finish the drawing sheet, they show it to Ms. Carlin, then put it in the Finished Basket at the front of the room. They get a coloring sheet from the shelf and head back to their tables. Ms. Carlin continues moving about the room, reminding children to stay in the lines or to turn their papers as they cut. Some are still working on the drawing sheet when others are halfway through the color sheet. The children talk to one another as they complete their work, comparing crayons and size of glue bottle. Those who work quickly place their work in the Finished Basket, put their materials back in their pencil bag, and go to work at Math tubs on the floor. Ms. Carlin will check all of the papers and place them in each child's work folder to go home at the end of the week.

When he finishes both papers, Alex yelps "Hah!" pops up from his chair, and puts his pencil back in his pencil bag. He bounds from the table with a whooshing sound, puts his paper in the basket with a flourish, and bounces to where his friend Jimmy is stacking inch blocks to make a tower. "I can build taller than you!" he says with a broad smile and proceeds to prove his point.

"Learning to Write"

Sitting with her legs crossed, Annie rests her weight on her arms that are bracing her behind her back. A slight smile crosses her face and she cocks her head to the right as she listens to Ms. Carlin.

"...Now, I'll give you the paper—you need brown paper, black paper, and red paper. Look—are they all the same size? No! Which circles would be the bear's eyes?" Ms. Carlin holds up two black paper circles each the size of a half dollar.

"The little ones," the class responds in unison.

"And which would be the nose?" holding up baseball-sized brown circles.

"Big ones!"

"Where do the ears go?" Ms. Carlin holds them on top of her head, looking very much like Mickey Mouse. "On the top?"

"No... on the sides."

"OK, let's get started." Ms. Carlin stands up and gathers up the different sized pieces of paper that the children will cut into circles to make a picture of a bear. Children scramble in front of her to form a column of bodies that push and bump each other. Annie looks blankly at Bob as he tries to get in front of her so that he can stand with Jimmy. Then she raises her eyebrows and shakes her head no. Bob sighs, frowns, and goes to the back of the group to wait his turn.

In front of her, Ms. Carlin has a sea of arms reaching for paper. Over and over again she puts together the sizes of paper that they need, saying them out loud as she makes a pile for each child. "One big brown, two smaller browns, two little blacks, and one little red." As they get their papers, they head to their tables and pull out their pencil bags. Pencils, scissors, and glue come out of the bag and the class sets to drawing circles.

After all of the paper is handed out and the children are sitting at their tables, Ms. Carlin raises her voice and interrupts them briefly.

"When you are finished, you are going to write a story about your bear—and you might want to say, 'My bear.' We need to figure out how to spell that, don't we. My bear. What letter makes the sound 'mmmmm'?" Ms. Carlin turns to the chalkboard, picks up a piece of chalk, turns back to the group and reiterates, "mmmmm."

Annie immediately pipes up, "M!" and the rest of the class follows her lead. Ms. Carlin turns and writes a large M on the board.

"What's next? My. [dragging out the sounds] What makes the sound 'eye'?"

Again, Annie is the first to speak, with several others trailing after her. "I"

Ms. Carlin writes the I next to the M. "My... OK... what's next? We have a new word, bear... bear... What makes the sound 'buh'? Buh-air."

"B" the group answers. Ms. Carlin leaves a space between the I and the B. She turns to the group again.

"Air. What would make the sound 'ay' [long a sound]? Bear [exaggerated]"

"A!" the class says with an enthusiasm that indicates that they are surprised to know the answer.

Turning to write the A, Ms. Carlin says, "Good... A... Buh—Ay—R... What letter makes the sound 'rrrrr'?" She turns and smiles slyly at them and there is a tense silence that fills the room for several seconds. Annie frowns and without making a sound her mouth moves as if she is making the sound 'rrrr.' She smiles and says, "'Rrrrr... R!'"

"Nice job, Annie! 'Mm-eye... buh-ay-rr'... My bear. You might want to start off your story with My bear and tell us something about your bear... First, you are going to cut your bear out and glue him together and then come up to the front, get a piece of paper and write a story about your bear. Everybody OK? Let's get going." With that, Ms. Carlin starts to circulate around the room, reminding children to turn their paper as they cut circles, to use only one drop of glue, to remember to write their names on the bear. They work at various paces, some children flying through the cutting and gluing as if they were on fire; others talking as they work and taking great care to make things symmetrical and even.

At Annie's table, Josh, Jill, and Jack, are working on their bears. Josh and Jack joke back and forth about their scissors and threaten to squirt each other with glue. Annie watches them as she works, laughing but keeping busy. She is the first one done with her bear at the rectangle table and she goes to show Ms. Carlin the final product.

"Very nice, Annie. What do you need to do now?" Ms. Carlin comments as she helps Penny hold the paper as she cuts.

"Write a story?" Annie ventures, looking about 95% sure of herself.

"Right... the paper is up at the front of the room, and you can put your bear on top of the shelves to dry... Did you put your name on it?"

Annie shakes her head yes and places her bear on the edge of the shelves. Then she gets a piece of paper, and returns to her table. The others are still cutting circles. Annie gets out her pencil and below her breath, she repeats "My bear... my bear." She taps her pencil on her head, then starts to copy the words off of the board. Starting at the left, upper corner, Annie copies 'MI BAR.' "My bear... (wwwent)... (wwwent)..." At this point, Ms. Carlin comes up to the table and sits down next to Annie. She doesn't say anything until Annie looks up from her paper with a perplexed look on her face.

"Looks like you've already gotten a good start on your story. What are you working on now?"

"Went... My bear went..."

"OK, went... what letter says the sound 'wuh'? Went"

"W?" Annie says and writes it on the paper.

"Went... What's next? 'Ent, ent... wuh-ent'?"

"N"

"Went-t"

"T"

"OK, what else?"

"Hmmmm... (softly) My bear went... to the park!" Annie chirps smiling. The other children at the table now seem to take notice, sitting and listening as Ms. Carlin and Annie talk.

"To... how would you spell to?"

"T" Annie turns and writes the T on her paper. "The... how do you spell the?"

"The is hard. It starts with the same sound as Thursday... a T and H together say, TH"

Annie writes TH. "Went to the ... park... park."

"What would park start with? Puh-ark."

"P" Annie answers with her head down writing. "Park."

"What letter makes the sound 'rrr'?"

"R" Annie says and as she writes she says, "Park... 'kkk'... K!"

"Good job!" Ms. Carlin says as she pats Annie on the back. "How are you guys doing?" she asks of Jill, Josh, and Jack. "Fine!" Jack replies as he sticks the last ear on his bear. "So, tell me about your bear," Ms. Carlin asks and the process of writing starts all over again with him.

Ms. Carlin's View of Her Program and How It Works

Ms. Carlin had had a lot of experience with kindergartners; twelve years of experience to be exact. She had seen many kinds of programs come through the schools and she developed what she thought were some very solid ideas about how young children should be taught. To understand how she ran her classroom, I will start with a brief description of the activities in which Ms. Carlin typically engaged her students. The following was the schedule for the Fulton afternoon kindergarten:

Fulton Daily Schedule

12:30	Arrival
	Talk time

	Opening:	Helper
		Attendance
		Individual greeting

	Calendar:	Yesterday, today
		Number of days in school (counted with sticks, pennies/dimes, number tape, tally)
		Weather

	Show & tell

1:00	Language Arts activity introduction
	Language Arts activity: story writing, handwriting, reading
1:40	Math tubs
2:10	Recess
2:30	Activity time [computer: Mondays]
3:05	Clean up
3:15	Dismissal

The kindergarten day started for Ms. Carlin's students when they entered the classroom at 12:30 sharp. Ms. Carlin had a policy that children who arrived at school earlier than 12:30 remained outside the classroom. Parents were gently but firmly reminded of this in the beginning of the year and there were few problems after the first couple of weeks. Upon arrival, the children went immediately to sit in a circle at the front of the room to participate in the opening. Opening activities were relatively traditional for a kindergarten. Ms. Carlin tried to take some time for the group to share things; she called this Talk Time. The helper for the day was announced, attendance was taken, and while attendance was sent to the office, she greeted each child individually by going around the circle, shaking hands and asking how they are doing. The calendar activities were from Mathematics Their Way, talking about yesterday and today, the date, counting the number of days in school and representing that number in various ways. Show and Tell came next, with children assigned a day to bring something that represented the topic of discussion for the week. The topic was usually a letter of the alphabet. Plans for the day were discussed at this point, then Ms. Carlin gave instructions for the Language Arts activity, which was done as in a large group. Language Arts activities were typically worksheets to reinforce a concept and/or writing tasks. As children finished the Language Arts project, they had their work checked and went on to Math activities, which were individually or small group oriented and for the most part, unsupervised. Recess followed the Math period and then children had Activity Time, which was a free play period. When Activity Time was over, it is time to clean up and go home.

Examining the activities that took place in Ms. Carlin's classroom, tasks could be sorted out in a number of ways. First, activities could be classified as loosely academically oriented or socially oriented. Academically oriented activities focused on readiness skills and were primarily from the subjects areas of Language Arts/Reading and Math. Socially oriented activities were educationally related (i.e., were derived from the Core Conceptual Objectives for the district) but focused on interpersonal relations and communication. A crude categorization of the activities could be done as follows, with time allocated to that activity in parentheses:

Academic	*Social*
Calendar (10)	Talk Time (5)
Language Arts (40) (worksheets, writing)	Greeting (5)
Math Their Way (30)	Activity Time (35)
Show & Tell (10)	Recess (20)
Total 90 minutes	65 minutes

My discussion of social activities will be brief and mainly focused on the time allocation for various activities in the class-room. Although there were approximately 50% more minutes allocated to academic activities than to social activities, this allotment represents a greater amount for social activities than one would think from the Core Conceptual Objectives, the Report Card or from my discussions with Ms. Carlin. We very rarely discussed activities such as Activity Time (the free play time) and I never saw her talk about them with parents in conferences.

Talk Time was discussed by Ms. Carlin in terms of the language opportunities it provided, so it was one of the activities that could be seen as having a dual role in the classroom. While it was a part of her program that took a substantial amount of time in her kindergarten day, social activities were not perceived by her as a part of her kindergarten program that provided crucial information on readiness.

Another way that activities in Ms. Carlin's program could be sorted was by the underlying message that structured the task. Within the academic tasks, two general kinds of activities could be identified using this scheme. The first was what I will call "doing it right" and the second could be described as "mastering content." Sometimes a single activity would have both of these components; other tasks concentrated on a single dimension, usually mastering content. The two vignettes are illustrative of these categories and I will use them as examples to explain how they differ.

Ms. Carlin used worksheets of various kinds to reinforce concepts that she introduced in class. These worksheets were typically Language Arts and Reading Readiness related and focused on tasks like coloring, tracing, cutting, and handwriting. The class usually did at least one worksheet every day; I observed the children doing as few as one and as many as four during the Language Arts/Reading period. Most of Ms. Carlin's tasks that used worksheets were structured very much like the task in the vignette. Ms. Carlin introduced the activity, gave instructions to the whole class (if there is more than one worksheet, all are introduced before the group got started), the children went to their tables to complete the worksheet, Ms. Carlin circulated around the room and gave very specific feedback, then the worksheets were deposited in the Finished Basket. At some later point, Ms. Carlin checked each paper, making any comments she felt were necessary for parents to understand their child's performance (including requests for work at home) and she placed them in the child's folder to go home at the end of the week.

The main message in doing worksheets in Ms. Carlin's class was "doing it right." By doing it right, I mean completing the process as Ms. Carlin explained it, in the correct order, and coming out with a product that Ms. Carlin felt was acceptable. In the vignette, Ms. Carlin explained to the class how to complete the triangle worksheets after a quick review of the other shapes they had covered. She set up the lesson by telling the class that some

of them were having a hard time drawing triangles so she decided
to give them a triangle drawing paper so that they could get more
practice and learn to do it correctly. She then gave *very* explicit
instructions about the process of drawing a triangle; where to
start and in what order to make the sides. She asked for a
reiteration of the process from the class, then went onto the instructions for the next worksheet. When the students were sent
off to do their worksheets, Ms. Carlin moved about the room to
supervise and give feedback to individuals. This feedback included
verbal praise or reminders and working with individual children
when they had problems completing the task as she had described
it. For example, in the vignette, Alex was making beautiful
triangles, but not in the way that Ms. Carlin had explained in
her instructions. She stopped him, erased several of the ones he
had completed at the bottom of the page and verbally reminded
him of the process: starting at the top, doing the two sides and
then connecting the bottom. Ms. Carlin routinely used an eraser
or gave children a second worksheet when they were having
problems; she did this so that they would have the opportunity
to do the task right. In addition to monitoring their work as they
completed it, children were normally asked to show their papers
to her before placing them in the Finished Basket. This allowed
Ms. Carlin to check them for accuracy so that she could catch
any mistakes that she might have missed as she circulated around
the room; the papers were checked again and marked by Ms. Carlin
before they were placed in the children's folders.

When I asked why it was so important for Alex to follow
her instructions for drawing a triangle when the final product
looked better than most of those done using her process, Ms. Carlin
answered that while the product is important,

> So is picking up the pencil and most importantly, following
> directions—wait until we start the handwriting! Writing over
> a line is really hard, but the most important aspect is *follow-
> ing directions as given in class* [emphasis added]. They need
> to listen and follow instructions so that they can get the process
> down correctly.

This highly specific approach to feedback gave Ms. Carlin
information about individual children, which allowed her to rank
and compare performance on most classroom tasks. It also gave
children in her class clear boundaries of acceptable academic
behavior, with easily expected consequences for going outside

those standards. Evaluation was public, both in the case of Ms. Carlin setting up the worksheet by telling them that she was giving them the paper because they had problems making triangles and in the individual feedback children received as they worked. Finally, it allowed parents to have additional information about their child's performance from the comments she wrote on the worksheets. Ms. Carlin could structure the way that parents interpreted their child's progress through frequent feedback. Ms. Carlin took this as far as adding instructions which were missing on a worksheet, so that parents would know whether their children did it right.

In contrast to work that focused on doing it right, were more open-ended writing activities that occurred almost daily in Ms. Carlin's class. Related to the current classroom theme, the children were presented with some kind of topic (exercise, Johnny Appleseed, wishing wells, and in the case of the vignette, bears) and sent off to write about it. Ms. Carlin used what she calls "the writing process," which involved children learning to write by writing, starting with them putting down any type of symbol (picture or character) to represent their thoughts, and moving to the use of letters to represent words. She saw the writing process as very much a developmental process, with stages that children went through as they learn and grow. She expected her students to start at various points of this developmental process and to progress at their own rates. The content covered on many of the worksheets was seen as part of the writing process, providing structured practice on letter-sound association and handwriting. If children could hear the sound when doing the worksheet, they should be able to incorporate it into their writing at some point.

The only group guidance given by Ms. Carlin was a kind of springboard to writing, in which she had the class spell some word or phrase that would be helpful in writing the story. In the vignette, they worked together to spell My Bear. The group spelling provided students with an idea for how to start their stories and also modeled the writing process by having Ms. Carlin pose questions on sounds within words and having some children (usually those more advanced in letter sound association) venture answers. They were then free to incorporate those words into their story; in this particular case, everyone used these words as the first two words in their stories.

The children in Ms. Carlin's class did not go through the draw-a-picture-then-dictate-a-story stage that is so prevalent in many kindergarten classrooms. Ms. Carlin felt that the dictation mode discouraged children from trying to write on their own: "It makes them feel like they haven't done a good enough job—it's hard enough to get them to write in the first place." If she wanted to remember what the child said the story meant, she waited until they handed it in and then wrote her version on the back of the paper in small and lightly written script.

Many children had difficulty with this format at first. They adamantly said they didn't know how to read, so how in the world could they write? On the day that the class did the bear stories, I sat with Jack as he argued just that. I asked him what he wanted his story to say and he replied, "It went to the park." When I asked him how he would write that, he replied with exasperation, "I don't know how to write. I only know the letters in my name." When I reminded him that there were some words on the board that might help him out, he brightened a little bit and settled down to writing them. After that, we worked on identifying the first sound in each word and Jack wrote down what he thought each of those was. He finished by reading his story to me, surprised that it came out as "My bear went to the park." (written, MI BAR W T P] When I discussed Jack later with Ms. Carlin, she told me that he was really resistant to experimenting with his own writing, not willing to guess or make things up. She later said that she did not think that he was very much of a risk taker.

Ms. Carlin kept the writing papers in a folder for the entire year and shared them with the parents when they came in for conferences. She used this opportunity to explain the writing process to the parents and to give them a picture of what stage their child was in developmentally. For example, this is what Ms. Carlin told Matt's mother at their November parent-teacher conference:

> This is his writing folder. At the beginning of the year, Matt was at the stage where he would only draw pictures—that was how he told his stories. That's where a lot of kids start the year. [She pages through the writing sample, which is arranged in chronological order from the start of the school year]. Then he graduated to writing some letters. He wasn't at the point of copying any letters—you know we sound out some words together and put them on the board and he didn't use those words. He was using his *own* letters to write his *own* story—so they were mostly the letters in his name. [She picks up a paper that looks like a piece of popcorn.] This is the day we made popcorn. We

were writing about things that we could hear, when we were talking about our five senses. He wrote "I HRD" and we had put that on the board to help them come up with things that they could hear. [paging on to the next paper] Here he goes back to using the letters that he knows, not copying from the board the words that we sounded out. Kids tend to go back to previous stages sometimes—you know it's like when they learn to talk— sometimes they do things that seem more babyish, but they just need time to practice. [She closes the writing folder] Matt is really showing great progress in his writing… he is just a little afraid to take risks. With all of the sounds that he has he should be sounding out more words on his own but he is not a risk taker so he doesn't take that step. But that's OK. It'll come.

In conversations with parents at conferences, Ms. Carlin interpreted the writing process and how individual children progressed within it.

How were Doing it Right and Writing activities different in Ms. Carlin's class? The most obvious difference were their foci. For Doing it Right activities, the focus was on completing the process correctly as defined by Ms. Carlin and producing a product that was acceptable to her. In contrast, writing was both a means and end unto itself. Ms. Carlin saw the process as open ended and developmental and accepted what the children gave her. There was no wrong answer.

In terms of evaluation of performance, the two were quite different. When students were doing worksheets, evaluation was very public, and occurred through verbal praise, erasure of incorrect or inadequate responses, or by being given a whole new worksheet when things were really a mess (as was the case with Andi on October 17 when she scribbled all over her coloring paper and Ms. Carlin had her do it again). There was feedback given to children, in class; and there was feedback given that was written on worksheets and shared with parents. With writing activities, verbal praise only was given in class.

Ms. Carlin sent Doing it Right papers home in the folders each week, with written comments to help guide parental interpretation. She kept writing papers at school in a folder for the entire year (and dated each paper with a stamp); making a chronological record of each child's progress in writing. The meaning of the writing process and a child's individual stage within that process was then communicated to parents by Ms. Carlin in face-to-face encounters, at conferences.

These two types of activities resulted in Ms. Carlin defining individual children in terms of characteristics that were related to the tasks' attributes and foci. For example, Ms. Carlin defined children in terms of their ability to follow directions, which was the focus of the Doing it Right papers. In our final interview in May, Ms. Carlin picked up on the fact that I had written the vignette about Alex and used it in an earlier draft of my case for Fulton. This incident described in the vignette occurred in her class in September:

> Ms. Carlin: This is kind of interesting too. Here the thing with Alex doing his triangles and stuff? He *still* can't follow directions.
>
> Int: Why do you think that is?
>
> Ms. Carlin: He can't process it and get it together. He's one of the only kids in my class that can't put a story in sequence. It's real important and I was really working on that in the beginning. You know with some kids, Alex especially, I was kind of questioning whether he was just blowing it off and doing it his own way or whether he just can't—*he still cannot follow directions!*
>
> Int: And that's a pretty good indicator?
>
> Ms. Carlin: That is a good indicator. It's kind of funny though cause I was thinking about it later and I thought [he was going to have trouble with] handwriting and he did a have real hard time with some of those things... Starting off on the side instead of on the dots, I mean *everybody* knows to start on the dots now. And he still starts off on the side sometimes. And even with his good artistic ability, some of the letters, he has one heck of a time. It's kind of interesting to see that now. You picked right up on that and now it's still to this day, he's still having trouble following directions. I have to really watch him, make sure he's understanding what to do and going through things.

She had cued in on Alex's problems with going through the process of drawing triangles in September; the problem could be distilled to a general difficulty with following directions. Ms. Carlin felt that she still had to watch him very closely to make sure that he did things according to the plan.

Later, when she talked about the kinds of classrooms these children needed to go into for first grade, she said that Alex would need a room with a lot of structure. She compared structure to a classroom that was run on a center model, where children made their own choices about what they would do when. Some phrases she used to characterize those few children who would need a more structured program were "It's just those few that, some of them are more definitely more oriented towards others... need a lot of reassurance and stuff." The need to have structure was related to difficulty following directions in Ms. Carlin's mind. She saw children like Alex needing a special kind of classroom to have success.

Ms. Carlin also used ideas about writing to define children. When I asked her whether the students were where she wanted them to be in terms of growth and skills, each child she mentioned was discussed in terms of writing. For example, Andi had been relatively impulsive and domineering at the first of the year, very interested in everyone else's business. Ms. Carlin was particularly pleased with her progress:

> Well, Andi and her writing. I can read things that she's done now when she does her writing. She still doesn't know—well, I haven't retested her for this quarter but last quarter she still didn't know quite a few letters. She's writing now where you can read it. Just about everybody's writing now where I can pretty much pick up what they're writing.

She also mentioned Andrew, who had been retained the previous year and had come in with skills that were not very well developed:

Ms. Carlin: Andrew has come a real long ways. He does real nice. So he's really come a long ways. And he's funny cause he's one that's always putting Y down for the W sound so this week it's been a big deal [Note: This week was Y week, in Ms. Carlin's class.] We'll say, "OK, what do you hear at the beginning of 'with'?" and he goes, "Y!" And we go, "Y???" And he just laughs and he says, "Oh, I mean W." So he's finally catching up on some of those, too. But he was having a real hard time at the beginning with letters and sounds and he's just really come along nice."

Int: Did that just happen all of a sudden?

Ms. Carlin: Yea, pretty much. That sort of happened after
spring break pretty much. Like he's finally gotten
all the stuff together.

As mentioned before, Ms. Carlin gave a great deal of feedback
on writing to the parents in the parent-teacher conference. Of
each fifteen-minute conference, at least five minutes were spent
talking about writing. The feedback tended to be related to an
explanation of the writing process and each child's individual
stage within that process.

Table 10 summarizes the differences between Doing it Right
and Writing activities in Ms. Carlin's classroom:

Table 10
Characteristics of Doing It Right
and Writing Activities in Ms. Carlin's Classroom

	Doing it Right	*Writing*
Focus	On completing the task correctly as defined by Ms. Carlin and producing a product acceptable to her	On doing writing which Ms. Carlin defined as open ended and developmental
Evaluation	Public and occurred both in class (with opportunities given to fix mistakes) and at home (with comments written on papers by Ms. Carlin)	Verbal praise only
Child work	Shared with parents weekly by sending home in the folders	Kept at school and shared with parents at conferences
Interpretation	Parents did alone, guided by Ms. Carlin's comments	Ms. Carlin interpreted writing for parents at conferences
Children defined	In terms of following directions	In terms of their stage in the developmental writing process; as risk takers

In addition to Ms. Carlin defining children in terms of their
writing ability, many of the children defined themselves in terms
of writing. I interviewed children in groups of three or four and
asked them to describe things they did in kindergarten and to
characterize those things as easy or hard. Easy activities were
all over the map; from playing house to jumping off bridges. Easy
activities were classified as play. When I asked children to tell

me about things that were hard in kindergarten, many (7 of 10) of them told me that writing was the hardest thing in their class. For example Dennis told me that writing stories was something that was hard for him to do in kindergarten. He focused on not being able to write the things that Ms. Carlin wanted him to write:

Int:	Tell me about something that you really have to work hard to do in kindergarten.
Dennis:	Writing stories
Int:	What about stories is hard?
Dennis:	I can't write all the things she tells me.
Int:	Like what does she tell you?
Dennis:	Like bat.
Int:	How do you figure that out?
Dennis:	Cause I look at the board.

Josh told me that he thought he would get better in first grade: "If we get into first grade, they'll tell us more about writing." Table 11 gives summaries of comments made by children who mentioned writing.

Table 11
Children's Descriptions of Writing as Hard

Name	Description
Dennis	Can't write all the things she tells me
Josh	If we get into first grade, they'll tell us more about writing
Tom	I have trouble writing words down sometimes
Matt	Writing stories is hard
Sally	Writing is hard [How will it get easy to write?] I'll get rid of my cold… I tried to write my ABC's but I messed up. I put the M in front of the A!
Hilary	Trying to figure out if you're right or wrong, the letters.
Tammy	[How will it get easy to write?] Just don't force yourself to do it. Just learn by your ownself. Just write things down, just write letters down and you have to think about it.
Hannah	Writing… I make things wrong… Somebody has to help me.

I asked seven children what Ms. Carlin wanted them to learn in kindergarten; five of them mentioned writing. None of the children mentioned that their parents wanted them to learn writing in school; they said their parents focused instead on being smart or nice, coloring pretty, not losing their coat, or adding numbers.

From conversations with the children in Ms. Carlin's class, it appeared that writing was a very important task in kindergarten. In addition, it appeared that it was a task that gave them trouble. Although Ms. Carlin presented writing as an activity that was open-ended, without specific right answers, the children appeared to have imported the criteria used for Doing it Right worksheet tasks. They thought it was hard and they worried about not being able to do it right.

Ms. Carlin's Thoughts on Readiness

During my time in Ms. Carlin's classroom, she often spoke about readiness. Whether or not my research focus on readiness set her up to interpret many of the events in her classroom in that manner is unclear. In any event, readiness was a recurring topic of conversation.

On my second visit to her classroom on September 8, Ms. Carlin discussed how she assessed readiness at the beginning of the school year:

> One of the main ways I find out about how ready kids are is having them do this:

How they do on this tells me a lot, you know about things like perceptual readiness. The kids who cut it out and put all the pieces in a pile—those are the kids I say, "Hey, this kid may not be ready." You know Tom? When he did this, he did a beautiful job cutting and pasting everything on the background and he had the one small circle left over. He threw a fit! He couldn't figure out where it went. I talked to him about it, showed him the background and showed him where it went, but he said, "But I can't put it there now!" He just couldn't figure it out! We do it again in the spring and you can really see the difference in what they can do between those two times.

Ms. Carlin used this activity, which involved perceptual motor awareness and problem solving to get an idea of how ready her students were. Looking at this after working with Ms. Carlin for less than a month did not give me great insight into how she thought about readiness. What kind of impact would the judgment that came from this activity have on the class' kindergarten experience? How would she use this information in thinking about individual children?

In the course of the year, I was able to gain a greater perspective on how she thought about the issue of readiness. Ms. Carlin brought the subject up frequently enough that I found myself building a mental model of how she incorporated information about children to make decisions about readiness. Ms. Carlin's model of readiness appeared to have nested parts. The first two parts could be described as the the *child* within the *setting*. Ms. Carlin placed much of her attention on the child when thinking about readiness. Within the child, readiness had two parts: a maturational component and an environmental component.

The *maturational* component to readiness, which was seen as inside a child, was linked to biological functioning and growth. This Gesellian idea came up a number of times, when Ms. Carlin gave me examples of readiness or when she talked to parents about it. For example, Ms. Carlin told me of an experience with her son that she felt was a good illustration of the idea that children must be ready to do things. Her four-year-old son had been totally unable to draw until last summer. No matter what she did, he just could not do it. That summer, her family went on vacation and among other things, they went to see Mount Rushmore. After the vacation was over and they were back at home, Max sat down at the table and told his mother that he wanted to draw Mount Rushmore. He wondered if she would help. He proceeded to sit for a long time, drawing the monument and had been drawing things ever since. She concluded that he had not been ready to draw before this summer, but when he got to the point that he was ready, there was no stopping him.

The maturational idea was communicated forcefully to parents during parent/teacher conferences in November. In all five of the conferences I observed with Ms. Carlin, she mentioned this idea in one context or another. For example, when talking with Andi's parents, Ms. Carlin suggested some handwriting activities that they could do at home. Andi's mother said:

> Mrs. A: It's kind of good, working with her. If she doesn't want to, I don't want to have no knock down drag out fight with her about it.
>
> Mr. A: But there are times when she needs to know things and that she has to do the stuff.
>
> Ms. Carlin: Well, so much of this has to do with her development—if she is not ready to do something, it won't help to try to make her do it. You need to watch to see if she is interested.

Ms. Carlin later talked to Andi's parents about how she checked to see if children could conserve number by playing a game with beans: she would put three beans in her hand and have Andi count them, then switch them to the other hand. If Andi could tell her that she still had three beans without counting them again, then she was able to conserve. Ms. Carlin then went on to tell them how conservation was developmental (which over time, I came to see that she defined as maturational) and was very much like losing teeth:

> That's a purely developmental kind of thing and most kinder-gartners are at about two beans at the start of the year. There is nothing you can do to hurry her up, you just have to wait. It's like losing teeth. Now she is ready to learn higher things. She counted to 39 at the start of the year and now she's all the way up to 58.

From the way that Ms. Carlin talked to parents about readiness, it is not surprising that they did not focus on it in interviews with me at the end of the first quarter of kindergarten. Ms. Carlin did not set readiness as a goal to be achieved or as a prerequisite to come into kindergarten. Instead she described it as a characteristic that she used to guide instruction; something that they could not do anything about but also something that they should not worry about too much. Ms. Carlin interpreted the readiness level of each child for the parents and suggested general types of experiences that they could provide for their child at home. She reinforced the idea that educating their child was the school's job, but that they could do things to reinforce what the school was doing.

For Ms. Carlin, the maturational component of readiness was related to the child's inner functioning and there was little any adult could do to change it. Adults could not make a child more ready if it was this maturational type of readiness, just as adults cannot hurry along the process of children losing teeth.

The *environmental* component was that part of readiness that was the result of the child's life experience and the kinds of exposure s/he had to various materials and activities. The environmental part of readiness was amenable to manipulation to some extent.

Ms. Carlin discussed how she saw this environmental aspect of readiness one day early in November. We were cleaning up at the end of the day, when Ms. Rodriguez (who taught kindergarten with Ms. Carlin in the past) came in and they began to talk about the class' progress. They were looking through a set of papers that Ms. Carlin was going to share with her parents at conferences that week. They talked about the difficulty that Ms. Carlin's class was having with handwriting that year. In her class, Ms. Carlin usually started handwriting worksheets in October to go with her Letter of the Week instruction. The class used d'Nealian workbook pages, which focused on tracing and writing upper and lower case letters on sets of lines. The children were having real problems; having a hard time finding where they should be on the paper and needing much guidance in the form of extra marks on the paper for tracing rather than writing on their own. Of particular concern was a new student in her class named Ramon, whose c's on his "C" paper turned out looking like randomly placed pieces of macaroni without regard to the lines on the paper. Ms. Rodriguez commented that "Handwriting was just so developmental, that some of them just need an extra year to be able to do things like write letters correctly." They continued through the papers, which included four worksheets that they had done that week. There was much variability in their work. Ms. Carlin shook her head and said, "I hate those cut and paste worksheets, but the kids just can't do them yet. They are really having a hard time."

When making comments on my fieldnotes for that day, I asked Ms. Carlin several questions. I was confused by what I saw as a contradiction. On the one hand, Ms. Carlin often told me that children cannot do things until they are ready. Using that logic, I would anticipate that she would delay instruction altogether when the class was having problems. Instead, I observed her using a number of different variations on the instructional theme for a concept, trying to provide them with much practice. This is how I phrased my confusion:

> You've told me many times that kids can't do things until they are ready; you just need to wait. Yet with this particular group this year, they appear to be having problems with handwriting worksheets and you have to spend a lot of time erasing what they've done and having them do them over again or by using markers to give them structured practice so they don't get lost on the paper. Or you have them do cut and paste worksheets, which you don't like and they seem to have lots of problems with.
>
> ....If kids can't do things until they are ready, then why introduce them to things that they are obviously having problems with? Does that mean that they aren't ready for them? How could they be exposed to the same material in a way that would match their level of "readiness"?

To these comments/questions Ms. Carlin gave a long reply, which was very helpful in developing my understanding of her interpretation of readiness. These comments, which were dated in late November, focused primarily on the environmental aspect of readiness, tying it to the things that she had done in her class recently:

> With the children who are *still* having trouble orienting on handwriting sheets, I have begun using only the capital letter page [in the handwriting workbooks] and have those students work in the rice table and cornmeal and chalkboards first. Some of those having trouble on November 3 are doing OK. Usually, by this time some of the color, cut and paste sheets are phased out as the students show more control and they are [showing more control now]. Does [the children] having problems with

the work mean they aren't ready? Not necessarily. For some it does—sometimes it is exposure and becoming accustomed to paper-pencil tasks—Ramon for example is beginning to do very well with writing, coloring, cutting, etc. Remember what problems he had?

From these comments, I began to understand that Ms. Carlin thought of readiness as almost two tiered. The first tier, which she saw as affected by school experiences, was that environmental aspect. Children who came into Ms. Carlin's classroom who had not had the experiences that would prepare them for kindergarten were not ready, but they could be given extended exposure to materials and tasks that could make them more ready. For this reason, Ms. Carlin tried to give the children who were having problems with the worksheets more experience with them, providing them different types of worksheets to do or by using an eraser so that they could correct their work immediately. This fit quite well with the school policy for dealing with unready children, which provided an extended-day program for unready children, giving them more time and school experience.

The maturational aspect of readiness dictated that children who were not ready were given activities at a different level developmentally. Rather than continuing to work only with the abstract worksheets on which children were to trace and write letters, Ms. Carlin backed up to a concrete level of activity. She provided a variety of experiences to stimulate their visual-motor readiness by giving them access to rice, cornmeal, and chalkboards for writing. In addition, she chose to use only the upper case worksheets, which she interpreted as simpler than the lower case worksheets.

Included in Ms. Carlin's interpretations about readiness were ideas about the importance of pacing for young children's learning. Because she believed that children could not do things until they were ready, Ms. Carlin felt that it was vital for children to be able to do things at their own pace. She mentioned the idea of "going at your own pace" several times during the year. When I asked her how she worked to accommodate varied levels of ability in her class, Ms. Carlin talked about how the program allows children to work at their own level:

> I think the program we use handles it by itself. Cause we do the writing process and so the kids are all, you know, everything's experienced-based and then we're writing stories based on their

experiences and their writing is up there at whatever level they're
working at. And then we do <u>Math Their Way</u>, so they're pretty
much working at whatever level they are.

The advantages of the writing process and <u>Math Their Way</u> came
up again when we talked in October. This time Ms. Carlin explicitly
talked about pacing as something that children needed and related
it to pressure:

> That's why I like the writing process and the <u>Math Their Way</u>
> because all of the kids can be doing things and they can all
> be working at their own pace and nobody feels like they are
> totally pressured as far as learning things that they aren't ready
> to. Like I said when you have a class full of kids knowing a
> lot then those that don't , that aren't ready are really pressured.
> They're put under a lot of pressure. Which is too bad for them…
> I've had parents like that… I've had to slow down parents.

In situations in which expectations were geared to the more
ready group, those who were not as ready were at a disadvantage. They felt pressure to keep up and if readiness was as Ms.
Carlin described it, there was no way for them to meet the pace.
If they were not ready, they would not be able to do what was
asked. Because Ms. Carlin used programs in which children
worked at their own pace, that pressure was not going to be felt
by her students.

Ms. Carlin thought about the pacing issue at two levels. The
first level was the level of curriculum; she used the writing process
and <u>Mathematics Their Way</u> so that children could work at a
rate that is appropriate for them. In addition she thought of it
at the instructional level; she used large group instruction rather
than center rotation so that children had the opportunity to choose
their own rate. When centers were used, groups of children usually
rotated every fifteen minutes or so. Ms. Carlin used large group
instruction and allowed children to go to other activities when
they finished the main activity, such as a writing assignment
or worksheet. She explained how she saw this related to pacing:

> When I had more time, I did centers. I just feel, maybe it's the
> kids I'm working with, but I feel like the 15 minutes time change
> thing just drives me nuts and I see a lot of kids driven nuts
> with it… I see Hilary just going bananas in here… she would
> never finish her work. There are other kids like that that are

so careful and they take so much care and pride in their work, stopping in 15 minutes to change is really hard on them.

Interestingly, when Ms. Carlin talked about the programs that she used in her classroom, especially when she referred to letting children work at their own pace, she did not talk about the Doing it Right activities. Although she did allow children to work at their own pace when they did worksheets (pacing at the instructional level), the worksheets were definitely geared at a particular skill level. As a result, children may have felt pressure if they were not ready enough to complete the task at hand. This apparent contradiction was explainable in that she saw the Doing it Right Activities and the activities that allow children to work at their pace as related to different types of readiness. The Doing it Right activities addressed the environmental aspect of readiness, which were amenable to instruction by giving more exposure to certain kinds of experiences. The other activities were related to the maturational aspect of readiness, for which pacing was important.

The ideas of pacing and readiness came up when Ms. Carlin discussed how she goes about planning instruction for a particular group of children. She felt that her students this year had required different types of activities than groups that she had worked with in the past: "The readiness levels of some of the kids are a lot lower this year than I've been accustomed to in the past. So I've had to adjust things and work more individually with kids." Her experience with the handwriting papers had required much more instructional adjustment than she had been used to in the past. She found it necessary to incorporate many more concrete activities than she had recently but she was pleased with the results because the children seemed less frustrated and she had been able to get help from parents at home.

In looking at the big picture of how kindergarten curriculum has developed, Ms. Carlin had seen an increase in the pace at which concepts are introduced. Over the twelve years that she had worked in kindergarten, Ms. Carlin had seen changes in the concepts that formed the base of the curriculum:

> It used to be that I had to do a whole unit on colors because they [the students] didn't know their colors when they came into kindergarten. Now most kids come in knowing their colors. I have two kids that don't know their colors: Penny and Ramon. And so we're just constantly kind of working with them but

since there are only two in the whole class, it's kind of hard
to make one unit up for only two… It has changed a lot since
I first started twelve years ago. Now most kids know their colors…
that's not even so much of an issue for most kids to do a whole
unit. We used to spend the whole fall on colors and shapes. We
didn't start letters until January. Now we start letters earlier
and one of the reasons that we start letters earlier is with the
writing. Doing the writing we start working on the letters and
sounds then that helps them in their writing plus it's more
meaningful to them cause they are doing their writing.

During the time that I observed in Ms. Carlin's classroom, I only
observed one activity that focused specifically on colors. It was
a color mixing activity in which children mixed balls of red, blue,
and yellow playdough to make orange, purple, and green. Even
though they lacked the fine motor skills for writing, most of this
group came in knowing color, so Ms. Carlin was able to step up
the pace somewhat and delete coverage of concepts that were
geared to children who did not have as many skills.

At Fulton, children spent one week studying each of the shapes
listed on the district report card (circle, rectangle, triangle, square,
oval, and diamond). Using shapes as a launching pad for the
year, Ms. Carlin taught shapes in an integrated manner: "I take
one shape a week so we correlate art and writing and everything
else with the shapes and that's a good way to get them started
in their writing." By October, they were finished talking about
shapes and the children were expected to be able to identify any
of the shapes covered. In the past, colors and shapes had taken
up the entire fall. Now they were the meat of the first month,
with shapes the primary focus. Students were onto letters three
months earlier than they were before; presumably because they
came in more ready.

Finally, Ms. Carlin did think about readiness as something
somewhat external to the child, which in a way competes with
the maturational view of readiness. In October, I posed a question
about whether it made sense to think of readiness as an idea
of people in a setting that depends on the kinds of children, their
experiences, and their parents' and teachers' expectations. This
is how she replied:

Yeah it does. Especially if you're talking about the half-day
sessions versus the extended-day sessions and things like that
there is a definite difference… Judging from the socioeconomic

status of the school you will see those differences in expectations. Sometimes I think that it is too bad that too many expectations are put on kindergartners a lot of the time.

She went on to explain about how pressured children feel when they are in a setting with expectations that are too high. In our last interview, Ms. Carlin tried to define readiness:

Ms. Carlin: Let me see if I can say it sort of simply. Readiness would be your ability to cope with the situation at hand. How you can cope with it, how you can deal with it. If you can handle it or not. So like for children coming to kindergarten, you see kids who are ready to sit down in a group, ready to listen, ready to work in a group. And other kids who are not ready at that point, who gain that skill as they go though school. You see kids who are ready to do paper-pencil tasks, other kids who are not ready to do paper-pencil tasks. And now at this point of the year, how kids are ready to jump into reading and start putting letters and sounds together. And the same kind of things with math.

Int: Can you get kids ready?

Ms. Carlin: Pretty much, I think for the most part. Unless there is an emotional problem... With a lot of encouragement and a lot of positive and even some negative, sometimes you have to isolate them... I think it is trying to work with the individual and meet their needs. I think most kids you can pretty well do that.

For Ms. Carlin, readiness was in part an aspect of the setting that a child was in, which depended on the expectations and the individual attention given by the teacher. She defined readiness as the match between the demands of the tasks in the setting and some level of development within a child. That ability to cope was an amalgam of what the adults in the setting wanted for the child, the biological maturity of the child and the environmental aspect of readiness that the school could work on. At the end of the 1989-90 school year, all of the children in Ms. Carlin's class were promoted to first grade.

How Was the Meaning of Readiness Constructed at Fulton Elementary?

Families approached the kindergarten experience at Fulton with much hope and good feeling; parents saw kindergarten as a beginning of an opportunity for children to make something of themselves. Their knowledge of the kindergarten program at Fulton was general in nature and they were uninformed about the nuts and bolts of school expectations or performance requirements. There were no systems within the Fulton community to acquaint participants about these types of school information. Within this context of hopeful expectation, children came to school when they were age eligible. The parents depended on the school to interpret their children's first school experience, taking a supportive, but reactive role in the educational process.

Ms. Carlin worked within an open, professional setting where she was not a sole teacher left alone with twenty-two students. She had colleagues available to develop ideas and materials and they shared responsibility for meeting the needs of students. She also thought of kindergarten as a place to get a good start, trying to help students become socialized to the school experience. Seeing her role as the person responsible for getting children ready, Ms. Carlin provided children with highly-structured activities that included both immediate feedback to the child but also feedback to parents so that they understood what was happening in school. In addition, the class participated in activities that were open ended to allow children to work at their own level and pace. The rules, processes, and criteria of the Doing it Right and Writing activities were very different and reflected Ms. Carlin's understanding of how children come to be ready for school. The Doing it Right activities, which focused on worksheets of various kinds, addressed the environmental aspect of readiness, which she felt was amenable to school intervention. The focus of these types of activities was following directions, which Ms. Carlin used as a marker of readiness. In contrast, the open-ended activities in the classroom addressed the maturational aspect of readiness, which Ms. Carlin felt was fixed by the child's internal growth and development. Children were defined in terms of their ability to write, both by Ms. Carlin and by their peers in class. Ms. Carlin emphasized the ability to put together sounds to make discernable words, while the children focused on being able to put down the right words. In a way, both Ms. Carlin and her students melded the criteria of the Doing it Right activities with writing activities so that there was, in fact, a right way to make a story. The public value of writing was combined with the public value of Doing it Right so that children interpreted their ability in one with the criterion of the other. A child's ability to do these things correctly was not used as a key to promotion to the next grade; instead it was used as a marker for instruction, allowing the teacher to know where to start teaching.

In this context, parents waited for and used the information provided by Ms. Carlin to understand what their children did in school. Ms. Carlin worked to form an image of each child through the feedback provided on worksheets and through communication of writing abilities at conferences. The children in her class incorporated the rules for work into their understanding of going to school. Ms. Carlin constructed a model of child readiness in the context of her program so that she could meet each child's needs instructionally and interpret the school experience for parents. Readiness, though used frequently by Ms. Carlin to understand her students, had instructional implications that varied according to the activity and whether she considered it environmental or maturational readiness.

CHAPTER 6

❧

NORWOOD

Along Norwood's Main Street is a blend of the old and new. The street is lined with antique stores, restaurants, a feed shop, and a Grange Hall. In front of these businesses are Saabs, Volvos, and every sort of mini-van imaginable. At mid-day, mothers and their pre-schoolers wander up and down the street, meeting friends for lunch or running errands as they come from their morning nursery school session. Mothers know each other through their children's activities: Brownies, soccer practice, and dance lessons forge bonds via common concerns and interests.

Norwood was an old rural town with a suburban feel; it had moved from a center for farm families to the home of corporate families of a nearby high tech plant and of commuters to the two midsize cities. Norwood was not a self-contained community, its residents were dependent on the nearby, larger towns for things like groceries, movies, and purchases like cars. There was a blend of old homes, condominiums, and newly constructed, executive homes that housed the mostly professional, white-collar families of the area. A couple of years ago, the homes in Norwood were awash with "For Sale" signs; the result of a downturn in the high tech field that forced layoffs and transfers. This upheaval had stabilized somewhat and there was merely a normal amount of moving going on.

In some ways, the families in Norwood harkened back to an earlier time. Many of the mothers in the community did not work outside the home; they spent their days actively involved in their children's social and academic lives. They went to aerobics, played tennis, ran carpools and playgroups, and volunteered at school. The fathers were executives, managers, medical professionals,

lawyers, business people. They lived upscale lives, providing every
advantage they could imagine for their children. Most of the
children coming to kindergarten had been to pre-school, they had
travelled, and had libraries that rivaled some pre-schools. Mrs.
Sunden, who taught kindergarten at Norwood Elementary,
described the parents this way:

> Well, we're really lucky at Norwood because a lot of the parents
> are really involved with their children and... I don't know if
> this is right to say but there's more money and there's more
> parents who get their kids involved in activities and just spend
> time and a lot more mothers that don't work.

Norwood Elementary was nestled in a residential area of
ranch homes. Approaching it from town, you first saw a large,
busy playground surrounded by a fence to keep balls and toys
in the school yard. The parking lot was always full and cars lined
the street along the side of the school. A Science Garden was
quiet and awaiting the next class to check on projects that lined
the ground. The school was housed in a sprawling, single-floor
brick building that was much larger than it looked from the
outside. The main door led to the office and the library, gym,
and music rooms were also within the school's core area.
Classrooms were at the ends of long hallways that fanned out
from the center.

The children who attended Norwood Elementary had every
advantage that a middle class environment could give. Few of
the families (8%) were eligible for the federal Free and Reduced
lunch program and there was no extended-day kindergarten or
Chapter One program at the school. Children with special needs
were mainstreamed in regular classes for the most part; parents
of disabled children had worked hard to keep their children in
their neighborhood school.

Budget reductions resulted in cuts in staffing at Norwood as
in other Thomas elementary schools; aide time was no longer
available to most teachers for anything but recess time. This
situation made Norwood teachers especially dependent on parent
volunteers to run their programs as they had in the past. Parents
ran enrichment programs such as Great Books, they worked center
activities in classrooms, and took groups of children to the library
or the Science Garden to do projects.

The school had a close relationship with its families. The
parents expected to have a stake in their children's education

and liked to be kept up-to-date on school news. The principal, John Hamilton, sent out a monthly newsletter with information about all past and upcoming events at Norwood. There was a lively Parent-Teacher Organization at Norwood, which involved families in all aspects of school functioning. Most school programs, such as Back to School Night or the yearly Christmas program, had a large number of family participants, whether they occurred during the school day or in the evening.

The kindergarten through grade six staff at Norwood was one of the most stable in the district. The teachers had been there for a long time and had established reputations in the community for the most part. They were much like the school's families; middle-class men and women who were actively involved in the educational process. The kindergarten staff at Norwood was younger than the rest; all three kindergarten teachers were under the age of forty-five. There were three sections of kindergarten at Norwood and each teacher worked in a kindergarten position half-time. Jack Presby taught kindergarten in the morning and art for the rest of the school in the afternoon. Lynn Evert, in her first year in the Thomas District, also taught morning kindergarten. Monica Sunden had taught for five years at Norwood and was responsible for the afternoon program.

Kindergarten at Norwood

Most children coming to kindergarten at Norwood had been in some kind of pre-school program; usually a Monday-Wednesday-Friday morning type of program with a traditional nursery school focus. The few that had not gone to pre-school had parents who had made a conscious decision to raise their children at home, with a mother who had left the workforce either temporarily or permanently. The stay-at-home children were almost as busy as those attending pre-school through their involvement in various sports and community activities like swimming or soccer.

Norwood was a community that anticipated the kindergarten experience in a multitude of ways. Parents actively sought out the advice of preschool teachers about whether their child was ready for kindergarten; they checked with friends to compare notes and experiences vis-à-vis the school. The Community School program ran a pre-school in the summer, housed in the kinder-garten rooms to ease the children's transition into the elementary

school experience. There were few surprises once families brought
their children to school on the first day of kindergarten.

The discussion of the kindergarten experience at Norwood
begins with a vignette of a group of pre-school mothers talking
about the upcoming year. It focuses on the ways in which
expectations about kindergarten were communicated among
parents even before the formal program begins.

"But Is He Ready?"

The hallway is bright and decorated with nursery characters.
It's too cold to stand outside so a group of mothers huddle next
to the classroom doorway. Waiting to pick their children up from
the morning pre-school session, their talk about the hottest topic
of the day—kindergarten enrollment.

"Well, how old is he?"

"He'll be five in August—he is a full month older than the
deadline," Garth's mother Anne replies with a puzzled look on
her face. She is standing against the wall with the other women
gathered around her.

"But that'll make him one of the youngest in his—"

"And do you know what they do in kindergarten now?"

"Isn't it pretty much like pre-school, with more kids?"

"No way," Kristin, a tall blond woman in jeans and a hand-
painted sweatshirt, says laughing. "Do you remember what we
did in kindergarten? Some clay, some paint, snack and rest, right?
At Norwood, they need to know their name, they have to know
their phone number, they have to know all this stuff. *Before* they
can be in kindergarten!" The five women shake their heads
collectively in frustration.

"Sounds like before you can even start, you have to know
how to read and stuff like that."

"But Garth knows how to write his name, he knows his colors
and most of his shapes—"

"Have you talked to Sandy [his teacher] about it?"

"Well, she did mention that she thought he was a little young.
But I figured that by September he'd be ready."

For the first time this morning, Jean speaks, looking very
serious. "I just know that with our oldest, I had to make the same
kind of decision—he knew a lot but was a summer birthday. We
went ahead and put him in and I've always regretted it. I think

that he would have had a lot easier time if we had just waited... He was smart enough to go. That isn't the issue. It's more a thing of attention span, being able to sit long enough to listen to what they tell you. Feeling more secure about what you are doing. You really have an edge if you are a few months older, especially at this age... It's one of those things you can't go back and change. Pushing them just doesn't seem worth it when you can let them be on the top by waiting a—"

The door opens and a gaggle of four and five-year-olds tumble out of the yellow classroom. They are raucous and full of news from their morning in school. Some are clutching easel paintings, others wear colored macaroni necklaces. Garth's mother looks at him with new eyes, comparing him to his classmates.

"Maybe he isn't ready..." she thinks to herself.

Getting Ready for Kindergarten at Norwood Elementary

Although most of the Norwood children have been to pre-school, there is something very special about kindergarten; it's almost as if people think about kindergarten as the start of *real* school. This is school that really counts. When I talked to parents in the month before the start of the school year, one theme resounded with almost a single voice. Because this theme was so strongly held and because the environment at Norwood was well developed even before the enrollment of most children in kindergarten, the discussion of parental anticipation of the kindergarten experience will be made separately from that of discussion of parents' thoughts about kindergarten during the school year.

The parents at Norwood unanimously voiced concerns about whether their children were ready for kindergarten, either in the past or in the present. To a person, each parent mentioned readiness and one of its dimensions when I talked to them in August. For these parents, they wanted their child to start the school year ready for kindergarten.[3] In the sample of pre-kindergarten parents (n=6), there was an even division between parents of males and females. Three had held their children out the year before, entering them when they were six (two boys and one girl); two were in the oldest part of the twelve month kindergarten age range and one was waiting for her fifth birthday in the first week of the kindergarten year.

When asked about the kinds of things they were thinking about as their child's kindergarten entrance approached, talk of readiness was pervasive. It ranged from the concern of two parents who felt that their children were more than ready to go to kindergarten, to two who had held their children out the previous year and were confident that the extra year had made them ready, to the final two who were slightly concerned about whether in fact, their children would be ready when they came into kindergarten. Within the idea of readiness, the parents spoke of a tightly interwoven set of ideas; it was hard to pull apart each dimension separately because they seemed so interrelated.

For example, Alice's mother talked about how good she felt this year about Alice going into kindergarten. They had decided to hold Alice out the previous year; the following describes how they came to that decision:

Alice's Mother: I think that she is mature enough now. Last year she could have went to school—she'll be six in September. We waited the extra year, because we felt that she really wasn't ready.

Int: Can you tell me about how you went about making that decision? What kind of information did you use and what you saw as the pros and cons?

Alice's Mother: I think I just watched her, how she interacted with other children when we'd go to the park. A lot of it too was just her skills... it seemed like she wasn't catching on to coloring or scissor cutting. Most of it I think was just interaction with other children that she'd meet on a day to day basis... She'd kind of hold back a little bit. You know, she wouldn't go into a situation and feel calm about it; she'd kind of sit there and look at the kids and didn't know if she wanted to do what they were doing and it would take her a lot longer. I don't really want to say come out of a shell because she's kind of different than her brother was, she wasn't real take charge. Where now she's a little better, she'll go up and start talking to another child if you take her to the park. She'll tell you how she feels instead of just sitting there.

In addition to mentioning that her daughter was not ready the previous year, Alice's mother talked about a number of the other aspects of readiness. Because these elements were so interrelated, they will be discussed separately, with the hope that the reader will get an ever-broadening definition of what readiness was in the eyes of the Norwood parents. The words these parents used in describing readiness often had common meanings. The text in which they occur is preserved to help the reader make judgments about their meaning.

Table 12 gives examples of talk about readiness and includes each child's birthdate. The examples have been arranged from most confident about readiness to least confident about readiness.

Table 12
Pre-Kindergarten Parental Talk About Readiness

Child's Name	Birth Date	Talk about readiness
Sam	10/4/83	They [his preschool teachers] say he's more than ready for kindergarten; that he can do just anything that was ever asked of him. That he has a very good vocabulary and that he understands bigger words, he also is fairly enthused about what he's doing so he's able to follow through on that so they've never really had any problem with him.
Tammy	10/18/83	She's ready and I'm ready... I guess probably her maturity. I don't want to call it maturity, but I guess that's what it is. She's grasping so many things and concepts. She seems to have an excellent capacity to remember... Also ready in that she seems to be real inquisitive about things.
Alice	9/22/83	I think that she is mature enough now. Last year she could have went to school—she'll be six in September. We waited the extra year, because we felt that she really wasn't ready... I think I just watched her, how she interacted with other children when we'd go to the park. She seemed like she wasn't catching on to just coloring or scissor cutting. Most of it I think was just interaction with other children that she'd meet on a day to day basis.
Greg	2/17/83	Last year he would have been starting out with cold feet, which emotionally, maybe he just wasn't quite ready. Whereas now, I think that he is real ready.
Rick	5/27/83	I'm a little apprehensive. I'm not sure that he is socially ready; he's just not interested in school.

Table 12 *continued*
Pre-Kindergarten Parental Talk About Readiness

Child's Name	Birth Date	Talk about readiness
Alyson	9/4/84	Mostly if she's ready. She'll be 5 on September 4th and I've talked to the teacher and she seemed to think that Alyson was plenty ready cause she can say her alphabet or most of it and count and her name and stuff. She seems to be doing a lot better—she's been in preschool for two years. It's something that kind of goes through my mind. I'm kind of scared—this is my first time.

Looking at the ways that parents talked about readiness, some interesting patterns can be discerned. The parents most sure about their child's readiness had children who were in the oldest part of the kindergarten age range if overage children were not considered. Those in the middle were confident at the time of our conversations, but were worried enough last year that they held their children out. Greg would have been 5½ if he had entered kindergarten by age eligibility only, Alice would have been 4. Of the two parents who had some current readiness concerns, their views were quite different. Rick had been held out the year before and he still didn't seem interested in school. Alyson, on the other hand, seemed ready to her mother and to her pre-school teacher but her mother was worried that her birthdate, which put her in kindergarten at not quite five, would work against her. The age pattern was relatively consistent for these parents: older children were usually seen as more ready. For this reason, the next dimension of readiness discussed will be talk of child age.

When parents mentioned age (n=6), there was a concern that if children were the youngest in their group, they would have problems. Their discussions ranged from classroom observations of children who seemed young to talk of how delaying school entry would provide an advantage in sports. Alyson's mother was the only parent I talked to who worried about age this year, and Alyson was the only child at the young end of the kindergarten age range. Alyson had already been through one placement related to age in her pre-school. She was not allowed to go into the pre-kindergarten class because she had a September birthday; presumably the pre-school assumed that her parents would hold her out:

I don't know if she'll be one of the youngest kids in the class—
the other kids will have already been five. The pre-school she
goes to—they have a pre-kindergarten class and she didn't get
to go in that because she wasn't four yet; she wasn't ready to
go into that. I thought that she seemed plenty ready to go into
kindergarten. I went ahead and enrolled her and I thought going
three years to pre-school was a little much.

Alyson's mother described the class that her daughter attended
in pre-school as having a different curriculum than the pre-
kindergarten:

There were the younger ones, who were younger than her and
the older ones that were already four and then the inbe-
tween group where she was. Late September, October, later in
the year turning four. You know, they mostly can't be enrolled
in kindergarten so they went ahead and opened up a new
class. The kids in the pre-kindergarten class were learning to
write their name a lot and doing a lot with markers and the
kids in Alyson's class, they did mostly things with buttons and
beads. It was all for their motor skills... and they did some match
up the things that go together; you know, learning how to
draw lines.

The children in the pre-kindergarten class had a more academically-oriented program, which focused on skills that would be
useful the following year in kindergarten. The children in the
in-between group did what might be called readiness-readiness
tasks: things to get them ready to do the readiness activities to
get ready to go to kindergarten. Alyson was skipping the pre-
kindergarten class and going straight into the kindergarten.

Greg's mother's discussion of why they held him out was
not typical of the other parents I interviewed but is an interesting
story, nonetheless. She mentioned in her initial comments about
readiness that she had felt that he had not been emotionally ready
to go to kindergarten the year before; that he seemed to have
cold feet. Although there were several dimensions to her reasons
for holding him out, the main reason they chose to delay his entry
is a real example of redshirting[4]: Greg's parents wanted to give
him an advantage in sports when he got to high school. Her words
describe their reasoning best:

It was a tough decision with Greg because he has a February birthday and has just turned 6 now so he was 5½ last year. In a lot of ways he was really ready to start and I think that one of the main things we looked at was boys and sports and how important that can be. Our oldest daughter is in high school so we can see that another year of physical development and growth on a boy can make a big difference in how well they do in high school. One of the boys my daughter dated this last year was a junior and he was on the varsity baseball and basketball team. Which was really good as a junior; some boys don't make it. And even he was saying to his parents, his mother told me this, "Why didn't you hold me back a year?" And she said, "Well Justin there was no reason to. Besides, look how well you've done." And he said, "But look how awesome I could have been. If I'd just been a sophomore instead of a junior this year, playing this well. Maybe I could have been on varsity three years." That was one of the things. Plus everybody says how boys are so much later blooming in a lot of ways... Socially over this last year, he played several different sports, he wrestled and swam on the swim team for the first time this summer, played baseball and soccer three seasons now.

As the primary motivating factor for keeping Greg at home, his mother cited doing well in sports. This was a goal that was ten years away, but something that Greg's parents felt was worth the investment. Their sports orientation showed in his already lengthy history of extramural sports which included wrestling, swimming, baseball and soccer. Holding Greg out would make him more ready in sports later on.

The full range of comments on age can be seen in Table 13. Comparing statements about readiness and statements about age, there did not seem to be the same pattern as there was at Fulton (increasing concern with age related to an increasing concern with readiness). This could probably be explained by the fact that all Norwood parents voiced concerned about both age and readiness; there was less variability than with the Fulton parents.

Table 13
Parent Talk About Age

Child's Name	Talk of age
Alice	I guess I see that a lot of it is just experience with my son. I was a mother helper twice a month... just seeing the other kids in the class. You know, some of them, I felt, just were not ready for kindergarten... They just seemed young. To me, I guess, if the child isn't ready to sit down and listen, then he's going to be missing out on a lot.
Alyson	She'll be 5 September 4th and I've talked to her teacher and stuff and she seemed to think that Alyson was plenty ready cause she can say her alphabet or most of it... I don't know if she'll be one of the youngest kids in the class—the other kids will have already been 5.
Greg	It was a tough decision with Greg because he has a February birthday and has just turned 6 now so he was 5½ last year. In a lot of ways he was really ready to start and I think that one of the main things we looked at was boys and sports and how important that can be... Well, that was another thing, had we been back in Connecticut, we probably (we moved from there 3½ years ago), we probably would have started him at 5½. Whereas here, especially at Norwood Elementary, so many people wait until after their child's 6th birthday.
Sam	One of our kids had to go through some kind of pre-kindergarten testing only because her birthdate was only one week ahead of the cutoff date. So she actually started when she was four. None of the other kids have ever had to had that done. They just wanted to make sure if they were ready.
Tammy	As far as any anxiety there isn't any, there's just excitement for her. She'll be 6 in October, she just missed the cutoff so she's really ready for it.
Rick	Because of his age we held Rick back last year.

There was less unanimity among the parents about the other aspects of readiness. Closely related to age was the idea of maturity, an attitude or way of being that indicates that a child is old enough to handle a situation. Four of the parents interviewed before school started mentioned maturity as a concern related to readiness. Alice's mother worried about whether she was mature enough to handle being in kindergarten. Much of this came from her experience as a mother helper during her son's kindergarten

year, when she watched how some children just did not seem
to progress as the year went on:

> Like at the beginning of the year and the end of the year, they
> hadn't learned that much and I just kept thinking to myself,
> that maybe if they had been a little bit more mature and able
> to settle down and listen, that they may have gotten a lot more
> out of it... With a little bit of maturity that comes with being
> able to sit for a while and listen to things.

For these parents, maturity was being old enough to take
advantage of what the school offered; immaturity was being too
young to do that.

Maturity was seen as a way of behaving, having to do with
social readiness. Many of the parents (n=5) made a distinction
between academic readiness, which was related to knowing the
things a child needs to know to go into kindergarten (colors, ABC's,
numbers) and social readiness, which was a way of behaving.
None of the parents were really worried about their child's
academic readiness; in fact three of the parents prefaced their
remarks about their children with a phrase like "We didn't feel
he would have any academic problems..." Social readiness
involved feeling good about oneself, getting along with others,
behaving as the teacher expected, and being interested in school.
Children who were not socially ready were thought to have
emotional problems starting school, especially being shy.

The Norwood parents were worried about their children's
social readiness and considered holding them out because of it.
Five of the parents interviewed before school started talked about
holding out; which is not surprising because three of them had
done it the year before. Three of them discussed their reasons
for holding their son or daughter out. Sam's mother spoke with
some disdain about parents who let their daughter languish in
kindergarten even though she was doing poorly and was taking
teacher time away from the rest of the class. She said that the
"parents refused to help in a way that would have benefitted the
child best." Alyson's mother said that if her daughter's teacher
said that she did not think that Alyson was ready for kindergarten
then, "I'd go ahead and hold her back. I just feel like that if I
went ahead and kept trying to push her through and she wasn't
ready, I'd feel really bad. I'd rather hold her back another year
and have her be at the top of the class next time." Alyson's mother
made no distinction between academic and social readiness,

indicating that their difference was not prominent in her eyes. This quote brings up a benefit that three of the parents alluded to when they talked about holding out. If a child was held out, the following year s/he would be at least average in abilities and probably even above average.

Finally, two of the Norwood parents talked about experiences that they had with older siblings of their incoming kindergartner that had an impact on whether they thought about delaying kindergarten entrance a year. It should be no surprise that in both cases, these were parents who had chosen redshirting the previous year. Alice's mother talked about how remembering the difference between her son Ryan's kindergarten and pre-school experiences helped her make the decision to give her daughter an additional year before kindergarten:

> Ryan went to pre-school and it was really unstructured—the kids got to go more or less at their own speed, when they were ready. It was more of a fun time. And then when he hit kindergarten it changed. The only thing that I can think of is little soldiers, that was my impression of it. I decided that if she missed time in pre-school to develop her own sense for... I don't know. They had some structure but much more lenience. When you get into kindergarten and they've got their little tables with each project they've got to do—they have to do these things. While she's in pre-school, if she doesn't feel like coloring that day, that's fine, she could go make a puzzle.

Tables 14 and 15 show parental comments on the subdimensions related to readiness.

Table 14
Maturity, Academic and Social Readiness

Child's Name	Maturity	Academic Readiness	Social Readiness
Alice	If she's mature enough, to handle the social part of it, of going to school. If she feels comfortable in the situation.	As far as academically, you know, I have no questions there because I think she's ready there.	I think for me right now, it's just social. If she feels good enough about herself.
Alyson		She's a pretty smart little kid, she's pretty quick.	[In preschool] they did a lot of art and stuff and she really thought she came out of her shell quite a bit this year and that really meant a lot to me because Alyson was so quiet. You'd say hi to her and she'd have her hand in her mouth.
Greg		I don't know, Greg's pretty bright so we really didn't feel that he would have an academic problem to start.	Socially over this last year, he played several different sports... So we've seen him grow socially... So I think he'll go into this situation feeling more at ease, with more self esteem. So it was probably a benefit from the social point of view.

Table 14 continued
Maturity, Academic and Social Readiness

Child's Name	Maturity	Academic Readiness	Social Readiness
Sam	In the things he can do. Like write his name and he knows numbers & letters & tying his shoes, drawing & coloring & things that I see him do and his vocabulary has always been a little bit more mature than children his age. He's able to talk in complete sentences, sometimes in complete paragraphs and produces words that are a little bit more mature than an average 5-year-old.		I would like to have him also be able to get along with the other kids.
Tammy	[When you say that she is ready, what do you mean?] I guess her maturity. I don't want to call it maturity but I guess that's what it is. She's grasping so many things and concepts.		
Rick	We held Rick back last year and now he doesn't seem so immature.		I'm a little apprehensive, I'm not sure he's socially ready.

Table 15
Holding Out, Becoming Above Average, and Using Experience with Siblings to Make Decisions about Readiness

Child's Name	Holding Out	Becoming Above Average	Using Experience with Siblings
Alice	If it's time to hold them one more year.... some people disagree with me, but it just seems to me like if there's that extra year in there, it's good. Maybe some kids, they're never going to sit and listen, but it just seems from my experience it seems that one year has helped my kids a lot.	I think that she will know more and that she'll get the lessons or whatever they're teaching at that time. That's what I think, that she's going to be an average or a little above average child that is going to catch on to what the teacher is saying and learn.	Ryan went to pre-school and it was really unstructured—the kids got to go more or less at their own speed, when they were ready. It was more of a fun time. And then when he hit kindergarten it changed. The only thing that I can think of is little soldiers.
Alyson	[If her teacher said she wasn't ready?] I'd go ahead and hold her back. I just feel like that I went ahead and kept trying to push her through and she wasn't ready, I'd feel really bad.	I'd rather hold her back another year and have her be at the top of the class next time.	
Greg	We had him signed up to start school last fall and then decided to wait and start him this fall.	I do think Greg will do real well; he'll probably have no problem being at the top of his class.	Our 2nd one started very young, we started her at 4½—she didn't turn 5 until the following January. That seemed like a real good thing for the first two years and then when she was in 2nd grade, I left her holding her teacher's hand and crying several times during that year.... She was up to 2 years younger than some of the kids in the class.

Table 15 *continued*
Holding Out, Becoming Above Average, and Using Experience with Siblings to Make Decisions about Readiness

Child's Name	Holding Out	Becoming Above Average	Using Experience with Siblings
Sam	I can remember one little girl in particular—she didn't know how to color. She was actually older than some of the kids in the kindergarten but instead of pulling her out and letting her start the next year, the parents, because of her size and age, felt she needed to keep up physically with the kids. But she wasn't able to.... They kind of let her get by with what she could do and the parents refused to help in a way that would have benefitted the child best.		One of our kids had to go through some kind of pre-kindergarten testing only because her birthdate was only one week ahead of the cutoff date. So she actually started when she was 4. None of the other kids have ever had to have that done.
Tammy			
Rick	Because of his age we held Rick back last year.		

The parents at Norwood voiced a solid set of ideas about
readiness for kindergarten when I talked to them before the school
year started. They felt that children should be mature and both
academically and socially ready before starting kindergarten and
that this overall readiness was very much a function of age. It
was thought that children who were older within the kindergarten
age group would be better able to handle the demands of the school
program. In addition to age, the Norwood parents were concerned
about their children's maturity, which translated loosely to a kind
of social readiness, or the ability to work within a situation. None
of the parents were worried about their children's academic
readiness, although three were careful to distinguish it from social
readiness. Five of the parents discussed holding out as a strategy
for unready children and three of those hoped that it would produce
a child who was at least average, and hopefully above average
the following year. Finally, three parents used previous experience
with older children to gauge their child's readiness and shape
their decision about whether to enter kindergarten when s/he was
age eligible.

*Parental Expectations for their Child's Kindergarten
Experience at Norwood*

The Norwood parents did talk about more than readiness in
our August interviews. They also discussed their expectations for
their child's kindergarten experience. Of the five parents who talked
about kindergarten expectations (Rick's mother did not mention
them), three parents mentioned wanting their children to get a
good start in school. Alice's mother wanted her to learn "numbers
and the letters and basic words and that kind of stuff that she
really catches on and has a good base for her schooling." This
attitude is akin to seeing kindergarten as preparation for later.
Tammy's mother was interested in her getting "a good introduction to learning. Set some good basis to continue on." and Sam's
mother was convinced that kindergarten would set the foundation for further learning, "Certainly, that's a very formative year
of education even more so than the pre-school. That's where they
begin all their basics and if they aren't challenged at that age
then it may carry through for the rest of their schooling as being
unimportant and they don't care about it."
While the Fulton parents focused on wanting their child to
get a good start in a general way (developing skills they would
need, having a chance for social interaction, developing attitudes

for learning, getting prepared for later experiences), the Norwood parents were more likely to discuss particular school content. Four of the five parents talked about learning specific things in kindergarten ranging from academic skills like reading or knowing the alphabet and numbers to following directions or working with paints and clay. Sam's mother emphasized the importance of the teacher in the kindergarten experience and listed the types of characteristics she would like to see her son's kindergarten teacher have:

> I would hope that it would be teacher who would command the respect of his students... Secondly, I would like the teacher to have patience to realize that every child in there is an individual. That there may be some who have a little more difficulty than others but not try to keep the same pace so much that somebody is losing out. I would like that teacher to provide a challenge to the kids, keep their interest going in what they're learning... I would like the teacher to be willing to contact the parents if there is a problem with the child.

Table 13 gives a summary of the kinds of things that the Norwood parents talked about when they examined their expectations for their child's kindergarten experience.

Table 16
Norwood Parents' Expectations for
Their Child's Kindergarten Year

Child Name	Parent Expectation for Kindergarten Experience
Alice	Just that she learns basically her numbers and her alphabet. Hopefully that she will be reading fairly well. She reads a little bit now, but that she will develop that. Basically with the numbers and the letters and basic words and that kind of stuff that she really catches on and has a good base for her schooling.
Alyson	Learning more of the alphabet and writing it, numbers, writing them more. Maybe learning a few words. I'm not really sure what they teach but when I talked to the teacher she said they more or less work on their name, alphabet, and counting. Maybe their address, stuff like that... Alyson pretty much knows all that.
Greg	I know he'll be doing a lot more of things that he enjoys doing, like painting and working with clay and coloring... He's never had anybody sit down and say, "Let's do your numbers and let's do your ABC's." He'll probably really enjoy doing those papers that they do.

Table 16 *continued*
Norwood Parents' Expectations for
Their Child's Kindergarten Year

Child Name	Parent Expectation for Kindergarten Experience
Sam	Get them really geared up so that when they pass into first grade when they have to go to school for a full day, it'll be something that they look forward to.
Tammy	Well, as a good introduction to learning. Set some good basis to continue on... But some positive foundations I guess... continue her development and motor skills... Just to keep up that inquisitive mind. Have that grow and work on those memory skills.

These parents wanted their child's kindergarten experience to be a positive one and hoped that they would get a good start on lifelong learning as well as developing a solid foundation in skills such as knowing the alphabet and numbers. An interesting exception was Greg's mother, who talked about the more traditional kindergarten activities of painting, coloring, and playing with clay. This is almost a contradiction when one considers that she held Greg out (although the reasoning behind it was for sports) and when one examines how she described her understanding of the Norwood environment. In the following description, Greg's mother talked about the ambiance of pressure that permeated the life at Norwood Elementary. She derived this interpretation from things she had heard from friends and teachers at Norwood:

> We have a neighbor whose daughter's birthday is in March and she's a girl (people are less likely to hold girls out) and they waited until after her sixth birthday. [Her father, who teaches at the High School] made the comment to me "I would never put a child in kindergarten before they were 6, especially at Norwood Elementary"... Even the kindergarten teacher that I was hoping that Greg would get this year told me that there is pressure. He can feel it. It is incredible how pressured these kids feel to do well. And I'm not sure [if] it's because of the affluent area that we are in where most parents have a college degree or some kind of college behind them or what. The kids are just feeling that they need to do well.

Greg's mother's concern about the pressure he might feel at Norwood occured in the context of the information system that existed at Norwood. As shown in the vignette, parents saw each other often, talked to each other, and shared what they knew about the school and its expectations. In some ways, the communication of expectations was as important as the expectations themselves and seemed to represent the shared values that existed among the Norwood community members. Parents seemed to feel a responsibility to let others know the "rules" that worked at Norwood. This communication process, which will be discussed later in terms of parents interviewed during the school year, was also brought up by Andy's mother, who met me at the Norwood parent information meeting that occurred the evening before school started. After I described my study to the parents, Andy's mother approached me and described the dilemma in which she found herself in trying to decide about enrolling her August birthday son:

> Your study sounds so interesting. I am dealing with that stuff with my son, Andy. I've been trying and trying to decide whether to put him into school—he just turned five and seems in really good shape but everybody says that I shouldn't send him this year, that I should wait until next year. They say that I'll be doing him a disservice. I was really worried so we had him tested—man, was that a big deal! She spent three hours with Andy and then a couple of hours with us to find out about him and she ended up saying he was fine! Still everybody says that I'm wrong and that he'd better wait. He's little for his age and they say especially later, that being so little will be a problem. The big thing is sports, that he'll be too little—I don't want him to play football anyway. How can I make a decision now that will have an impact in seven or eight years? How do I know what to do?

In trying to deal with the information and feedback that she had gotten about enrolling a child with a late birthday, Andy's mother did what most middle class Americans do; she got a professional opinion. When this opinion concurred with her own about whether Andy was ready, she was still confronted with the disapproval of her peers. Her friends' anecdotal knowledge of age and readiness contradicted the data provided by the psychologist (which cost $700.00) and they continued to insist that Andy would be better off if he waited to enroll in kindergarten until the following year. To some, it may appear that Andy's parents bought his readiness. But they did what they felt was necessary to buck a pervasive trend among the Norwood parents. From data of the 1988-90 kindergarten cohort at Norwood, it was estimated that 14% of the male kindergartners had been held out. This was for the entire Norwood kindergarten group. Andy's parents chose to put him into kindergarten, relying on their gut feeling about how he would do in kindergarten *now* rather than wait for some later payoff in the form of sports excellence.

What did the attitudes of the Norwood parents regarding readiness, age, and maturity mean for the way that the kindergarten experience was constructed for their children? What happened in a classroom when a sizable proportion of the kindergarten population was older than would normally be expected? What was it about the nature of kindergarten at Norwood that motivated parents to hold their children out? In the next section, these questions will be explored by describing how Mrs. Sunden, the afternoon kindergarten teacher developed her program within the environment of Norwood Elementary. A vignette which tells of a conversation between Monica Sunden and her colleague, Jack Presby, sets the stage for that description.

"Working Toward First Grade"

At Norwood, the two kindergarten classrooms are connected by workrooms and bathrooms and the teachers bounce back and forth between the two rooms frequently during the day. Three half-day sessions are taught by three teachers: two who work half-time and one who is the school art teacher when he isn't teaching kindergarten. It's 12:10 and the classrooms are quiet—the teachers are between sessions.

"I just talked to Mrs. Meeker," Jack blurts as he flies into Monica's classroom. Monica doesn't look up from the mess on her desk. "Who's Mrs. Meeker?"

"You know, AJ's mom. From my class last year."

"Oh... OK... What were you talking to her about?"

Jack raises his eyebrows in an expression of knowing disdain, prompting Monica to get herself in gear. "Whose class is he in?"

"Milly's... Mrs. Meeker says that AJ is really unhappy. He just needs to be a normal six-year-old boy, not reading the 68 books they read in a year. So he's in big trouble in there. You know all the kids that were retained are in that class? They ended up keeping back eleven, didn't they? So he's with kids who have already had all of the beginning first grade stuff *plus* they know how to read. AJ comes home and asks his mom what is the matter with him because *he* can't read. It's a no win situation! So she's feeling bad, wishing that they had held him out like everyone had suggested. At least the extra year would have been fun for him. And he was really great last year!"

"Yeah, I've already been zinged a couple of times with their workroom comments on the kids we sent them this year—and I thought they were one of the best groups I've had in years. We've got to talk to John [the principal] about this—I don't think that they anticipated what would happen to the kids we sent to her when they're dumped in with kids doing this material a second time. They don't have a chance."

"Let's figure out how to present this and sit down with the boss!" is Jack's parting comment.

As Monica gets things together for the afternoon's activities, she can't get her mind off Aaron, in light of her discussion with Jack. "He'd drown in first grade here. He just wouldn't make it. It would be really hard. I don't really recommend kids to repeat in kindergarten, but for him, he might need that. They review in first grade the first couple of weeks and then they go... I don't know what it is, but he just doesn't seem like he is with us. What am I supposed to do?"

What is it Like to Teach Kindergarten at Norwood Elementary?

Monica Sunden was an energetic, thoughtful woman in her late twenties. In the fall of 1989, she rejoined the kindergarten staff at Norwood after taking a maternity leave in the spring of the previous school year. Teaching the afternoon kindergarten session at Norwood was prompted by the birth of twin sons; it takes some time to get out of the house with twins, so teaching the morning class was out. Mrs. Sunden had been teaching at Norwood for five years and was just starting to have the siblings of children from her first few classes. All of those five years have been spent with kindergartners and she had developed what she thought was a coherent and sound philosophy for her teaching.

At a parent information night for incoming Norwood kindergarten families, Mrs. Sunden talked about her philosophy of education and how she saw that philosophy carried out in the types of activities she arranged for her students:

My philosophy of education is that I want to help your child
feel good about himself, to be excited to be here learning. Those
are the two main things: to feel good and to be excited to be
here. I don't use a lot of workbooks in my program—we do a
lot of active learning: cooking and hands-on activities that get
them into learning. One of the main things I want them to learn
is that it is OK to make a mistake as long as they try. We do
a lot of invented spelling in my class, having them try to figure
out how to spell things on their own, especially from January
on. They should try to spell things the way they think it should
be spelled. One thing you can do is to have them do a grocery
list at home and write what they need at the grocery store, then
find it at the store. That's a lot of fun for them. Just to let them
know that it's OK to try and to be wrong. It's OK to make
mistakes. Another thing is communication. It's really important
in any grade but especially in kindergarten. If you have a problem
or a concern, please call me, either at home or at school. I'll
give you my home phone number, I don't care. I just think it's
important to talk when we need to.

In this statement to parents, Mrs. Sunden outlined the kinds
of things she tries to do for her students and their families as
a kindergarten teacher. Her two major goals for her program were
to have her students feel good and to be excited about being in
school. Feeling good was a prominent theme in Mrs. Sunden's
instructional activities and will be discussed later when specific
tasks are examined. Central to the idea of feeling good is that
it is OK to make mistakes. Mrs. Sunden felt that this was very
important for students like hers, who come from backgrounds that
emphasize attaining goals and excelling in school, to learn to
deal with not being right (an interesting contrast to the orientation
that Ms. Carlin takes at Fulton).

Part of the way that Mrs. Sunden worked to make children
freer in their responses was not to use workbooks. She felt that
workbooks were based on the assumption that there was one right
answer in a task and were actually rather boring media for
teaching young children. Again and again Mrs. Sunden spoke
of not using workbooks in her class; it was a very important part
of her identity as a kindergarten teacher. In discussions with the
first grade teachers, Mrs. Sunden underscored the fact that she
did not use worksheets with her students and that they should
not expect facility in completing them. Her infrequent use of
worksheets was also a critical way that she distinguished herself
from Mr. Presby, one of the other kindergarten teachers. While

Mr. Presby certainly did not use an inordinate number of dittos, Mrs. Sunden saw the number that he did use as one of the things that made them different as teachers.

Another way to show children it is OK to make mistakes was her use of invented spelling, a method of facilitating emergent literacy development. When invented spelling (or temporary spelling as it is sometimes called) is used, children are encouraged to try to think of the way the word might be spelled, using their knowledge of letters and sounds. Children form their own spellings of words and use them in their writing. Over time they learn to incorporate the traditional spellings of words into their writing, but the invented spelling is never portrayed as the right way. Mrs. Sunden saw the use of invented spelling as a way to allow children to be free in their language, encouraging children to express themselves in a way that is appropriate for them.

The use of invented spelling and active, hands-on learning activities were Mrs. Sunden's way to make sure that her students were excited about coming to school. It kept them engaged in the education process and helped to keep them interested in what she was teaching.

Finally, Mrs. Sunden pointed out the importance of communication to the success of her program. She felt it is such a vital part that she even gave families her home phone number in the hope that they would get in touch with her if they had concerns. This was a necessary action in the context of the relationship of the school and the community, which will be discussed again later.

When I asked Mrs. Sunden about the goals she had for her students, she focused on the expectations that she had when they came into kindergarten, emphasizing the fact that she really did not have a list of skills that were required for them to be in her class. Instead, she listed several skills that were handy, in terms of classroom management, for children to bring to kindergarten:

> My goal. First of all, I don't have any real expectations when they come in. A guy called me from a newspaper a couple weeks ago and said, "What do you expect your kids to know when they come in?" I don't expect them to know anything. I mean I'll take them wherever they come in. We'll work with whatever we have. I don't get too concerned about it. It's nice if they know how to write their name... It helps if they can tie their shoes and button their coat or zip up their coat... Just because when I have 25 kids and I need to zip 25 coats it's kind of hard so

if they kind of know those kind of taking care of themselves
then that's good. Kindergarten is such a growing year for them.
Even though they've been in playgroups and pre-schools, a lot
of times they haven't been with many kids yet... Just getting
them to get in line and get in a circle and getting them to get
along and make friends and be in a group. So I think kindergarten
is such a social year.

Mrs. Sunden felt that she could work with most children when
they came into kindergarten, especially if they had basic self-
care skills. According to her, kindergarten was a time for growing
and learning to be social.

Mrs. Sunden felt that other people would see her job much
the same as she did; that say, her principal, John Hamilton, would
want the kindergartners to like school. She also listed several
academic skills that would be found to be important to others
when they examined the kindergarten program:

I think a lot of people would just say they'd like their children
just to really like school and like being there and like getting
up in the morning and going. Academically, I would probably
just say teaching the kids the sounds and alphabet and writing
their name and recognizing their shapes and colors.

Mrs. Sunden hinted at the kinds of expectations held by
parents and other teachers at Norwood regarding kindergarten
when she talked about the escalating curriculum. As described
in the literature, the first grade curriculum had been put into the
kindergarten curriculum, resulting in an increase in expectations
for young children's performance: "I think the expectations in
all grades are—well, what they expected in fifth grade now they
expect in fourth grade and what they expected in second grade,
now they expect in first grade. They're putting a lot of pressure
on kids, I think."

The kindergarten teachers were a tightly knit group who
planned together and shared responsibility for preparing materials. Each of the three contributed to the effort with an area of
strength: Jack was an artist, Lynn had a large musical repertoire,
and Monica wrote all kindergarten communications for the group.
The three sessions of kindergarten covered the same material at
the same time as the year went on because they planned a calendar
at the beginning of the year and fine-tuned plans as topics arose:

At the beginning of the year, Lynn and Jack and I sat down, before the kids came and we had a general plan about what we're going to do. We took a calendar and wrote on those weeks the letters we were going to teach and then we took the science kits that are available and worked those in like "Sight & Sound" during S (except we didn't get that kit)... So [then] we do our calendar every month with our parent helpers and it kind of refocuses us for the month. We get together again and say, "We're going to do this and this and this."

For example, the October calendar, which all the kindergarten teacher sent home to the parents, had the following skills listed for the entire month:

Math: Classification—by color, shape, size, & length
         Patterning

Health: Happiness is Trying, Smiling, Sharing, & Caring

Science: Autumn Cornucopia

For each of the weeks, the following topics were listed:

Week 1   Letter of the Week: Hh
         Show & Tell: Something about fire or fire prevention

Week 2   Letter of the Week: Ff
         Show & Tell: Tell the class your name, address & telephone number

Week 3   Letter of the Week: Nn
         Show & Tell: Bring something that makes noise

Week 4   Letter of the Week: Pp
         Show & Tell: Share your decorated paper pumpkin

Week 5   Letter of the Week: Tt
         Show & Tell:

By using this calendar, the teachers focused their instruction and let parents know what kinds of things they are doing in class. The calendar was one of their main ways to get parental involvement through activities like Show and Tell.

Much of the kindergarten planning was done on the fly because Jack, Lynn, and Monica had very separate schedules. Mrs. Sunden described how the plans got worked out:

> When I come in, when I'm walking around setting up my room, we're talking about it. Or I'll stop or after school we'll talk about it. Then when the week comes up on Thursday or Friday we'll stand in here and talk about things we want to do for the next week and Jack will have some things and say, "Do you want to make this or this?" and I'll bring out my ideas and Lynn will have hers and we'll all kind of brainstorm there and then we just kind of pick and choose what we want to do. We just do our lesson plans then. If I have a project that they all want to do, then I just get it ready for everybody. Or if Jack has something, he'll round up the paper... In math, we're all kind of on our own. It kind of depends on where our group is... By the end of the year we're pretty much all finished.

At the end of the year, Jack, Lynn, and Monica all got together and pooled their budgets for the following year so that they could get materials that could benefit all three classes. It took some negotiation to get agreement on what types of things to buy, but they managed to come up with a common purchase. This kind of co-operation showed the common goal that all of the teachers had for their programs and the unity they displayed as a kindergarten staff. In some ways, it also showed how they pooled information about what students needed in order to go to first grade and made decisions between books and puzzles, for example.

Parental Influence at Norwood

All kindergarten parents at Norwood filled out an information form during the first week at school to help the teachers know their students. The form included emergency information, data about siblings, day care, interaction with others, skills the child had acquired, parental expectations and goals, and special information that might be pertinent to the teacher. Examining the goals and expectations that parents noted on Mrs. Sunden's information sheets, two types of goals emerged: social-emotional and academic. Of the social-emotional goals, two subgroups could be seen: interactional goals and personal feelings. Of the interactional goals, parents wanted to see their children begin to work in groups (1), meet other children (4), and communicate with others (3). Under personal feelings, parents noted wanting their child

to feel good about school and learning (5) an
garten experience (4). Under academic go
interested in reading (6) and writing (3). On
of incoming skills, the following were noted fo
in Mrs. Sunden's class:

Dresses self —	24	Tells time —	0	Kno from
Writes name —	21	Reads —	2	Recog ABC's
Recognizes 0-10 —	22	Ties shoes —	16	Dials te
Knows phone number —	15	Knows address —	24	

When I asked Mrs. Sunden before school started i
about her parents' expectations for their children's kind
experience, she referred back to the information sheet
types of expectations that parents had voiced in the past:

> We have a little piece of paper or information sheet we h
> to pass, asking what are your expectations for your child t
> year in kindergarten? A lot of the questions are about when th
> learn how to read. They really want them to learn how to rea
> or they're thinking that maybe that's the time. But, no, that's
> not one of our goals in kindergarten. We just help them *want*
> to learn how to read.

In contrast to parents in the past, only about one fourth of the
1989-90 kindergarten parents in Mrs. Sunden's class mentioned
reading as a goal for their child's kindergarten experience. When
asked later in the interview about other things parents were
interested in for kindergarten she broadened the scope of their
expectations to the social-emotional goals that were listed by
parents on the information sheets:

> They want them to like school. That's a real big one. I just want
> them to be able to like school and make friends and I think
> a lot of parents are worried that their children aren't going to
> behave. At conferences, [they ask] "Well, how do they behave?"
> "They're wonderful." "Really? They're not like that at home."

the match between parent and teacher expectations
;arten, it was much more synchronous than might be
rom what Mrs. Sunden had originally mentioned. Both
nd teacher were concerned with wanting children to like
id to have good relationships with their friends.
ints at Norwood had a pervasive influence, felt in the
it they talked about the upcoming kindergarten experience
ir children, in the way that they talked to the teachers
year started, and through their involvement as the year
on. They had the idea that they could have an active role
eir child's education and the school reinforced that idea in
vay that school people worked with parents.
The school year started at Norwood with the parent infor-
tion meeting held the night before school began. The meeting
s organized to give parents an overview of the kindergarten
ogram and to answer any questions that the parents might
ave. Parent volunteers in classrooms were requested and in-
olvement in the school parent-teacher organization was solicited
by the principal, John Hamilton. Parents were given an introduction to the kindergarten teachers that included personal and
professional information (like number of years in the district,
teaching kindergarten and number of children) so that the teachers
were connected to the community. An interesting comment was
made by Mr. Hamilton during a discussion of the kindergarten
screening (which at Norwood occured during the kindergarten
day in September). After Mrs. Sunden had described some of the
tasks that children would be asked to do on the screening, Mr.
Hamilton interrupted and admonished the parents, "Now don't
go home and have them do this over and over [touching his thumb
to each finger, which was one of the motor tasks]. Remember
that this is a screening so we just want to see where the child
is." From past experience at Norwood, Mr. Hamilton felt that
it was necessary to remind the parents that coaching on the
screening task was not necessary; that they should not interpret
this as some absolute measure of their child's ability.

This parental press to succeed was also shown when Mr.
Presby talked about how parents reacted to report card grades.
At a Kindergarten-Grade One meeting, the two groups of teachers
talked about the kindergarten report card. Mr. Presby recounted
the pressure he felt when parent tried to renegotiate their children's
report card grades: "And parents get crazy if their child gets an
S-. They try to talk you up to an S! And you know, I don't know

if this is fair, but a child really has to be outstanding for them to get an O." The parents at Norwood worked as advocates for their children, even willing to argue over kindergarten report card grades so that their child could have all the marks of success.

Unlike the school-dominated parent-school relationship that existed at Fulton, the relationship at Norwood was more inter-active, with parents making their needs and expectations known in concert with the needs and expectations of the school. The parents, especially mothers, were actively involved in their children's education, in every aspect of school life. Mrs. Sunden told me that she had more parent helpers for her class than she knew what to do with; many parents couldn't be scheduled as often as they wanted. The kindergarten teachers even allowed parents to bring younger siblings when they came to work in the classroom, as long as there was an attempt to get the young ones involved in the work of the room. This policy was very accommodating to the needs of parents and was not seen in other schools studied.

At conferences in November, all the kindergarten teachers gave parents a copy of the kindergarten report card (which is not marked until the end of the first semester), a list of Reading Activities in the Home, a list of Things To Work On for parents. The Things To Work On list had the following elements: (1) Address, phone number, birthday; (2) Printing first name; (3) Letter recognition of capital and lowercase letter along with letter sound for: M, m, H, h, F, f, N, n, P, p, T, t; and (4) Name, address and a first class stamp to send a card for grandparents day. Mrs. Sunden described how they used the opportunity of meeting with the parents to address two needs: the need to focus their attention on the curriculum as represented on the report card and the need to let parents know the requirements of the curriculum so that they could prepare their children:

> So if we make sure that we teach what is on the report card (and you don't want to teach *to* the report card)—we just did birthdays and knowing your birthdate and knowing your address and knowing that stuff for show and tell. But that's one of the report card [objectives] and we worked it in to be a fun Show & Tell type thing so it didn't seem like any big deal. But when we did our conferences, I told the parents, "This is what you need to do" ...I just want them to know so that when they come in after they've looked at the report card, they can have questions ready or whatever they need. We thought we wanted them to

know what to expect. What we were teaching and why we were
teaching it.

Telling the parents about upcoming skills that would be assessed
for the report card had two purposes: to get the kind of backup
support from home that makes teaching easier and to let the
parents know the rules of the game so that they won't be surprised
or disappointed when their child was tested. This kind of co-operation kept information more free flowing and reduced the chances
of power struggles between the school and the family when
children were measured against the objectives for the program.

Mrs. Sunden's kindergarten session started at 12:45 each
afternoon. This, however, was not the time that children arrived
in her classroom. During my visits to Norwood, children arrived
as early as 12:10 and there was usually a good number of children
there by 12:30. Parents would drop their children off if they were
on the way somewhere else, or would stop to chat with Mrs. Sunden
about how their child was doing in class. Mrs. Sunden was a
half-time teacher and her only preparation time was before and
after class. The early arrival of children caused problems for her,
in that she had a hard time getting business done in the office,
returning phone calls or running off materials. It wasn't until
the end of the year that she told children that they were coming
too early, in part because it seemed that the parents felt that
it was OK to bring their children early. In our last interview,
Mrs. Sunden described how frustrating it was to have children
arrive in so early to class:

> I have kids coming at 12:15 still. The other day Eric came at
> 12:30 and I just said, "You're too early." Yeah, I think 12:30
> is a little early. Ten minutes is not that big a deal, but it is
> when I'm not in here! I can't get stuff together. And parents
> come in at 12:30... They want to chit-chat and ask me this and
> ask me that. I can't get stuff done. That's how come [I really
> appreciate it when] Allie comes in and does her stuff and she
> goes and leaves her stuff for me... Sometimes I need to be running
> to the office and I need to make phone calls and I need to do
> stuff and I can't do it because like yesterday, Alyson and Eric
> came early at 12:30 and I really needed to run to the office but
> then a bunch of others started coming in early and I just couldn't.
> Because I don't feel like I can leave them because then when
> I come back, they're bonkers and then I have three parents
> standing here watching them thinking, "Where's Mrs. Sunden?"

It seemed that the status that Mrs. Sunden had at Norwood was as a provider of a service of which parents could take advantage. This was in contrast to the role of an authority that Ms. Carlin showed at Fulton that would not allow that kind of treatment. Whether this was personality-related, with Ms. Carlin being more assertive in these types of situations, was unclear. It had obvious ramifications for both teachers in terms of the duty free preparation time they had available.

In the vignette, a former kindergarten parent came back to talk with Mr. Presby about the difficulties that her son was having in first grade, trying to find ways that they could ease the way for him. This was a theme that came up several times during the school year at Norwood. Parents there were used to being able to manipulate the system so that they could get the best for their children. One of the ways that they did this, according to Mrs. Sunden, was by knowing how services and resources were allocated within the community. If they knew that, they were more likely to be able to get what they needed. Mrs. Sunden described how this tended to work, focusing on how parents looked for the "good" first grade teacher for their child:

> Yeah, this is the kind of area where [everybody wants to know] Who's doing better than what? Who's got more than what? Who's got this and who doesn't? Who's got what teacher? I hate this time of year, to tell you the truth, with the parents because they all come in and [want to know] "Who should so-and-so have next year for a teacher?" What are you supposed to say? It's really hard, they really put you on the spot. And they go, "Well I just think you know better than anybody cause you know how the teachers are." And I always say "I don't think that's true, I know them, but I don't really know their teaching style." ...It's really hard and they put all of us on the spot... The first grade teachers call them Looky Lou's. People who come. And The Shoppers. They think they're shopping. Which they really are.

The parents at Norwood were willing to put in the time to research who would do the best job for their child and would consult their kindergarten teachers, who had proven that they were trustworthy and useful. This put the kindergarten teachers in a bad situation, where they felt that they would seem disloyal if they recommended one teacher over another for their children. At Fulton, this kind of very personal confrontation rarely happened, as most parents readily took the placements that were advised by Ms. Carlin and the other kindergarten teachers. The dynamics of the parent-school relationship were completely different at Fulton and Norwood, with the parents at Norwood having much more power to affect the educational experience of their child, both at home and at school.

Meeting the Ever Present Demands of First Grade

A persistent chorus sounded at Norwood: the work of kindergarten was done with an ever mindful eye on the demands made by the first grade program. In the vignette, Mr. Presby recounted the problems that one of his former students was having in first grade. AJ felt that something was wrong with him because he could not read like many of the other children in the class who were repeating first grade. Monica was frustrated by the professional pressure she felt when comments were made about the preparation of first graders, which implied that the kindergarten teachers were not doing their job. The parents involved themselves through their quest for a good first grade teacher. From the comments and interactions observed at Norwood, it seemed that first grade had three related types of influence on the kindergarten program: curricular concerns related to preparation of students (Is Marcy ready to go to first grade?), professional concerns related to comments made about the success of the kindergarten program in light of student first grade performance (Did I do my job so that my class will be able to fare well in first grade?), and finally parental concerns that started early in the kindergarten year about where to place their children (Is Mrs. Borden a good teacher?). All of these influences worked to place a pressure on the kindergarten program which was not seen at the other two schools.

When Mrs. Sunden thought about how students were doing in her kindergarten, the expectations of first grade often seemed to loom over her, coloring how she interpreted things. In our first interview, she brought up how the first grade teachers and their style of instruction affected what she did in her classroom:

> First grade at Norwood is very academic and I think their expectations are way too high and they put too much pressure on the kids and I really feel sorry for them. That's one concern I have about sending my kindergartners to first grade... I've been in the workroom and I know what kinds of things they do....They just do worksheets. They have 5 or 6 worksheets

sitting on their table when the kids walk in. And they're all
laid out on the table and they have to be totally done by recess.
If they don't get them done, they have to spend recess [in the
classroom]. Therefore, you have a bunch of kids in at recess every
day… They know their job. They've been there forever. And it's
not that they're not nice, the kids like them and all that kind
of stuff and they're very nice personally… and they're probably
very good teachers but I just think they feel like that they have
a lot of pressure on them and it all comes here… I had a little
girl, Jessica… She just wanted me to do everything… Well, I
just can't—they would tear her up in first grade… I told her
parents, if she doesn't sit down and get busy with her work and
get her job done, her first grade teachers, you're going to be
hearing… that she's young, that she needs to be retained, that
she's not getting her work done.

Mrs. Sunden was frustrated by the experiences of the students
sent on to first grade because it was so different from what she
constructed for them in her classroom. The pressure on the
students that came with the expectations of the first grade teachers
made Mrs. Sunden uncomfortable and she even tried to explain
it to students before they were promoted into first grade. She
described how she told them that things were going to be different,
that first grade was much more difficult than kindergarten and
that they would be expected to do more. It did not seem to be
the kind of message most kindergarten teachers wanted to give
their students.

Even within her own classroom, Mrs. Sunden found it difficult
to work within the boundaries set by the first grade for performance. If she had students who were very advanced in terms of
regular kindergarten skills, it was difficult for Mrs. Sunden to
get help from the first grade teachers. She talked about having
a child named Michael the year before who could read at the
fifth grade level. Wanting to provide him some enrichment
experiences so that he would continue to grow in his skills, she
decided to consult with the first grade teachers on the types of
materials and activities she could use with him. Mrs. Sunden found
it to be another frustrating experience:

I went to the first grade teachers and I said, "What do I do?"
Not very often do I have a child who can read like that. And
I just wanted their opinion on some kinds of things I could do
to stimulate him so he wouldn't be bored and getting in trouble
and all that kind of thing. They just didn't really help me very

much. They didn't help me a whole bunch. They don't want them
being in any kind of first grade workbook or doing any kind
of first grade work so that when they go to first grade they can
go into what [the teachers] have.

Mrs. Sunden came to the conclusion it this was not fair for her
students to put the needs of the Grade One teachers before their
needs. Not knowing what to do or not wanting to cause conflict
was not a good enough excuse. She decided that the needs of
the student would become her first priority from now on:

> Really, I probably could have done more with him. I kind of
> feel bad that I should have, but I really wasn't sure what I should
> do or how far I should take him or I didn't want to step on
> anybody's toes. But I think that I really learned from that. I
> don't think anymore I really care. I need to do what's best for
> the child.

Part of the reason that Mrs. Sunden had not forced the issue
of getting enrichment activities or special placements for her
students in first grade was that she knew what went on in their
classrooms and she thought that it was inappropriate. Somehow
she would have to come to terms with the tension of wanting
experiences for her gifted students and not wanting to subject
them to less than appropriate education. Mrs. Sunden did not
have any children with the kinds of needs that Michael had in
her 1989-90 kindergarten class so the issue did not come up in
quite the same way.

What did come up was subtle, but persistent, criticism by the
first grade teachers about how the kindergarten teachers prepared
children in their classes. They were told in various ways that
they taught their students letter-sound association inappropri-
ately, that the students were too noisy to work, and that children
came in not knowing how to hold a pencil, all of which made
the first grade teachers' job very difficult. These messages were
received in a number of ways. For example, Mrs. Sunden talked
about hearing comments in the teachers' lounge or the workroom
about the long list of failings the current group of first graders.
These comments were often interpreted as implying that someone
had not done her or his job and no fingers were pointing at the
Grade One teachers. The kindergarten teachers were tired of it:

We've heard about things in the past where we've heard them say, "These kids don't know how to write their name." And we told them, "We teach them how to write their name." We do the best we can do and then they get what they get when they get to first grade and if they have a problem with what we are doing, we want to know about it. We don't want to hear about it via the lounge.

To try to take care of this gap in communication, the kindergarten teachers asked to have a meeting with the first grade teachers so that they could discuss the two programs. The meeting was scheduled during the normal grade level meeting time, one Wednesday after school. Jack Presby introduced the meeting to the group by explaining why it had been called:

I wanted to give you all a copy of our kindergarten report card so that you would have an idea about what we are required to teach. I thought we should get together to talk about what we are required to do and for you to let us know what kind of expectations you have and how you see the kids that we are sending you.

From this opening, the interactions in the meeting were such that the first grade teachers gave pronouncements related to how they would like to see things happen in kindergarten or on the types of skills they saw in their first graders. For example, when examining the report card, the following exchange occurred:[5]

Jean (1):   Do kids flunk if they can't do these things listed?

Alice (1):   I hope so! [much laughter]

Milly (1):   These first things listed in Behavior: Has good attention span; Listens attentively without interrupting; Follows directions. Star those! Those are the most important things for us. Those kids have to have those skills.

After espousing the need to keep language activities alive in the kindergarten (with extensive discussion of the kinds of activities that would provide this practice), Milly asked about the kinds of things they found it necessary to drop from the curriculum:

Monica (K): Well, we only have 2 hours and 45 minutes to get everything in.

Jack (K):	And we have to do things like health and science and social studies now.
Alice (1):	You do that first semester? We don't do that stuff until the second semester.
Jack (K):	We try to integrate it into what we are doing in the rest of our program but we really feel like we are hitting a hard wall.
Jean (1):	It seems like they are trying to put too much into the kindergarten curriculum.
Alice (1):	And you are incorporating first grade things— things that we used to do in first grade.
Milly (1):	I think that you kindergarten teachers are going to have to start squawking about what they are trying to get you to do.
Jean (1):	And things like social studies can wait until the second semester.
Jack (K):	Well, we try to incorporate the activities into the science kit into whatever we are doing.
Monica (K):	Right. When we were talking about the letter M, we did a Me unit, and we talked about magnifying glasses and magnets.
Milly (1):	Those sound like terrific activities but you are leaving out vital kindergarten activities. You don't need to do those extra things every day.
Jean (1):	Yeah, some weeks just don't do them.
Milly (1):	You're doing enough during the school year.

Although the first grade teacher voiced humanistic and relatively traditional values about the kind of experience they would like to see in kindergarten, these sentiments were very different from the stinging comments about the skills missing in their students.

Milly (1):	It used to be that we had a big middle—now there really is no middle.
Alice (1):	I don't have any readers. There aren't any stars except for two from out of state. There just seem to be more on the low end.
Monica (K):	Well, we aren't teaching reading in the kindergarten!

Jean (1):	The kids don't know their color words!

Jean (1):   The kids don't know their color words!

Jack (K):   Now they should know that; we work on that all year!

Alice (1):   Or they write their name in all capitals.

Monica (K): We are fighting that all of the time.

Milly (1):   And they don't know the alphabet letter names. They say things like "Ba" for B. We're not saying that you don't teach these things. You are just trying to do too many things and they are not ready.

Jean (1):   Last year, I had a group that was really wanting to read and to write. But this year, not really.

Milly (1):   I think that the kids we have this year are really sweet disposition-wise. Sweet and nice—no turds!

Jean (1):   But last year the kids I had really wanted to write.

Milly (1):   I think that this pencil grip stuff comes from expecting more from these kids earlier. We are trying to get them to use a pencil to write on their own. It's something that might better wait until the second semester.

Again and again, the first grade teachers talked about the shortcomings of their students. The children in their classes just did not fit their expectations for what a first grader should be doing. This was not just idle chatter either; these judgments were carried out in practice over the years. Of the first graders in the 1988-89 cohort, nineteen of them were recommended for retention in first grade (approximately one fifth of the group). Ultimately, eleven were retained and all of them placed in a single class along with a group of kindergartners promoted from the year before. That policy had repercussions demonstrated in the vignette, in that the children who had not been retained felt like they were behind their retained peers because this was their first time through the first grade material and they could not understand why they did not know it.

Readiness at Norwood—How Age Sets the Stage

One of the most important ways that people at Norwood understood children was by their age and markers of their age, such as behavior. Age was used in general descriptions of children, in discussions of children's ability, and in discussions of special programs. The concept of age was intimately entwined with judgments of readiness at Norwood and will be examined in that context. Outside Mrs. Sunden's classroom at Norwood was a bulletin board that displayed information the staff wanted to share with parents. All during the 1989-90 school year, an article from *Parents'* magazine had a place on that bulletin board that seemed to encapsulate the way that the Norwood staff and many of the parents thought about age and readiness. The title of this article was "Is Your Child Ready for School?" and led off with this teaser: "Age isn't the only factor. Lots of kids are developmentally unready—and pressuring them can bring long-term problems. But what choices do parents have?" (Bjorklund and Bjorklund, 1988). The article focused on the contradictory role that age can play in the assessment of readiness. On the one hand, the authors asserted that young children with summer birthdays might not be ready for school because of immaturity. In contrast, age was not the only indicator and the authors included a checklist "to help parents appraise their child's 'readiness'" (Bjorklund and Bjorklund, p. 116). This piece of writing represented how the Norwood community tended to talk about and act on readiness.

One of the first times I spoke with Mrs. Sunden, she described a couple of situations in which children were found by one person or another to be unready, and age came up:

> I was at a Discovery Toy party and a mom told me about taking her son to the doctor for the pre-kindergarten physical and the kid was just a mess the whole time—he had a fit. By the end, the doctor said, "There's no way this one is ready for kindergarten." And all along they had just assumed that he should go and now they are really worried and are trying to decide what to do. The parents look at me and ask, "What should I do?" [she laughs] All I can say is, "You know your child the best. Ultimately you need to make the decision." I guess I always figure that they could try putting the child in and see how they do. I had a boy two years ago who had a summer birthday and he came into my class and just couldn't cut it—he was having a really hard time. His parents took him out and then he went into school last year and he was a *completely* different little boy. He seemed happy and really ready to be there. You know when we had that developmental kindergarten program, that was really good for those younger ones. It's a less structured program that really seemed to fit what those little ones needed.

Mrs. Sunden gave examples of two children who were not ready for kindergarten: one, who was identified by his doctor and the other, who was "young" and just could not make it in her class. When he returned the following year, there had been a transformation that Mrs. Sunden attributed to having that extra year of growth. Age was the culprit: young children were at risk for problems because they just were not mature enough. This is the same idea that had been voiced in the pre-kindergarten interviews by Norwood parents but as I will show, it was less well-developed than the very coherent school model of age and readiness that was discussed by the teachers.

Approximately five years before, the Norwood staff had developed an alternative program to deal with children who appeared to come into school unready. With a population that did not qualify for the district extended-day program, they felt it was necessary to come up with structures to deal with children who did not meet the school performance expectations. The structures that they put together were a developmental kindergarten program, which had a less demanding program than the usual kindergarten class and also a transitional first grade, which emphasized the needs of children finished with kindergarten but unready to undertake the demands of the academic program in grade one. These two programs usually resulted in children taking three years to get through the kindergarten-grade one sequence (developmental K-kindergarten-grade one or kindergarten-transition room-grade one). I asked Mrs. Sunden to describe how these programs came about at Norwood:

> The teachers really wanted it because they could see the kids that were younger having problems like in the second and third grade. They were too young to catch up. It was really difficult for them. So the teachers could see, those who teach the upper grades, they could probably pick out the ones who are young.

As a response to children who might have later difficulty, the staff at Norwood concluded that they could stop these problems before they began by intervening and putting children who were young in a special class early on. Mrs. Sunden was the teacher for the developmental kindergarten and she described what her students were like: "I had a lot of—they were young. They just wanted to lay on the floor and I had a little girl who had her blanket. They liked to play in the water. They were very young... A lot of my birthdays were in the summer... They were more just really young." The reasoning behind the alternative program was maturational in nature and focused on age as the primary marker for readiness. The teachers were given Gesell Institute training to help identify children who were not ready and to provide a basis for developing the alternative curriculum that was necessary for the classes. With this maturational orientation, the only way to help students at risk was to give them more time to mature; in this case it was through an alternative placement that was less structured and demanding on the students.

In place for four years, the developmental kindergarten and transitional programs were discontinued according to Mrs. Sunden because "the parents were not supportive of it at all. I think it was OK until they said their children needed to be in it." The parents at Norwood had enough power to put pressure on the school to disband a program that they felt put a stigma on children who were placed in it. They were involved enough in the school to know what the program was about (in their view) and they knew enough about how to work the system that they had it removed from the school.

The maturational model for describing children had not been discarded at Norwood, however. Mrs. Sunden often used the idea of children acting young to describe their behavior. For example, this is how she talked about Alyson when I asked her to describe various students in an October interview:

> At first I thought, you know, she just turned five after school started... I thought this little girl is going to be really young and she *is* young in a lot of ways, but she is a really nice little girl. She gets along and is really polite but she knows what is going on. She writes her name, capital A and the rest of the letters lower case. She can recognize the letters and she is taking in a lot of information.

Even though Alyson came in with a September birthday, her behavior allowed her to overcome the "young" tag that normally was attached to a child with a birthday that close to the school enrollment cutoff. Because she could perform as a child who was not young, she was seen as ready by Mrs. Sunden.

In the Kindergarten-Grade 1 meeting that was held in October, Milly asked the kindergarten teachers if they were seeing immature children this year. In his reply Jack compared the younger and older children in his class and gave examples of how the young children act:

Jack: Oh, there are some older ones, the ones who are ready
               to go. Then there are the ones who have just turned
               five. Those are the ones we watch. Like my Daniel.
               He knows so much—about airplanes and everything
               but he can't keep it all to himself! He talks constantly
               and can't listen. He talks about things that have
               nothing to do with what we are doing. Really bright
               but into everything.

Milly: That's because he has no awareness of others. In
               that respect he is a 3½ year old but in his need for
               action he is at a 4½ level. Just no awareness of others.

Milly analyzed Daniel's behavior for Jack, putting it within a
traditional Gesellian age level framework which described
characteristics of children at various ages. The training that she
had received to work within the transitional program was still
useful to her to understand how children's behavior represented
their readiness level by age.

Mrs. Sunden rarely spoke of readiness as something that
guided her teaching. Unlike Ms. Carlin, who had a model of
readiness that she used in instruction, Mrs. Sunden used the
expectations of the first grade teachers and their curriculum to
calibrate her judgments. The focus of her assessments was often
related to child age, either chronologically or what she might call
developmentally (i.e., how old does the child act?).

Even though the alternative program had been disbanded,
the age model for readiness continued to be applied at Norwood
in less explicit ways. Some parents were choosing their own three
year track for their sons and daughters by practicing academic
redshirting, delaying entrance into school until children are six.
When this was combined with the relatively large number of
retentions in first grade (20% of first graders recommended, with
more than half of those actually staying back), the system seemed
to have readjusted to require children judged to be unready to
have some kind of alternative program at some point in their
early school career.

To try to get a better idea of the kinds of behaviors that would
be problematic for a child going into first grade, the kindergarten
and first grade teachers talked about specific examples of
things children might do. Part of the impetus for this discussion
was a specific child in Mrs. Sunden's class, Matthew, who had
many of what Mrs. Sunden would call immature behaviors:
sucking his thumb, rolling around on the floor, etc. She wanted

to get an idea of whether doing these things would impede his
progress in first grade:

> Mrs. Sunden: We talked to the first grade teachers a while back
>   and we gave them examples of behaviors that
>   we were concerned about and I said I had a little
>   boy who sucks his thumb all the time. Matthew
>   stopped sucking his thumb there for the longest
>   time; he never sucked it at school and his mom
>   and dad said he sucked it a lot at home. But then
>   all of a sudden, like after January, he started
>   sucking it again a lot. He just kind of went back
>   to it, so I didn't make any big deal of it anymore.
>   But they said, "Don't worry about that." And I
>   was saying how he was lying on the floor and
>   they'd say, "Don't worry about that." I was kind
>   of in shock that they weren't concerned about the
>   things that I was concerned about.
>
> Int: What kinds of things were they concerned about?
>
> Mrs. Sunden: They weren't even concerned about the kids
>   academically, which surprised all of us, that they
>   weren't more. Their main concern was that they
>   sit still and listen to a story and attend to a task.
>   And if they can't do that then they're worried.
>   They can't sit for like a half an hour or whatever
>   and listen to a story and do sharing and do that,
>   like our opening stuff, if they can't sit through
>   that then they're worried.

From this particular discussion, Mrs. Sunden was left with a
confused idea about what it meant to be ready for first grade.

The parents at Norwood came into the school with very
specific ideas about the kinds of experiences they thought their
child should and would have in kindergarten and they had a
way to measure whether their child was ready for that experience.
Within the school, the parental community was active in the life
at Norwood and exerted its presence in most aspects of the school
program. The kindergarten teachers worked together to develop
a coherent program for the kindergartners, and much of this work
was done within the scope of and in response to the expectations
of the first grade curriculum and its teachers. The people at
Norwood almost unanimously used some form of a maturational
model for understanding children and they used explicit policies

(like the alternative programs that were developed and then disbanded) and unstated policies (like the use of redshirting and retention in grade one) to meet the needs of children who did not meet the expectations of the school. With all of this going on around them, what was it like to be in kindergarten at Norwood? What was Mrs. Sunden's program like? These are examined in the next section.

To introduce classroom life in Mrs. Sunden's kindergarten, this section begins with a vignette focusing on one part of a day with her students. In this vignette, Mrs. Sunden introduces the topic for the day, circles, and then moves the children into small group activities through which groups of children rotated.

"Learning About Circles"

Mrs. Sunden watches her children listening intently for the shape they are holding. The voice on the record calls triangles, circles or squares. They pop up and sit down, smiling broadly. Not bad, considering this is only the fourth day of school. As the song plays, Mrs. Sunden is running through the plans for the week in her mind. Jack has given her the materials she needs for the art projects for circle day today and rectangle day tomorrow; all she has to do is get the triangles and squares ready for Thursday and Friday. No problem—her parent volunteer can get that together tomorrow. Since it is only a four day week, they'll hit diamonds next Monday.

Gathering up the shapes when the song is finished, Mrs. Sunden tells the children that they are going to start working in groups. Explaining that they will stay with their color groups, there are several activities that they will do today, switching from one activity to the next after a short period of time.

"Some of you will work with Mrs. Graue, making caterpillars out of circles. Some of you will be doing seat work... Today is the first day that we are lucky enough to have helpers from sixth grade. They'll be at the seat work table to help you, if you need help. Let's say good afternoon to the sixth graders."

"Good afternoon, sixth graders," the group says in unison in a sing-song tone.

"What shape is this?" Mrs. Sunden asks as she holds up a big pink construction paper circle.

"A circle."

"That's right, it's a circle. You'll be coloring and cutting out this picture of a bird and gluing it on this circle." She holds up a picture of a bird with a worm in its mouth that has a dotted circle around it. "If you work with me—you'll come to what we call the teacher's table right here [pointing to a table] and we'll be talking about shapes. If you are at free choice, you can take any of these shapes to build other shapes or anything you want. You can use these shape templates to draw with or you can listen to the Gingerbread Man story in the listening center. Are you ready to give it a try?"

Mrs. Sunden then calls the children individually to go to an area and start the activity. There are about seven children in each group. Each activity lasts fifteen minutes, then the groups of children rotate to another. As the first group attacks the caterpillar task, they confidently draw circles on small pieces of construction paper then cut them out with scissors. With a little encouragement, almost the right amount of glue is used to make the circles stick to the background paper. The children then decorate the caterpillar with antenna and grass. It seems that they could go on with this project forever, adding circle after circle to make the world's longest bug. When they are finished with the caterpillar it goes into their cubby to take home.

At the free choice table, the children seem to go from one choice to another, trying out their options. They try stacking the pattern tiles, using the shape templates for drawing, and using the listening center. They tend to go together in clumps, with one child making the decision to check out another activity with a couple of others trailing behind.

At seat work, the sixth graders watch benignly as the children color the bird and cut it out. Supervision is needed only for the gluing process so that the children don't flood the table with the white gooey stuff. This appears to be a social activity for the sixth graders, who chat back and forth, sometimes competing for the attention of the kindergartners.

Mrs. Sunden sits on the floor with a group, talking about shapes. They work on sorting shapes of various colors and sizes and talking about their attributes—which ones are round, which have points, which have four sides. Mrs. Sunden makes mental notes about the kinds of things the children say about them and it seems that almost everybody has a pretty good grasp on the concepts.

After about fifteen minutes, Mrs. Sunden asks the children to freeze. She then reassigns the children to new activities, telling them that if they were at the art table, they can come work with her, if they were with her they can go to free choice, if they were at free choice they can go to seat work, and if they were at seat work they can go to the art table. When they are unfrozen, the children move to their assigned area with a minimum of confusion. It takes a minute to get the ball rolling again, but each group then dives in and gets to work.

The Kindergarten Experience in Mrs. Sunden's Classroom

In contrast to Ms. Carlin's kindergarten program, Mrs. Sunden's classroom did not have the very distinctive set of activities such as "Doing it Right" and "Writing", with their separate rules and criteria for success. Mrs. Sunden's program had a single focus for the most part, in that she organized her instruction through projects that taught various concepts. For example, when the class was learning about the letter B, they learned about bears, they went Bumper Bowling; all content areas tended to focus on the unit at hand. For this reason, the description of her first grade preparation program will examine how these content areas were developed within the project orientation.

The schedule of Mrs. Sunden's classroom started officially at 12:45, but as mentioned earlier, children often arrived earlier than that. During the period of time before 12:45, the children explored around the room, playing in the housekeeping corner, the writing center, working puzzles, or playing among themselves. During the hours of the formal kindergarten session, the choices made in terms of child activity and materials were made by Mrs. Sunden for the most part. She provided some leeway for students by putting more than one type of activity at the free choice table, with their selection confined to the things on the table. Occasionally Mrs. Sunden announced a free choice period that included any materials in the classroom; this occurred no more than once a week.

The daily schedule for Mrs. Sunden's class shows the variety of types of activities included in the Norwood kindergarten program:

Norwood Daily Schedule

12:45-1:00	Opening Attendance, Calendar, Weather, Pledge, Person-of-the-Day
1:00 - 1:15	Alpha time/Alphabet Adventure
1:15 - 2:20	Small group work Seat work, Free Choice, Parent Helper, Teacher
2:20 - 2:30	Clean-up and/or begin Show & Tell
2:30 - 2:45	Recess
2:45 - 3:10	Health/Science/Social Studies/Free Choice
3:10 - 3:20	Show & Tell, Story, Sharing Time, Author's Chair
3:20 - 3:30	Clean-up & Dismissal at 3:30

Within the small group activities, Mrs. Sunden did math two times a week, reading readiness two times a week, and writing once a week at the teacher table. In terms of analysis of the time allocation in Mrs. Sunden's classroom, it is difficult to do a single breakdown of different kinds of activities. Content areas were interwoven within the unit topic being covered in the class and the activities that comprised something like seat work varied from academic to social depending on the day. Probably the most obvious characteristic of Mrs. Sunden's schedule is the fact that her students did not have a regularly scheduled free play period during the day. Even free choice varied in its focus, sometimes being academic, other times being clearly social. Materials for free choice were always chosen by the Mrs. Sunden, the name came out of the fact that they usually had a variety of materials from which to make their selections. When the kindergarten teachers were asked what types of things that they had given up in the classes to incorporate the ever-broadening objectives of the kindergarten curriculum, Mrs. Sunden replied "We've given up a lot of kindergarten stuff. Things like free play and free choice."

When Mrs. Sunden formally started the kindergarten day, she asked the children to meet her at their circle spots. These were spots in a circle at the front of the room that had been assigned by Mrs. Sunden at the start of the year. She assigned them in a boy-girl pattern, trying to separate children who might have problems sitting together. The first order of business was choosing the Person-of-the-Day, who worked as a helper, taking attendance to the office and being the first in line whenever the group moved from place to place. Choosing the person of the day was a random event, facilitated by the Magic Pencil, which Mrs. Sunden used to point to the Person-of-the-Day's name. Children were clued to the Person-of-the-Day's identity with statements like "This person is a boy" "This person is wearing red shoes."

Next was the calendar, which was completed in the Math Their Way style, with the addition of the "Word of the Day," which was left in a balloon by the morning class. Each class left a word that started with the letter of the week and the other class tried to guess what it was from hints given by the teacher. They often used this later in the year as practice in decoding, leaving key letters out of words. The Person-of-the-Day was allowed to choose a song, which involved some kinds of whole class sing along actions. Mrs. Sunden's class used musical activities such as this more than any of the other classes I observed; they were all from records.

In the Alphatime or Alphabet Adventure part of the day, the class did activities related to the letter of the week, either using a Letter Person story or song or listening to a story about a character beginning with the letter of the week. Sometimes this was used as a springboard for the small group activities.

Small group activities were run as described in the vignette: the class was divided into four groups (of about seven children each) which rotated through the four tables set up each day. Seat work (or independent work) was usually some kind of writing task; either a ditto to teach letter writing or dictating a story to an adult. The focus was working semi-autonomously. Free choice usually had two or three activities available for the children to do. Activities such as using a magnifying glass or playing with magnets were at Free Choice during M week. At the parent helper table, children completed an art project that went with the topic of discussion. In the vignette, the children made caterpillars out of circles to go with the circle theme for the day. As mentioned previously, at the teacher table, Mrs. Sunden worked on math or reading twice a week each or writing once a week. Each small group worked for about fifteen minutes, then rotated to another table.

The remaining part of the school day was flexible and depended on the length of the activity chosen. All activities were done in a large group format. Show and Tell was usually done during several pieces of the day and focused, again on the topic under discussion. During N week, the children were to bring something that made noise, during T week, they brought tricks. Children are assigned a day of the week for Show and Tell, but no formal mechanism was used to keep track of who had or had not brought things to talk about. After a child had presented something, the class was allowed three questions or comments. The child called on those with raised hands who might ask a question about the Show and Tell item or might say something like "I like that."

One way that the activities in Mrs. Sunden's classroom could be sorted out was by size of group: things were done either in a large group format or small group format. Large group activities had the teacher as the focus, with individual student engaged at her invitation. Large group activities were usually done with children in their circle spots, with Mrs. Sunden sitting or standing at the edge of the circle. From this spot, she ran through routines (like the calendar), gave overviews of the day's activities, or read stories. One of the salient aspects of large group activities was the emphasis on children raising their hand and being called on to gain access to the floor. Mrs. Sunden gave much positive reinforcement to children who followed these guidelines and typically ignored children who did not follow these conventions. Specific instructions for activities were rarely given in the large group setting; instead, those were given at the small group level. Large group activities included opening, alphabet activities, Show and Tell and stories.

Children were not grouped by ability in Mrs. Sunden's class, which was a change from earlier in her career. Previously, she would ability group for the first part of the school year then mix the groups up later. However, the previous year she tried heterogeneous groups and found that they worked really well:

> I knew where each kid was, but I think the kids who are really doing well can help the kids who aren't. Sometimes they can talk to them in kid language and stretch it a little bit. And it does a lot for the kids that have a lot of ability to be able to do things like that. So I didn't ability group at all last year. I thought the kids really helped each other that way. I like doing it much better that way.

When she comprised small groups, Mrs. Sunden just tried to balance the groups by sex and to separate children who interacted poorly in class. She enjoyed these heterogeneous groups and saw them working well in her class.

During small group, Mrs. Sunden introduced various concepts and checked for mastery. They did group sorting activities, patterning, worksheets, writing, and letter recognition activities. This small group interaction was very important to her—it gave her a chance to do assessment and interact on a one-to-one level with her students:

> I just feel like I know my kids better when I work in small groups. I know them more individually and I can see their work habits better. When I do large group situations all 23 want your attention at that time. They all want you to draw their circle and they all want your help right then. I just couldn't get to all 23. Even when I do large stuff, it's frustrating.

Working in small groups made Mrs. Sunden feel closer to her students. This was especially important because she wanted them to feel good about their work and the small group format allowed her to intervene before children got into trouble. She gave an example of doing a free hand reindeer art activity, where the children were given no patterns to trace:

> I don't get too worried about what they look like but the kids get upset. Just like Jared [who had gotten confused trying to cut two antlers out of a piece of paper and who ended up very frustrated.] And you can catch things like that and you can teach them something instead of having them cut it out and say, "Oh." Then have it be all wrong and all you're doing is giving out more paper instead of helping them fix it. Because I can't help them fix everything they do wrong when I'm with a big group.

The small group format was used for many activities in Mrs. Sunden's classroom because she wanted the children to feel good about the things they made and did—they worried about making mistakes or having something that did not look good. This pressure did not come from Mrs. Sunden, who only made negative comments when she thought that children were not trying their best. Trying to get children past the fear of making a mistake was one of Mrs. Sunden's main goals:

> The beginning of the year the kids come in real quiet and shy and they want things done for them and they're constantly looking for approval. "Am I doing this right?" But as the year goes on, they get to be so much more independent. They don't ask as many questions and they aren't as worried, I don't think about whether things are right or wrong.

Much of the focus of the kindergarten program at Norwood originated in the demands that were made in the first grade program. Because the first grade teachers had very specific and relatively rigid requirements for student skills and abilities, activities and materials were chosen in the kindergarten with those requirements in mind. "If you don't do what they think the kids need, we hear about it. And not from them but we hear about it via the grapevine." Mrs. Sunden related why she felt that she could not rely solely on Math Their Way for their math program and needed to combine it with the use of a mathematics basal program:

> We just start at the beginning of the teacher's guide and kind of work through it. D.C. Heath. Plus I do Math Their Way. For me, Math Their Way, I just needed something more structured for math. I did Math Their Way one year and I didn't feel like I had a grasp of what they knew and I needed to make sure that I got all these things taught because of my curriculum. Because I had to make sure that they could write their numbers to ten and Math Their Way doesn't really make sure that they know that. It's fun if they do but if they don't... It comes back to us. We have to show that we've done all that stuff.

Because of the accountability pressures that Mrs. Sunden had to deal with related to content coverage, the small group format provided a good assessment opportunity for her class. Her focus on the numbers 1 to 20 was interesting because the district objectives for that area only required children to identify the numbers 1 through 10 but the district report card listed 1 through 20 for writing numerals. Mrs. Sunden interpreted the requirements of her program to include the broader objective, extending from 10 to 20.

Learning letter sounds and putting them into words was a major task in the Norwood kindergarten, with much of the instructional effort placed in that area. Unit activities were for the most part oriented to letters of the week; the class began the study of the alphabet in the third week of school. The order of presentation of letters came from the Alphatime Program, which starts with the letter M. Mrs. Sunden explained that she used the Alphatime loosely, using the letter people to introduce each letter. In addition, each child wrote a Zoophabet Book, in which stories were written about imaginary animals for each letter of the alphabet. The activities used to introduce and reinforce alphabet learning worked to integrate many areas of the curriculum.

Children learned to write letters of the alphabet through large group instruction which involved Mrs. Sunden drawing upper and lowercase letters and having children volunteer words that began with that letter. During the week the children did a worksheet in which they practiced writing the letter; the worksheets were not checked for accuracy but were sent home the day they were completed. Formal assessment of letter writing occurred later in the school year during individual testing.

Writing experiences began at Norwood with children dictating stories both in groups and individually. With group dictation, the class started with a title and then built a story together. The activity was teacher led. Individual stories were dictated for class books containing stories and illustration by each student. These stories were put together and bound as a book for use in the classroom. In October, Mrs. Sunden began to transition the class into writing their own stories using invented spelling. For some children there was much resistance to using invented spelling because they said that they did not know how to spell the words correctly. A low pressure environment in terms of writing seemed to ease much of the children's fear.

After Christmas, the pace of reading readiness instruction increased slightly with the introduction of several activities that reinforced letter sounds. The first was a game called Around the World in which pairs of children sat together and were flashed pictures of simple words for which they were to offer the beginning letter. The child who said the letter correctly first moved to the next child in the circle and were presented another picture. The child who identified things correctly moved around the circle, going "around the world." This was a very public practice in and assessment of the ability to identify initial consonant sounds. Mrs. Sunden said that the children loved it and when I saw the class playing in January, there was obviously much excitement generated.

The other activity was for children to play Hangman to learn to decode words. Hangman was sometimes played in a large group (especially initially, when the children were first learning to play) and later pairs of children went to the chalkboard to play during free choice times in the classroom. When I interviewed children in January, many of them talked about playing Hangman.

The use of these types of activities for reading readiness instruction was very different than those in the other classes studied. They were less contextually oriented than say the writing activities in Ms. Carlin's classroom and as such, could be seen as much more difficult. They had a competitive spirit, which took full advantage of the achievement orientation that seemed to drive many of the Norwood students, which Mrs. Sunden had mentioned previously.

Norwood Students and Their Perceptions of the Kindergarten Experience

I interviewed many of the students in Mrs. Sunden's class in January to find out how they were thinking about being in kindergarten. Two different methods were used to elicit information from the children. During small group time, Mrs. Sunden gave me access to a center so that I could ask groups of children questions. Each group of seven was asked to draw a picture in response to a question (What do you learn in kindergarten? What is easy in kindergarten? What is hard in kindergarten? What do you need to learn to go to first grade?) Each group was asked only one question. After children finished their pictures they dictated the text to go with it. This was a common writing activity in their class so they were quite used to it. Later, I took small groups of three or four children in same sex groups out of the classroom to ask them a set of questions about the things that they were learning in kindergarten and what Mrs. Sunden and their parents wanted them to learn.

When asked what kinds of things they learn in kindergarten, Mrs. Sunden's students did not focus on any particular aspect of the program. Dennis told me that he learned that the earth moved slow; Ida learned letters, reading, and writing; Tammy learned to write, but thought that her parents would teach her reading; and Eric told me that he hadn't learned anything yet. Four of the kindergartners told me that drawing things was easy; other answers focused on hanging coats up, walking, and singing. Things that they found hard in kindergarten were varied as well. Drawing was cited by three of the thirteen students, while others thought making things out of clay, cutting things out, and coloring big were difficult. Andy had an interesting answer to the question, "What is hard to do in kindergarten?" "I have a hard time reading. You have to learn how. In first grade probably the teacher will teach me. Evan Scott won't learn—he has brain damage. The teacher is very nice." Somehow, Andy had hooked up the idea that learning had to do with how well your brain works and he knew that Evan Scott could not learn because he had what someone had told him was brain damage. I do not know how he defined brain damage.

Probably the most consistent set of responses came from Mrs. Sunden's students when I asked them what they needed to learn to go to first grade. Of the seventeen students who answered this question, eleven said that you had to learn to read to go to first grade. Most of the students I talked to interpreted their job in kindergarten to be learning to read and they had very vivid ideas about what would happen if they did not learn those things. When I asked Eric and Dennis what would happen if they did not learn to read, this is how they responded:

Eric: Um, my teacher will say I'm not going to be in first grade, I'm still going to be in kindergarten.

Int: What do you think Dennis?

Dennis: I'll get in trouble.

Int: And what will happen if you get in trouble?

Dennis: Um, we'll have to put our heads down.

Int: How would you feel if you didn't go on to first grade?

Eric: I would feel pretty sad. What happens if I was nineteen, what happens if I was a hundred years old and I was still in kindergarten?

Int: You think that could happen?

Eric: Yeah!!

Ida told me about how her brother had stayed in first grade for two years because, "he had trouble reading and there was something wrong with his eyes and so now he has green glasses."

Jared, who had been held out of school the previous year because his mother felt that he had very immature behavior, interpreted what you needed to do in kindergarten in terms of how other people would react to you:

Int: Jared, what do you think you have to learn to go to first grade?

Jared: Read and be good and sit down and be still.

Int: What if you don't learn how to read?

Jared: If you don't know how to be good then you'll be a
          bad boy.

Int: OK, then what will happen?

Jared: Then you'll have to wish that you were good... Nobody
          will want you if you're a bad kid.

Jared seemed to be investing much of his self worth in how others
thought he was behaving in school. He defined his goodness in
terms of whether he could sit down and listen and read. Considered
in the context of how Jared's mother thought about the payoff
of the extra year for year (which will be discussed in the next
section), the way that he thought about himself seemed to be a
setup for failure in that any negative feedback from others would
be internalized by Jared as meaning that he was bad.

*How Did Norwood Parents Talk about Their Children
and Kindergarten After the First Quarter?*

As at Fulton, I made arrangements to interview parents when
they came for parent teacher conferences in November, at the
end of the first quarter of school. I attended a set of evening
conferences that would allow interviews with a broad range of
parents. Six interviews were scheduled, with five parents coming
in for their appointment with Mrs. Sunden. All interviews but
one occurred before the parents met with Mrs. Sunden and the
conversations tended to focus on the types of things that parents
were thinking about after their child had been in kindergarten
for the fall. Three were the parents of sons, two had daughters.
Two of the boys were overage for kindergarten. Johnny, who had
moved to Norwood in the summer, had spent the previous year
in a special pre-kindergarten program designed for children
perceived to be unready. Jared had been held out by his parents
and had spent what should have been his kindergarten year in
pre-school. Both Mitch and Jennifer were born in January, so
they were relatively older and Susan had a May birthday.

In the pre-kindergarten interviews, Norwood parents discussed readiness as a multidimensional idea that included
maturity, age, social and academic readiness. Examining how
parents in the November interviews talked about their children's
kindergarten experience so far, three of the five explicitly discussed
readiness in one way or another, a fourth talked about it in a

roundabout way and the fifth did not mention it at all. The group
of parents could be most sensibly divided into two groups: those
who spoke of readiness freely (n=3) and those who did not (n=2).
How were the two groups different? Those who did not speak
of readiness did not speak of talking to other people in the
community, and did not discuss any kind of belief about age and
how it would relate to their child's competence at school. Their
most salient characteristic was probably that they had not been
in the Norwood community very long; each had moved to Norwood
within six months of the start of school. Because they had not
been a part of that community for an extended period of time,
they had not had the time to incorporate the language and beliefs
that characterized Norwood parents. They therefore did not have
readiness as a template for interpreting their experiences and their
child's skills and abilities.

These two parents were also very different, however. Johnny's
parents were greatly concerned about his progress. He had gone
to a pre-kindergarten program the previous year and they had
been told that he would move to a more normal ability level with
that extra year. This is how his parents described the decision
progress that led to the extra-year placement in New Jersey:

Mother: He went to two whole years of nursery school... and
          then at the end of nursery school (they always test
          them with the kindergarten screening) I guess half way
          through the last year of nursery school they tested him.
          And every time you would go into the conferences,
          they'd say, "Well, he's behind in this... and he's not
          paying attention... and he's not really doing what we
          are asking him to." So we got to know these teachers...
          She had recommended that he not go in, that he spend
          another year in nursery school and I didn't think that
          would be too good. The town had the option of kin-
          dergarten or pre-kindergarten with only ten children
          in the class... So he went there, he did in the middle
          to the lower end of the class, not at the very bottom
          but in the lower of the middle end. He liked it so I
          thought that was positive, he was with kids his own
          age and it was just like kindergarten except not as
          much stress on grades... It was good, we were glad
          we sent him there... The teacher didn't think it was
          a maturity thing. The Child Study team did, they felt
          that they should wait a year until he was in kinder-
          garten and try again. They thought maybe in half a
          year...

Father: That's the frustrating part, you don't know who to
            listen to ...

Mother: Yeah, you know you have a feeling yourself that there
            is something that needs to be done and they come in
            for five minutes and they play with the group at that
            moment and they say, "Well, he's just a little
            immature."

Johnny's parents made very general comments about how they
had been persuaded to try an alternative program for his normal
kindergarten year. The only thing that they really focused on
was the maturity aspect: they had been told that he was immature
and that an additional year would alleviate that particular problem. Johnny had been in Mrs. Sunden's class since September
and his teacher was concerned about him. At his parent-teacher
conference, Mrs. Sunden expressed her concerns about his grasp
of material presented thus far in the year (primarily letter sounds)
and the way that he just did not seem hooked into what was
going on in class. In the following exchange, Mrs. Sunden and
Johnny's parents discussed what they thought should happen
next to help him out:

Mrs. Sunden: And he needs to know those sounds to begin
               reading—that's the first big step he needs to take.

Mother: I hate to go through another year without some
               kind of special help. I've been reading about
               Learning Disabilities and he has a lot of the
               symptoms...

Father: But before you were afraid of the ramifications
               of going that route—you didn't want him labelled
               at such an early age.

Mother: I don't want him labelled, but if that's what it
               takes, whatever. He needs to learn to read. He
               already went through pre-K, we have given him
               that extra year. Both the teacher and I saw that
               he just wasn't catching on, but the experts just
               told us that the saw immaturity. His teacher was
               worried about him and had the team come in to
               observe him. They came into class for five minutes
               and for that five minutes he was on his good
               behavior—so they said that he was just immature.
               What can they tell in five minutes?

Mrs. Sunden: You already waited a year. Plus he's big. It would
               be really hard to keep him back another year.
               You know, there are times when we'll be talking
               and I'll ask him a question about what we're
               talking about and he'll say something that is not
               related at all.

The extra year had not provided the payoff that Johnny's parents
had been led to expect; he was still lagging behind his classmates in most areas. They had come to the conclusion that
something more was needed at this point, even if it meant risking
being labelled. They did not frame their interpretation of his
difficulties in terms of readiness; instead, they could feel the
difficulty that he was having and wanted to find something more
tangible than immaturity to define it. Even though Johnny had
experienced a special placement related to readiness, his parents
did not talk in the same way about it as some of the parents
that I will discuss later. After this conference, a Special Education
referral was scheduled and Johnny received various services
throughout the year.

Talking to Jessica's parents was much like my conversations
with the Fulton parents. They had been excited about her coming
to kindergarten, especially in terms of the social opportunities
it would provide. When I asked them what they had been thinking
about in August before Jessica started school, they focused on
interacting with other children: "Most of all, how she was going
to get along with a bigger group of kids. She's been around in
a pre-school situation for two half-days and then she was off when
we moved out here. So she didn't have that much a connection
with kids until we started school." Talking about how things had
gone so far during the kindergarten experience, they discussed
their excitement over how much she had learned about letters
of the alphabet and writing and counting. They had come to terms
with the fact that other children were starting to go through
beginning readers but that Jessica had shown no interest or
aptitude in trying them. Mrs. Sunden had persuaded them not
to push her too much. They were just interested in Jessica's
continued progress and that she would continue to like school
as much as she did now.

The three parents who discussed readiness in our interviews
tended to focus on three dimensions: discussion of age, description
of readiness, and experiences with older siblings of their kindergarten age child. Susan's parents, in some ways, seemed prisoners

of Norwood philosophy. They had been told by various friends and neighbors about the importance of age and were very worried about how that might impede Susan's kindergarten experience. In addition, Susan's mother had been told that kindergarten had changed a lot recently and that there was a lot to learn. In turn, the school apparently expected children to come in with all kinds of skills that formerly would have been the work of the kindergarten year. Her parents talked about how they got the information that was the basis of their concern about enrolling her this year and the kinds of things that helped them decide to go ahead and put her in school.

> Father: We were concerned before school started about whether Susan was old enough because she just turned five and some people would say that she needs to be six to start kindergarten. But I think that if she needs to be six to start kindergarten, they'll be eighteen when they graduate and I don't think at the other end it's a good situation to have somebody that old graduating from high school. I felt that we just needed to see how it goes. She was doing pretty good at home.

> Mother: [Her pre-school teachers] felt that Susan was ready for kindergarten. But I talked to several other moms that actually kind of scared me because they made it sound like kindergarten, they cram a lot into it. Which I think they do, a lot more today than what they did twenty years ago or thirty years ago... But I was really concerned hearing all that as far as what is expected of her and if she could do alright with all of it.

> Father: I think that it's better that she is in kindergarten... Than another year of pre-school. I think that she would have gotten bored with another year of pre-school. We may be pushing her a little bit, with kindergarten, but I think that it's not too much if she gets frustrated once in a while.

Susan's parents tried to balance what they had heard from their friends and what they heard from her pre-school teacher with their gut feelings about what kind of impact holding their daughter out would have. They opted to go ahead and send her. But even after making that decision, they were still confronted with evidence that made them have second thoughts. Susan's mother talked about things that she learned by being a volunteer in Mrs. Sunden's class that continued to stir up their fears about Susan's age:

Actually, from being around Susan's class, I was filing some forms one day and it had all of the kids ages on them and I was kind of surprised to see that a lot of them were quite a bit older. Like a good year. Then that goes back to the moms that I knew that had kept their kids or put them in for two years of pre-school versus putting them in. So... I played with the idea at first of holding her back a year.

Susan's parents felt however, that she was ready for school and that she would do OK. They thought that it was silly to make the decision that she was not ready until they had given her a chance to prove herself. Even if parents were saying that the curriculum was arduous, they wanted to give their daughter the opportunity to go to kindergarten that fall:

A lot of this stuff that we were hearing were these people who had moved into the area in from somewhere else with younger kids. They said that at Norwood Elementary they have to know their name, they have to know their phone number, they got to know ALL this stuff. *Before* they can be in kindergarten. Sounded like before you could even start, you had to know how to read and stuff like that... Some parents [seemed to be getting] wrong information. I believe when we had the discussion about whether she should go or not, I said try it. The worst you could do is hold her back a year. [do kindergarten again]... Rather than saying no, she's not ready for it—how do you know she's not ready if you don't give her a chance?

Through all of this trauma of trying to make these decisions, Susan's parents found that they were very happy with their daughter's kindergarten experience. She was learning a lot about letters and numbers and seemed really content with how the year had gone. Her parents were a little bit surprised about the instructional pace in terms of the kinds of things the children were learning. When I asked them if they were learning pretty much what they had expected Susan to learn, her mother replied:

Yeah, I think so. Maybe a little bit faster than what I thought. I mean, from talking to other people, they said a whole lot is crammed into them in that first year but from being here right in the beginning you see how everybody is so new. They are all just getting to know each other. I guess I didn't expect it to happen this soon. I guess I just expected them to be more just friends and get to know each other before it really got going.

In some ways, Susan's parents bucked the redshirting trend at Norwood, taking in a lot of advice and watching their daughter very carefully to make sure that they had not made a mistake. What is very interesting about all of this is the fact that Susan's early May birthday was really not near the cutoff at all. Susan was five years, three months old at the start of the school year and a full four months older than the entrance cutoff. Yet her parents interpreted much of Susan's kindergarten experience in terms of the impact of age and readiness.

Mitch was a classic case of a later birthday, which allowed his parents not to worry about readiness and age. But they still talked about it. When I asked them what they had thought about as kindergarten approached in August, his mother replied, "I didn't have any particular worries about what he could accomplish because he seemed more than ready. He's a January child, so he's older." Later, I asked her to elaborate on that a little bit:

> I guess that I was secure about it because he was older. We had one son that was not older and I elected to go head and send him, and I've always regretted it. I think that he would have had a lot easier time. He was smart enough to go. But it isn't the issue. It's more a thing of attention span, being able to sit still long enough to listen to what they tell you. Feeling more secure about what you are doing. You really have an edge if you are a few months older... for a child a few months can make a big difference. I was advised by friends that since he was a boy not to send him. But of course, we just felt like he was ready, look at all of the things he knows. It's one of those things you can't go back and change. He's always been a little bit immature. He's been one of the younger ones in the class. Not one of the behavior problems, just difficult paying attention. He does OK but school is just a little harder.[6]

Mitch was a very capable boy, who though not outstanding, did not have difficulty with any of the tasks presented in Mrs. Sunden's classroom. Although his parents did attribute it to some extent to his general hard-working nature, much of the their interpretation was related to the fact that he was "older" in the kindergarten class and would therefore have the automatic advantage of age.

Jared, who had been held out the previous year, was probably the most interesting case overall. Jared's mother had used two roles she played to make her decision to keep him out an extra year. As a mother, she knew that she wanted him to have the best experience possible. As the director of one of the pre-schools in Norwood, she had professional experience that she used as a lens to interpret whether Jared was ready and what she should do if he was not ready in her eyes. At the beginning of the year in Mrs. Sunden's class, she had been a little bit concerned about whether Jared would be able to pay attention and settle down. She wondered if he could be in the classroom and sit still and not get too excited. This came after he had spent an extra year in pre-school. I asked her how she made the decision to keep him out of kindergarten the year before:

> Just experience. I own the pre-school down in Norwood. I've seen a lot of kids who are young fives or late fours who go to kindergarten and they're just not ready for it, especially the boys. So just from what I've seen plus he has an older brother also that was the same thing, he was just along the borderline and I kept him the extra year and I was really glad that I had done it. So I guess it's just that I've seen when people start them when they are age eligible but they are not maturity ready that it's not worth it, it's just too much of a struggle for the kids. Just let them wait a year.

Most of her concern a year ago had focused on his school behavior: how well he could sit and listen in a group. When she described how he had appeared to her the year before and how he had progressed in the meantime, Jared's mother went into a long explanation of how the body's match with brain development affected a child's readiness:

> Last year there was no way he could have sat still long enough during group times without popping up and just blurting things out or just fidgeting. He's gotten that a little more under control since last year. Temperament-wise... when he would be disappointed with something it would just rock him a lot more while now it's a little more OK. Just typical growing up things where a year can make all the difference in that age. For their brain to catch up with their body. A lot of the time, what I've seen with little kids is when their body is going through a growth spurt their brain just kind of takes a back seat and the child is like they can become very emotional or they can become no emotion when their body is going through those growth spurts. You can just tell that something is going on with their body. All of a sudden their personality is different, when their body is going through something new. With other children, I've seen

when you start them too early, if they are not real social kids...
and they are real shy, they're just overwhelmed by school. They
just don't get the hang of it until maybe the year is over. Then
they've already gotten this bad feeling about school and they
don't feel good about it. If they would have waited that extra
year, they might have been a lot more confident in their interactions with other children and they would have been ready for
it. I see a lot of that in the pre-school.

Jared's mother's model of readiness was the most maturational
of any of the parents that I interviewed, at Norwood or elsewhere.
It was a very good match for the model held by the staff at Norwood
Elementary; one that focused on biological maturation as the
mechanism for the development of readiness. She was also very
aware and concerned about behaviors in the classroom such as
being able to sit and listen. These were exactly the types of things
that the first grade teachers had mentioned as behaviors that they
thought the kindergarten teachers should worry about when
thinking about sending kindergartners to first grade. Readiness
became a characteristic of an easy to manage child.

In looking at the approach taken by the three parents at
Norwood who discussed readiness, three dimensions emerged: age,
descriptions of readiness and experiences with older children. From
their talk, it appeared that the communication network had
significant impact on how they thought about readiness. What
others told them shaped the way that they interpreted their
children's abilities and how they they anticipated the way that
their children would fit in the school. Again, it is interesting to
note that the families interviewed who did not talk about readiness
had only recently moved to Norwood and had therefore not
developed the very local meaning of readiness that was characteristic of the Norwood community. Table 17 displays some aspects
of the longer term Norwood residents' ideas:

Table 17
How Did Parents Who Were Concerned About Readiness
Talk About It At Norwood?

Child Name	Age	Readiness	Experience with Older Siblings
Jared	I've seen lots of young 5's & late 4's, not ready especially boys… I've seen when they start them when they are age eligible but not maturity ready.	If they would have waited that extra year, they might have been a lot more confident in their interactions with other children and they have been ready for it.	He has an older brother… was just along the borderline and I kept him the extra year and I was real glad that I had done it.
Mitch	He's a January child, so he's older… I guess I was secure about it because he was older.	I didn't have any particular worries about what he could accomplish because he seemed more than ready.	We had one son that was not older and I elected to go ahead and send him and I've always regretted it… He was smart enough to go. But it isn't the issue. It's more a thing of attention span, being able to sit still long enough to listen to what they tell you. Feeling more secure about what you are doing.
Susan	We were concerned before school started about whether Susan was old enough because she just turned five and some people would say that she needs to be six to start kindergarten.	[Her pre-school teachers] felt that Susan was ready for kindergarten.	

The Meaning of Readiness at Norwood

The meaning of readiness developed at Norwood was surprisingly coherent and highly communal. Based on a maturational belief about readiness, much of the interpretation of children in the school and community was done on the basis of age, with the assumption that relatively younger children in a kindergarten group would do less well than relatively older children. Parents were socialized by their friends about the importance of being the oldest in the group. Their reasoning ranged from the demanding nature of the curriculum, development of more mature behavior, to being the biggest and most powerful in sports. Only Johnny's parents discussed academic ability; for the most part the concern was framed in terms of how their child behaved.

This maturational model was shared with the parents by the staff at Norwood. With a tradition of nativist (biological) thought in the school, the staff developed extra-year programs to deal with children who did not meet school performance expectations. Developmental kindergarten and transitional first grade classes were offered because the staff had seen the difficulties that younger children had later in their school careers and they wanted to alleviate some of those difficulties. When the official programs were discontinued, an extra year of pre-school or home learning was used to allow additional growth and development so that children would be more ready to meet the challenges of first grade.

First grade at Norwood was seen as fiercely academic and this curriculum level was interpreted both in terms of its rigor and in relation to the strength of will and the political power wielded by its teachers. The first grade teachers were a closely knit unit at Norwood who made explicit pronouncements about the performance of their students, which translated into implicit judgments regarding the work of the kindergarten teachers. Mrs. Sunden interpreted what she did in her classroom in terms of the demands of the first grade program. She came to make decisions about children with those demands in mind. She told me about Aaron, who was having problems in school paying attention and learning the concepts that they were covering:

> He'd drown in first grade here. He wouldn't make it. It would be really hard. I don't really recommend kids to repeat in kindergarten but for him, he might need that. They review in first grade the first couple of weeks and then they go... I don't even know if he could do it all day. He's going to have to have a lot of growth before the end of the year.

In our last interview in May, Mrs. Sunden told me that almost all of her students were going to first grade next year. They had been a fun group and she had really enjoyed them. Two of her students, Aaron and Juan, would be going to first grade in the morning and then kindergarten in the afternoon. They were not ready for first grade, but they really needed to be in school all day to get more exposure to school activities. These were working-class children, one of whom had very limited English. Their experience coming into kindergarten had put them at risk because there were so many things that they just had not come in contact with. For children like these, the school took an interventionist approach to help them get more ready for school. It was an intervention that had been used before with children who needed to be in school rather than be at home so that they could become more ready. The expectation was that they would go to first grade full time the following year. The extra-year program was still alive at Norwood, although through a split grade arrangement.

CHAPTER 7

ROCHESTER

If you asked people in the area to describe Broadview, they would invariably tell you that it was a working-class community. Much bigger than either Fulton or Norwood, Broadview's character was a little more difficult to discern. It seemed brawnier and more diverse; with less long term tradition than Fulton and more heterogeneity than middle-class Norwood. The town had a variety of factories and production facilities that provide employment for the Anglo and Hispanic families who lived within its boundaries. Broadview was unpretentious and honest, with people who had pride in their town.

The downtown used to be the center of the community, with shops lining Main Street. All of the buildings were still occupied in this downtown area, but they were no longer the homes of the main merchants. They had moved for the most part to the malls that dot the edges of town. Broadview divides itself now into East and West, with enough people so that services like recreation centers can be supported in several parts of the city.

Broadview was the heart of the Thomas School District, with most of its schools within the town's boundaries. There was a mixture of old and new schools in Broadview and recently there had been adjustments to the attendance boundaries so that instructional services could be provided more efficiently.

Rochester Elementary sat at the bottom of a grassy hill at the edge of Broadview. At the top of the hill were the homes of Wolf Bay Estates. With large, perfectly manicured lawns, these homes had views of the town and the mountains in the background. Middle-class Anglo professionals lived in this subdivision, with experiences and expectations much like the parents of

Norwood. They were active in their children's educational lives and spent much time working with their children so that they would have the tools to succeed. At the bottom of the hill were tract homes and apartments for the working-class members of the community. They were modest homes, often rented, with wire fences separating the yards. Many of these people worked in the turkey plant in the center of town, coming home at all hours of the day, depending on their shift.

With its position between these two neighborhoods, Rochester Elementary joined what could be seen as groups of people with different interests and experiences. The school served neighborhood children in grades kindergarten through grade three plus children from the Clarendon School attendance area who were bussed in to Rochester. Clarendon and Rochester were paired, with Rochester providing K-3 services and Clarendon providing 4-6. The Clarendon students were much the same as the Rochester students, with fewer affluent children in the group. To make provision of instructional services most efficient, Rochester was named a bilingual center and provided bilingual classes at each grade level K-3. Because of this arrangement, Rochester's student population was very diverse. It included children from Wolf Bay, who had been to several years of pre-school (in the traditional nursery school format of three mornings a week focussing on play), the children of working-class parents who were second generation Hispanic-Americans who had spent their pre-school years with babysitters or in day care homes, and the children of first generation Mexican-Americans in the country either legally or illegally who were having their first exposure to English in school. Looking at the demographic information on the school can be misleading; although 50% of the students at Rochester were eligible for the federal Free and Reduced program, it is important to keep in mind that approximately one third of the students came from families that were quite affluent.

While the teachers at Fulton and Norwood found it necessary to provide a more accelerated curriculum because their students were entering kindergarten with knowledge what had traditionally been thought of as kindergarten, I was told by one of the Rochester teachers that a large part of the student population at Rochester had changed in the opposite direction. From what veteran teachers had told her, the kindergarten program and children had undergone a transformation in the last twenty years that had a dramatic impact on the focus of instruction in general:

All I know is that teachers like Martha will say, "Ten or twenty years ago, when I started, we expected them to come in sit down, be quiet and to listen and to be polite. I mean we expected all of these things and they were that way. And we did seatwork. GOBS of seatwork. And we expected them to color and to cut and to be quiet." ...Even in other schools, that supposedly have upper middle class populations, even they say, "They don't come to us the way they used to." Maybe they aren't as articulate as they used to be and whether that's an influence of TV, or mothers working, whatever it is that sociologists are saying, I'm not sure... Now I can't say that I've seen it. In the four years I've always been in extended-day and consequently the kids that I get are already designated as needing extra help. It used to be they would come in knowing their letters, quite a few of them, then it was the minority that came in like a lot of our kids.

The students at Rochester had a variety of needs and the school had developed programs to try to meet them. Rochester was a Chapter One school, providing additional instruction to children who were performing below a certain level. Within-class bilingual instruction was provided at each grade level and each bilingual class had the additional resource of an bilingual aide for approximately two hours per day. A Head Start class was housed in the school. Rochester also had two extended-day kindergarten classes which worked to try to shrink the gap between the children coming into kindergarten with many school-valued experiences behind them and those who were seen to be at risk. Mrs. Ramirez, one of the extended-day kindergarten teachers, described how the program was put in place at Rochester:

Part of the thought behind the extended-day program was how can we close the gap between these children who come in needing so much and they've got this tremendous span to cross as compared to this child who comes in all ready with all this background, knowing all the things that they need for school. That's how they got the extended-day.

The staff could see that children coming in without certain experiences were going to have difficulty keeping up with their more privileged peers, so they asked the school district to allocate funding for extended-day classes at Rochester. The program had been in place four years at Rochester.

In addition to the development of the extended-day kinder-garten program, the staff at Rochester had been working to put into practice their commitment to finding solutions for children who did not fit the standard performance expectations. There had been a move away from using retention as an intervention for children who were behind their age group:

> The trend has been to not retain kids. So it may be that you are looking at them thinking that they are going to have a hard time but you're not retaining them because they don't have the certain knowledge base that you think they should have... So we need to do something else. That's part of how we got the extended day. We said, "OK, we're getting all these children coming in at a lower level than we had seen them previously. What are we going to do with them because we can't retain all of these kids. We can't retain 40 kids."

In looking for options that did not include retention, the teachers at Rochester found it necessary to draw wider boundaries of "acceptable" performance at each grade level. Teachers began to work together to find ways to meet all children's needs, rather than those in a specific range around the mean. This approach required more communication among staff and a commitment to shaping educational experiences so that they were targeted to a broader range of students.

The staff at Rochester was known throughout the district as one of the most active of any of the schools. The teachers liked to be involved in the decision-making and were not afraid to voice their opinions on most subjects. Principals did not stay at Rochester for very long and in the fall of the 1989-90 school year, a new principal, Paula Birch, began her first year. Mrs. Birch was not bilingual and deferred to the bilingual staff on most matters that concerned their programs. The staff members at Rochester were friendly and interested in any new people coming into the school; Rochester was the only school where I was regularly greeted in the hall or engaged in conversations by staff other than the kindergarten teachers.

Kindergarten at Rochester

More than at Fulton or Norwood, telling the story of the construction of the meaning of readiness at Rochester is really telling the story of a particular teacher, Isabel Ramirez. This strong, articulate, committed woman guided my way to an understanding of the bilingual kindergarten experience at Rochester in a way that did not happen at the other two schools. The fact that her classroom was part of the bilingual program made me very dependent on her to translate and interpret the kindergarten experience at Rochester; not being able to speak Spanish made me rely on her. This reliance ranged from not interviewing any Spanish-speaking parents in my August, pre-kindergarten parent interviews (because many of them had not registered in the spring for the fall kindergarten program) to relying on her to translate conversations that she had with children. This reliance should not be seen as a limitation to the study, however. Parents and children were interviewed through the use of an interpreter. I felt that I was a part of the kindergarten experience at Rochester in much the same way that I was at Fulton or Norwood. In presenting the story of the construction of readiness there, I found that Mrs. Ramirez' voice predominated. Her voice will be the primary one heard in this description; the story is rich enough that her voice is enough.

Rochester Parents' Thoughts on Their Children's Kindergarten Entrance

A sample of Rochester parents was interviewed in August as their children approached their kindergarten year. Unfortunately, none of the parents I interviewed had children who would have gone into a bilingual class. The sample drawn was a school sample, representing all the parents who had registered their children for kindergarten in the spring. Of the ten parents sampled from Rochester, none was Hispanic. When the sample was pulled, I did not realize how different the parents in Mrs. Ramirez' class and the other parents in the school would be. In looking at how the parents interviewed were anticipating this big step in their child's life, I have taken the view that these data provide a context for understanding the particular meaning of readiness that evolved in Mrs. Ramirez' class. The examination of these interviews shows how the expectations were set for the general population of Rochester Elementary and will set the stage for how the bilingual program fit into the setting.

Five parents were interviewed in the month before their children entered kindergarten. Two were parents of sons, three of daughters. Nathan and Charley had been held out the previous year and had July and September birthdays respectively. Erin and Leslie had October birthdays, making them almost six when the school year began in August. Brittany was four when she started kindergarten.

When asked about their thoughts as they approached their child's kindergarten entrance, these parents responded in a manner much like the Norwood parents. Four out of five of the parents spontaneously mentioned both age and holding out in these interviews and there was a sense that the informal community information network was at work at Rochester to provide parents with the structure to interpret their child's kindergarten experience in the context of age.

For example, Leslie's mother focused on how other parents' actions made her think about putting Leslie in school. When I asked her to describe how parents talked to their children going to kindergarten, her comments centered on age:

> The only thing is the age thing. I have a friend who has a boy who was five last May and she could have sent him but she didn't because teachers at the school he's going to say that boys socially are not ready. So she had decided that she was going to keep him back so he's already six in May and he's just going to go now... Everybody else has talked to this one, this one, and this one and I don't talk to anybody so I just have to hear what everybody else has to say. I think that each kid is different so I really don't think that you can say that this is good for everyone. For so many years you don't have to worry about that then all of a sudden, it's like, Where are they going to go to school and at what age?

This sounds much like the environment at Norwood, where parents discussed their child's kindergarten entrance in terms of relative age and they pondered whether they should pay attention to the formal entrance age or to the informal age that results from holding out. Even the children at Rochester had a sense of the older age for kindergarten entrance. Nathan's mother told me about how one of Nathan's friends took care of helping him understand that he was going to sit out his official kindergarten year because of his age:

> When it got brought up, one of his other friends was in the back seat and he answered it for me beautifully. He said, "Nathan, you can't start kindergarten, you have to be 5½." Because *he* was 5½. And that's really true—to get a good start boys really should be 5½ to start. And that ended that.

Table 18 summarizes the manner in which these Rochester parents
discussed the upcoming kindergarten year:

Table 18
Rochester Parents Talk of Age and Holding Out

Child's Name	Birth-date	Age	Holding Out
Nathan	7/16/83	Well, when we put him in pre-school—he's an August birthday—we always knew that that would be a question... He's also big for his age, so he looks older than he is so sometimes people expect him to act one way when he is actually acting the way he should for his age. I talked to [his pre-school teacher] a little bit about it and she said that she knows that there were some kids that shouldn't start when they are border-line birthday, but felt that Nathan could. But when I talked to her at the end... she agreed that it would be better if he waited.	We struggled with it right up until probably April the year before he would have started. We pretty much looked at that year during pre-school and watched him to see how he felt. And being a teacher, I teach 2nd grade and I talked to parents who have done it and never regretted it and a lot of parents who didn't do it and wished they had. I would have, if I make a mistake, I'd rather make it on the safe side than on the other.
Charley	9/27/83	I have Charley, he's almost six, he's an older kid because he almost missed the deadline by a little ways and I decided I wanted to keep him back and make sure he was ready for kindergarten.	My parents are both teachers and my mom works in elementary school and my brother was one of the kids who started and then they had to hold him back in 3rd grade, they didn't have to but they did. Because he just wasn't doing well. And he did wonderful after that... I just felt like if I could have him a better start from the beginning, he might be better off all the way around.
Erin	10/17/83		

Table 18 *continued*
Rochester Parents Talk of Age and Holding Out

Child's Name	Birth-date	Age	Holding Out
Leslie	10/24/83	I just think she'll do so much better; she will turn six in October so she missed the deadline last year [Did you think at all about trying to get her in last year?] No because I've heard so much that you're not supposed to push them and people that I know that have had children that turn five even before the deadline still kept them back a year.	Everybody was trying to decide that if they were going to send them immediately when they turned five or if they were going to hold them back until the next year... I don't know if holding him back was the right thing or not.
Brittany	9/12/84	She's five in September, there's a choice, I don't have to start this year. They don't start till the end of August and she'll be four, so technically, she can start but it's not required. So I'm kind of unsure about that.	[What do you think will happen if they (her kindergarten teachers) decide that she's not really ready?] She'll start next year.

Four of the five Rochester parents felt that age would have an impact on how their child would do in school. Three of these parents had children who would have been in the youngest part of the kindergarten age cohort if they had entered when they were age eligible. The redshirting parents felt that they were now more ready and were more confident because they would have the advantage of age. Brittany's mother was slightly concerned about the fact that she was starting at age four.

Their expectations of the upcoming kindergarten experience varied considerably. They ranged from the second grade teacher who knew what the curriculum was going to be like and was a little worried that her redshirted son, Nathan, would be bored after sitting out a year, to Erin's mother who assumed that it would be much like pre-school but not as much play. Table 19 summarizes their discussion of the kind of experience they were anticipating for their children:

Table 19
Rochester Parents' Expectations for
the Kindergarten Year

Child's Name	Expectations for the Kindergarten Year
Nathan	I guess because I'm a teacher I know more of what to be looking for. A lot of the curriculum has been changed because they don't see a lot of papers coming home... I'm more prepared for the whole language thing and the math manipulatives... I hope he won't be bored—only because he's had the two years of pre-school—he knows his letters and sounds and he is starting to read—I just hope that he can extend himself in the curriculum enough that he's not bored.
Charley	I was real impressed with Rochester, that's where he is going to. I went to a teacher conference and I was real impressed with the staff.
Erin	She was in pre-school last year so I kind of just assume it's kind of the same thing. Not as much play as they did in pre-school. More learning than pre-school... More of the alphabet and more recognition of numbers and of course her letters and the social part of it—getting along with other kids.
Leslie	I hope that she comes out knowing the things that are expected of her so that she doesn't have to struggle in first grade.
Brittany	Well, she went to pre-school, and they told us there that they needed to be able to write their name and know their ABC's and count to ten and be able to button her own jacket and put on her shoes and things like that.

Parents interviewed at Rochester sounded much like the Norwood parents when they discussed ideas like age and holding out. Of the five interviewed, two had held their children out the year before. They were worried about what would happen to children who were in the youngest part of the kindergarten age group and almost all of them had thought about or heard about holding children out so that they could be older. In the 1988-89 kindergarten cohort at Rochester, it was estimated that 22% of the male kindergartners had been held out. It was a pervasive practice and one that was obviously a major part of this community's ideology.

As mentioned previously, these parents did not have children in Mrs. Ramirez' classroom. Their views are presented as both context and contrast to the environment that was constructed in the bilingual extended-day kindergarten at Rochester. At this point, I turn to Mrs. Ramirez and her classroom, opening with a vignette of Mrs. Ramirez thinking about her students.

"And Then There are My Kids..."

Peeking out the door, Mrs. Ramirez watches one of the half-day kindergarten classes walk to the library. In two neat lines, they move quietly behind Mrs. Jones. Chuckling, Mrs. Ramirez compares them to her class. They are getting better but for some reason, the lines of her children seem to undulate with a life of their own.

At the classroom door, she sends the children out to recess. They tumble out of the room, heading for the playground equipment. Again, she thinks how different the two sets of children are. In the other kindergarten, they can have children coming in that are reading. They have all those basic kindergarten skills and are ready to go on. And their parents are asking, "You know, my child is reading, so what are you going to do for my child?"

And then there are my kids. They are here because they are behind. They don't know their address, they don't know their phone number, they don't know their colors. Forget numbers and letters, that's just like a world away. And their parents are different. They say things like, "Well, I didn't know that I was supposed to talk to my child about colors. I didn't know that reading was important to them." ...They have travelled. They go to Mexico annually. And that means that they are out of school for maybe two or three weeks. And in the public school system, there is nothing that draws on all of the experiences that they have. So they come back and it's like, "OK, that's really nice that you did that but we're in school here and this is what you need to go to school. So can you repeat this story? Now I'm going to do some design and I want you to copy it." And that could be really irrelevant to the child, but that's what we judge them on. For some of these kids, you might say that they are not ready to be in school. What this child needs is another year at home. But then you look at home and say, "Nope! That's OK. What this child needs is to be in school." Because at home there is nothing happening.

Mrs. Ramirez

Describing the extended-day bilingual kindergarten at Rochester is inseparable from describing Isabel Ramirez. A small dynamo whose vibrant personality is the heart of the program, Isabel was in her early thirties and in her eighth year of teaching. Four of those years had been in kindergarten at Rochester. Isabel had a four year old daughter who attended the Community School pre-school at Rochester on Monday, Wednesday, and Friday and a one year old son at home. She spent her lunch hour three days a week picking Janie up from the babysitter's to bring her to pre-school. That cut a thirty minute lunch very short.

Mrs. Ramirez' view of herself and of her job at Rochester were inextricably intertwined. She saw her job as different from the other three kindergarten teachers at Rochester because of the nature of the bilingual program:

> If you were to say, "What are you?" I would say, "I'm a bilingual teacher first." So my top priority is bilingual education. Extended-day is real important and I've told Martha [the other extended-day teacher], "If I have to fight for something, I'll fight for bilingual ed. You fight for the extended-day."

This concern with bilingual education had at its base her commitment to developing a sense of ethnic identity among her students. In Mrs. Ramirez' mind, her job was to foster a sense of self worth within a system that saw her students as different. She used her own experience to ground her approach to teaching:

> I lived in North Dakota and there were no Hispanics. So it was more of a novelty. My dad came in to teach Spanish and it was some big thing. It was so neat. I went to Mexico and it was just cool! It was something that I never once felt ashamed of. When I went to Arizona as a young adult, I was asked, "What are you? Are you Anglo or Hispanic?" It was really different to me. It was like, "What do you mean?" There was a definite line, you needed to be one or the other. So *they* know what you are. I said, "Well, my name is Isabel Ramirez and you can decide what you want." ...I think what happened to me as a young adult, happens to these kids when they are little. At two, they've already figured out what box they belong in. Before then, probably. They know what box they're in. And they've also decided whether this box is desirable.

Although she saw herself as culturally different as she was growing up in North Dakota, Isabel never felt it to be a marker that was undesirable in any way. In fact, it seemed to provide her with some kind of capital to trade as a child. It was a shock to be pigeonholed when she got to college and she felt uncomfortable with it. With sadness she saw it happening to her students at a very early age, even before they got to school.

Being Different at Rochester

Many of the parents at Rochester had the middle class experiences and expectations of kindergarten that I saw at Norwood; they knew the rules of the game and they knew how to work the system to get what they wanted for their child. These children came into school with a constellation of skills and abilities that were a good match to the expectations of the middle class school. Their teachers developed certain expectations and standards to match this set of skills. In many schools, these children would be the ones who would set the standard for everyone in the school. Over time, however, the staff at Rochester found themselves unsure of how to work with children entering school without those skills and abilities. They needed new ways to meet a broader set of needs. At this point the extended-day program was developed:

> We were getting a large number of children coming in not ready for kindergarten. They were unprepared as far as our expectations. And consequently, since they came in lower, they left kindergarten a little bit lower. So you could feel the ripple effect all the way through. There was concern among the kindergarten teachers and first grade teachers... the kindergarten teachers were saying, "They come in, you've got the ones here who can read and then you have the ones who don't know their name. It's too hard. We don't know how to deal with this span. It's too difficult."

The extended-day program's purpose was to deal with an increasingly heterogeneous population at the school. In addition to developing multiple programs, Mrs. Ramirez described how there was not just one set of expectations for children at Rochester. With two extended-day classes and four sections of half-day kindergarten, the kindergarten teachers had come to an understanding about where children should be and what can/should be done for them during their kindergarten experience:

Well, we have talked about this before. The half-day teachers say, "You know, our expectations are just so different." And they *are* different. For one of the other kindergarten teachers, they may have this child that they consider very low, a very good candidate for retention. And if they were in my classroom, I wouldn't even *dream* of retaining them. Because they would be in the middle. Because I would have five that would be much lower than they were. We've talked about it before and haven't come to any kind of conclusion but it is something that we are aware of and we have been discussing it as a team.

Why were the expectations so different for the children in Mrs. Ramirez' class? In almost every way, the children in her class were seen as different. They did not come from the houses on the hill; they had not been to pre-school; they did not know their shapes and colors. Many of them did not know that they have a last name. But their lives had not been empty up to the point that they entered kindergarten:

> Usually they come to my classroom with a wide range of experiences. However, they are not the experiences that the public school system values. A lot of my kids are bilingual. Or if they're not bilingual, they would have the opportunity because they are in a setting where they hear a lot of the other language... Their experiences don't go into the middle class Anglo society. White America doesn't know about their life at all. And it's real different. So when they come to school they are not middle class white experiences. Maybe they went to the zoo once but they haven't gone to the museum. They haven't been to Washington, D.C. or they haven't been on a family vacation to California to the beach. They went somewhere else. Maybe they went to Mexico and maybe they even had to work in the fields, so they can save up money so that when Christmas comes.

In addition to being behind their peers in a general way, the children in Mrs. Ramirez' class were seen as essentially different from the rest of the student population because of their ethnic and cultural difference. Their families lived lives that are not like those of the main stream, middle class. They did not fit in.

The most obvious marker of difference was their language; many of the children and their parents did not speak English. When the parents came to school to register for the fall school program, their children were immediately set off from the rest of the group. Their screening was done separately, by special staff

(Mrs. Ramirez and Mrs. Perez, one of the bilingual aides). If they were thought to be Spanish-dominant, they were immediately placed in Mrs. Ramirez' class. They were assumed to be unready because language posed a barrier to their learning.

There were slots for twenty-two children in Mrs. Ramirez' program and the children needing bilingual services were assigned to her first. If there were still openings in her class and there were English speakers who need extended-day placement, they were put in Mrs. Ramirez' class. In the past, Mrs. Ramirez had parents pull their children out of extended-day class when they saw that their children were the only Anglos in the group; this did not happen in the '89-90 school year. Of twenty-two, five children were English speakers, with two of them being fairly bilingual. Any communication between the school and her students' parents was done through Mrs. Ramirez; as will be seen she was the link that joined the families to the school.

Parents from Mrs. Ramirez' Class

Like the parents at Fulton, the parents of Mrs. Ramirez' students were working class people. Mrs. Ramirez described them as employed at the local turkey plant, as custodians, welders, carpenters, mechanics, mothers at home on welfare. When she thought back over all of the parents with whom she had worked at Rochester, she said that she did not think she had ever had parents who were college graduates or who worked in a white collar job.

Their school experiences were quite varied, from those who have gone through about sixth grade in Mexico, to those who have been through high school in the States. Many of her parents took night courses in English, "so that means that they're working and they go to night school, and then they have their family... They do the best they can. And it's hard." The experiences that they had in school had been unpleasant for the most part. Mrs. Ramirez found this to be one of the most difficult parts of her job to turn around:

> They don't like, it a lot of them. They will say things like, "Well, I hated school and those teachers and they made me feel like this ..." And they're the ones who are real hard to get to. That their attitude will really make a difference. [I tell them] "Your child is going to want to be like you." So if dad didn't like school, I want to be like dad. "Yeah, I hate school and school stinks."

Mrs. Ramirez' parents were more disconnected from the school than even the Fulton parents when they presented their child at the school door in August. Part of that disconnection could be due to their previous bad experiences with school; they had good reason not to be overly interested in interaction with the school. It could also be due in part to the language barrier they faced; they had a voice only through Mrs. Ramirez. Finally, they were disconnected because they did not approach their child's first school year with a well defined set of expectations. When I asked Mrs. Ramirez to describe her parents' expectations, she told me that they did not have any:

> They don't, I don't think. Or their expectation is that they'll graduate from high school or maybe they'll drop out. Or you seem to get parents who don't seem to even think about it Or they may say, "I want my kid to like school." or "I want my kid to finish school." "I didn't graduate, so I want my child to graduate." But mostly I think they want their child to like school. " I want them to like school. I want them to be happy." A lot of the parents were drop outs or they had a very hard time in school and they didn't like it.

Like the Fulton parents, these parents had a general idea about their child's kindergarten experience: they wanted them to be happy. They did not have a list of skills that they thought that their child would need or a list of skills with which they wanted them to come out of kindergarten. They were not making plans for college as their child went off on the bus for kindergarten; they wanted them to graduate from high school. Education was the business of the school and they did what they could to get their child to school so that education could start:

> When I look at my parents, most of them haven't been thinking about what do I need to do to get my child ready for school? And so they just say, "Well now you're five and so now you go to school. And at school is where you're going to learn all these different things"... It's not that they're not concerned. And it's not that they don't want success for their child. But it's just really that they see it as the school's job. "Here's my child, now you teach him."

Mrs. Ramirez' contrasted her parents with the other parents at Rochester. The parents from her class had a very simple set of expectations for their child's school years: they wanted them to like school and they wanted them to complete it. They tended to stand back, not trying to put forward any agenda of their own. The school was seen as the authority.

The parents from the other extended-day class (whom I did not interview) had more experience with the schools and they had an idea about how to get the things they wanted for their children. Mrs. Ramirez contrasted the two sets of extended-day parents and focused on how the other extended-day parents interact with the school:

> Our classrooms are a little different in that she [the other extended-day teacher] has, she has parents that have been here awhile. So she has Hispanic parents that have gone through the system. Whether they had success or not. They've had experience with the school system. So they tend to... try to manipulate the system. They will say, "You don't like my child. You know, my child said that you did this and you made him cry and he came home crying and how dare you do that!" So she gets phone calls from the parents. And they come in very threatening and say, "I want my child pulled out." and it's like "Fine, why don't you come in and observe and after you spend a day with me and your child in my classroom, then you tell me if you want to pull them out." Well that never materializes. That's just a lot of threats or angry phone calls or angry words. Whereas my parents, a lot of them haven't been through the system in the States so they don't do that kind of stuff.

They had been a part of the school system and knew generally the kinds of things they needed to do to operate in its structure. Although they did not always carry through on their threats, they made an effort to assert what they saw as their rights and responsibilities as parents.

The parents that I interviewed before school started formed the third group at Rochester. They were Anglo. They knew what to do and they had opportunities to be involved in the life of the school. Mrs. Ramirez described them as follows: "They're the ones that are fortunate enough to be able to be the mother helpers, to be in the classroom, they're probably the ones that are in PTO... [They are] more involved... And their expectations are higher."

What kind of educational impact came from the fact that Mrs. Ramirez' parents were so disconnected from their children's definition as students at Rochester? It meant that they did not have power to negotiate for their child in the same way that other Rochester (or Fulton or Norwood) parents had available to them. Because they were not part of the construction of the meaning of readiness at school, they were dependent on and left it to the school to construct and interpret a meaning for them. Probably unbeknownst to most of these parents, their children started their kindergarten experience labelled as unready; that was the reason they are assigned to Mrs. Ramirez' class. Working from this starting point, the school redefined the concept of readiness within the extended-day program. This role fell primarily to Isabel Ramirez, who worked to close the gap, both for her students and parents. How she did this is the focus of the next section. The discussion of the extended-day bilingual kindergarten at Rochester, which had features that were very different from the other two classes studied, begins with a vignette of a small group of children trying their hands at scissor cutting in Mrs. Ramirez' class.

"Scissors"

A feeling of quiet concentration permeates Mrs. Ramirez' classroom. Children in small groups are scattered around a room which buzzes with activity and intention. Groups converse in English or Spanish or sometimes a combination of both. Today a small group is having its first encounter with a specific scissor task: cutting out shapes to make a turtle from construction paper. Rosa, Estela D., Armando, Pedro, and Berta sit together at a low rectangular table with Mrs. Ramirez, who supervises them as well as a group working close by on the floor with Rig-a-Jigs. Not much conversation occurs among the cutters—they appear to be consumed by the unfamiliar task. Although most five year olds at Rochester Elementary have had lots of experience with scissors, these children are using them for the first time. And *it is hard*. Watching them work, Mrs. Ramirez is again reminded of the difference in starting points for her extended-day class compared to the half-day classes. Like night and day.

Rose looks up from her paper, which has the edges snipped off but does not really resemble a turtle. When she first picked up the scissors, she tried to use them with two hands. Now she is chopping with one, but keeps finding her thumb below the paper, which is by most standards upside down. She exclaims, "But this is hard!" "Oh, I know, sweetie. But just try. Do your best." A warm smile from Mrs. Ramirez seems to recharge Rosa's spirit and she goes back to cutting.

It would be nice to be able to say, "Can't cut? Then shouldn't be in school yet," muses Mrs. Ramirez. But what good would it do? If you see what it would be like for them at home, then you realize that this is *exactly* where they should be. Their homes are rich, exciting places, but they just aren't having the experiences that the white middle class school expects of them. We spend the year trying to make these kids feel good about themselves and trying to close the gap between them and the children in half-day kindergarten. It just doesn't make sense to set up standards that the kids have to measure up to before they come in. I just take them where they are and tell the first grade teacher what that point is when the year is over. Working together is the only way to make school a good place for these children.

Closing the Gap

Extended-day kindergartens were district sponsored programs in the Thomas School District, with the purpose of providing additional instructional time and resources to children seen to be at risk. Schools within the district were identified as having students with special needs and funds are allocated to provide the extended-day placement, above and beyond the half-day reimbursement provided by the state. Using an early intervention rationale, the district provided more instructional time (5 hours, 45 minutes versus 2 hours, 45 minutes) and more staff (most classes have some aide time available to them).

Children were screened, when possible, before the school year started in August. The district used a screening device from the Early Prevention of School Failure (EPSF) Program, which assessed children in the areas of auditory, visual, language, fine, and gross motor skills. Each child's performance was compared to a national norming group for his/her age and then rated as considerable strength, moderate strength, average, moderate need, or considerable need. At Rochester, placement in the extended-day program was determined by ratings of considerable need in two of the following areas: language, visual, or auditory skills.

The EPSF curriculum was used in the extended-day program. It was keyed to the skill areas assessed in the screening process and arranged by visual, auditory, language, fine and gross motor skills. This was in contrast to the district curriculum, which was developed with a content area focus, such as math, social studies, etc. A copy of the EPSF curriculum can be found in Appendix 6. One message that could be taken from the skill organization of the EPSF curriculum is that the focus of school experiences was on the child skills, rather than on the subject matter. There was the sense that instruction was oriented to providing remediation for specific skill deficits, using an environmental perspective, which empowered the teacher to provide experiences that would move the child up a skills ladder.

In comparing the EPSF curriculum to the Thomas District Core Conceptual Objectives and the report card, it is obvious that the EPSF objectives included skills that were at a more basic level than in the other two curricular documents. This makes sense in that the EPSF program was remedial; its purpose was to increase the readiness level of the children coming into first grade, therefore it should have started with more elementary skills. In addition, the EPSF objectives were more concrete, dealing for the most part with bodily movements, manipulation of objects, and attaching language to concepts rather than orientations to subject areas (such as, "The student will demonstrate an understanding of the concept of 'reading' as a communications process"). There was considerable overlap between the EPSF objectives and the district curriculum; they were organized differently, however. The district objectives focused on subject matter, while the EPSF objectives were grouped according to a skills organization. This points attention in different ways. The district objectives oriented the teacher to the material to be covered, while the EPSF objectives pointed to the deficits in measured child skills. The least overlap occured in the areas of fine and gross motor skills, which were not discussed in very much detail in the district objectives.

Instructional activities were keyed to the objectives, with a scope and sequence that was relatively linear in terms of skills acquisition. Skills levels were assessed and children placed along a skills continuum; that level provided the starting point for their instruction. Classroom activities were then provided and children intermittently assessed to determine whether they have acquired each skill. In addition, activities were sent for children to do with their parents at home that reinforced skills that were being worked on in school.

In what follows, I describe the types of activities that Mrs. Ramirez used in her classroom and the specific structure of her program. I begin with a vignette of the part of the day she called modality groups.

Mrs. Ramirez' Extended-day Kindergarten—How She Works to Close the Gap

"Modality Groups"

After going through attendance and collecting lunch money, Mrs. Ramirez gets the children ready to go off into their modality groups. Because it is the middle of October, they don't need much direction to get them in their groups and settled down. Today they are working on language. Grouped by language level, they have varying proficiency in either Spanish or English and their instruction is geared to their dominant language. One set of children heads off with Mrs. Perez, the classroom aide, to go on a walking tour of the school to talk about various areas in the building. Another group settles down at the listening center after Mrs. Ramirez reminds them that they will talk REALLY loud if they try to talk while they have the headphones on. Because they are supposed to be listening, they should probably not be talking.

Mrs. Ramirez settles on the floor with a group. She shows them photos that have colorful scenes on them, with people doing a variety of things. Holding up a picture of a boy talking to a dog who is standing behind a spilled glass of juice, Mrs. Ramirez asks them in Spanish what they see in this picture. Also in Spanish, the children identify the actors and objects in the picture and with probing questions, they talk about what the picture is about and what might have happened before. Next Mrs. Ramirez shows them a picture of a two bowls of cat food, one with four cats around it. Mrs. Ramirez asks what they see in the picture. "Cat," replies Rosa. When asked the number of cats, Arturo answers "Four." "Why are the cats not eating from the other bowl of food?" Juan Leon says, "That lady told them not to eat from the other one." "There's a dog over there," suggests Ernesto.

I work at a table with six children on a worksheet that says, "You Drive Me Crackers Sorting Sheet." On it are a square, circle, oval, and a rectangle, which they are to color then cut out. Talking about the shapes as they color, the focus is on either color or shape.

"What color do you need, Juan?" I ask.

"Red," he replies and reaches into the cookie tin filled with crayons. He swishes his hand through the crayons until a red comes to the top.

"So what are you going to color red?"

Pointing to the oval, he replies, "This one."

"What is that?"

"Um... a circle?" he suggests.

"This one is a circle," I reply, pointing, "That's an oval."

He turns to Helena and points to the oval on her sheet. "Ovalo," he says with a smile on his face. By this point Javier is hacking away at his shapes with a pair of scissors, apparently perceiving some kind of competition to complete the assignment. Intermittently there are arguments about the more exotic colors, whether red-orange is really red or really orange. They spend time comparing colors and trying to come up with the shade that it is closest to.

As they work it appears that they assume that each shape should be a different color. "You're doing two the same color!" Margarite exclaims with a shocked look on her face. Juan replies, "No way," as he colors both the circle and triangle red. The conversation flows between English and Spanish, sometimes in mid-sentence.

When the groups rotate through the activities, they line up and move quietly and quickly. Two of the groups do not come to work on the shape worksheet with me, but work with Mrs. Curtis, from Chapter One, talking about body parts and clothing. In between groups, Mrs. Ramirez quickly checks her plans on her desk. Working on patterning in a large group before recess will reinforce shapes, she thinks to herself, a Positive Action activity after recess, then group work during High Scope time to reinforce colors and shapes again. Color and shape dominoes or bingo should work for one group, making pictures with pattern tiles for the second group, and sorting objects by color then shape for the third group. As she heads back to her group, she feels good. Hitting this stuff over and over seems like the best way to get it to stick in their minds. If they don't get it now, that's OK because we'll keep talking about it throughout the year. They've grown a lot since the beginning of the year. They're doing great!

Rochester Daily Schedule:

8:45-9:45	Opening
9:00-10:00	Modality groups
10:15-10:30	Recess
10:30-10:50	Positive Action
10:55-11:30	Student lunch
11:45-12:15	Rest
12:30-1:30	High Scope
1:30-1:45	Recess
1:50-2:25	Varies by day (math, PE)
2:30	Dismissal

The day started in Mrs. Ramirez' class at 8:45, when the bell sounded and children came in from the playground outside. Quietly, her students hung up their coats and school bags and sat down at the square, an area marked on the floor where the children sat in assigned spots. Depending on whether it was an English or Spanish day, Mrs. Ramirez would do the opening activities in the language for the day, greeting each child and collecting lunch money. The pledge would be said over the intercom and then Mrs. Ramirez would introduce the activities for modality groups. Geared to the EPSF curriculum, activities focused on either language, auditory, or visual skills. Children were grouped on two dimensions, the first being language (Spanish or English). They were then typically grouped according to ability on the skill that was the day's focus (language, auditory or visual skill). At times however, groups were comprised heterogeneously by EPSF skill to allow students to interact with others not working at their level. Mrs. Ramirez ran one group, Mrs. Perez another. For the first thirty minutes, Mrs. Curtis, a Chapter One teacher worked with a group of English-speaking students. There were usually four groups rotating through the activities that Mrs. Ramirez had set up, some adult supervised, some independent. The adult-supervised activities used during modality groups were from the EPSF curriculum and focused on a specific skill. Instruction in the small groups occurred in the groups' native language.

After modality groups came a transitional time that usually involved a group math activity, then recess. Before lunch the class

participated in a Positive Action activity, which was a school
mandated program to teach positive self concept. Mrs. Ramirez
accompanied the children to lunch, then they had a thirty minutes
rest period. High Scope (described later) was next, and during
that period, three adults were available in the classroom: Mrs.
Ramirez, Mrs. Perez, and Mrs. Cullen, the speech-language
pathologist. Another recess followed High Scope, then a math
or physical education activity. After this very full day, children
were dismissed at 2:30.

All of the structures and provisions for the general extended-
day program were in place for Mrs. Ramirez' class, but in addition,
her program had the focus of language. Different from the
language area in the EPSF curriculum, which focused on delayed
language development in English speaking children, Mrs.
Ramirez' class was a bilingual class in which children were often
given their first exposure to the English language. Therefore, she
had two major forces shaping the development of her program:
the EPSF curriculum and bilingual education practices. As
mentioned earlier, Mrs. Ramirez defined herself as a bilingual
teacher first.

More than at Fulton or Norwood, the instruction that occured
in Mrs. Ramirez' class was directly related to the incoming needs
and ongoing progress of her students. At Fulton and Norwood,
the teachers had a general curriculum structure that dictated when
they would cover most major content (when they talked about
the letter M, for example). There was the assumption that most
students would have mastered the content at the end of classroom
discussion and the class moved on to the next topic. Due to the
nature of the EPSF curriculum, there was constant iteration
between assessment and instruction, with Mrs. Ramirez' children
moving to the next level of skills only when they had mastered
the previous level. When I asked Mrs. Ramirez how she went about
planning as the year went on, she focused on the the various
curricula to which she must attend:

> I think pretty much, the EPSF curriculum. Because it is pretty
> much scope and sequence and so you start with skill one and
> you go from there. Now what impact, say, what books I choose,
> kind of goes along with what the other kindergarten classes are
> doing... I know kind of what they are doing. And then we have
> our kindergarten curriculum, which you have to do. So once you
> do all that, there doesn't seem to be that much time left over...
> I do look at the report card and I do know that we have to cover

shapes and colors and all of those kinds of things... Some of
it is not part of kindergarten objectives... but it's what kindergarten has covered in the past... For example, kindergartners
do not have to know their letters. It's not one of our objectives...
but kindergarten in the past has covered letters, still covers letters,
and probably will always cover letters.

Mrs. Ramirez was the only teacher who mentioned the fact that
there was a mismatch between the Core Conceptual Objectives
and the report card. She chose to focus primarily on the EPSF
curriculum as the guiding document for her program.[7]

Beyond the curriculum structure, Mrs. Ramirez looked at the
skills that her students had in making grouping and instruction
decisions. She used the results of the EPSF screening to make
initial groupings by skills area, worked with the children on
particular skills and then shifted groups around as needed:

> I put them into groups... I'll say, "I have language here and
> I have these six who are in considerable need, I'll put them in
> one group. I have these who are in moderate need, I'll put them
> in one group."
>
> I tend to do the activities that are suggested and when I'm done
> with all of the activities, I look at the chart. I kind of average
> it out or I may take a testing day. OK, we've looked at this
> for a while and I look at their sheet, for the most part, everyone
> looks like they have S's, they look like they've got it, so I'm
> going to test this skill. That's the score that I use. And then
> I shift kids around... There are three different groups. There
> are groups for language, groups for visual, and they're also
> grouped for auditory. So the sheets that I have are what dictate
> which kids go together that day. And then that's when I'm
> working specific skills with certain groups. So let's say it's an
> auditory day, I have my considerable need kids and moderate
> need auditory kids and we're doing two different things. And
> the next day it will be visual and so groups will change. And
> then once the chart fills up, the skills sheets, then I look at that
> too. I might say, this is a considerable need group but Javier
> has all S's he's doing fine. Let's try moving him out of there
> and putting him with the moderate need. Then I might say
> Ernesto is really having a hard time, maybe he needs to redo
> that skill so I move him to the considerable need group, depending
> on how they did. It could be we get on a skill that is hard for
> them, or they plateau for a while, before it clicks, they need a
> little longer doing it than the rest of their group. That's how
> it works.

Depending on what skill they were working on on a particular day, the groups that children found themselves in were comprised by dominant language and skill level. Dominant Spanish speakers *usually* worked with other Spanish speakers and with children who were working at the same level and pace as they were. Children who had considerable needs in visual skills were not necessarily those with needs in auditory or language skills so from day to day children did not work with the same classmates. In addition, Mrs. Ramirez sometimes used mixed ability groups, so that children with more developed skills could serve as role models. This was frequently the case in language groups so that children could hear and use a variety of levels of language in their modality groups.

Mrs. Ramirez oriented her instructional practice according to what she felt her students needed at a particular point in time. Groups were formed so that children working at the same level could participate in activities that would strengthen their skills. Other times mixed ability groups were formed for modelling. These strategies were used so that Mrs. Ramirez could provide children the special things she thought they needed in her class. Beyond moving through the EPSF curriculum, Mrs. Ramirez talked about three other things that she thought her students needed in order to close the gap between them and the other students at Rochester. She worked to provide them self acceptance, concrete, hands-on activities, and mechanisms to pull their parents gently into the life of the school during the kindergarten year. I will discuss each of these tactics in turn.

Both Mrs. Sunden and Ms. Carlin talked about how they worked to help their students feel good about themselves. That is standard kindergarten philosophy. Mrs. Ramirez was no exception. When I asked her to describe herself as a teacher, in addition to being a bilingual teacher, she replied:

> For my kids, it's a lot of acceptance. They're still in that touchy feely stage where they need lots of hugs. And validation of their self worth, that they are important. They can do things. Oh, to give them the feeling that, "Oh, I can do this. I'm a pretty smart kid." For me to say, "Yeah, you did a super job." So that they feel good about themselves. You need a sense of humor and patience. I want them to try.

Mrs. Ramirez was in sync with the other teachers in her commitment to helping children develop good self concepts. This commitment was heightened, however, because she saw them as coming into school identified as different from the rest of their agemates. Her students, because they were culturally and ethnically different from the rest of the middle class, Anglo community at Rochester, needed to learn that it was OK to be different; in fact, it could be something to be proud of:

> I guess the first thing that I do is use the language, Spanish, in the classroom. Because, one, it says it's important. If nothing else, I want them to feel proud of who they are. To think, "Oh, how neat. It's OK to use my name Helena, I don't have to be Helen in school." Or just be proud of who they are because they cannot change it. It's going to be that way forever. I don't even do too much with the transition into the middle class Anglo society, because they already know. They already know that they are different. They know that there is this world out there that uses English and there is this one way. They know that. And so what I am trying to tell them is that, "You don't have to be exactly like this. It's OK to keep some of this." So they don't feel that "OK, I can't use any Spanish and I have to be Helen." I try to say, "It's OK. Helena is a beautiful name. You know what my name is? My name is Isabel." "It is? Oh, how neat."

This sentiment was backed up by her actions in the classroom. As I worked in Mrs. Ramirez' classroom, I saw her providing a very even balance between English and Spanish, never privileging one over the other. Whole group instruction in the classroom alternated between Spanish and English; Mrs. Ramirez called them English days and Spanish days. In this way, the students found that one language (and the culture surrounding it) was not more important than another, at least within the walls of her classroom. She still found it necessary to deal with the language chauvinism that existed among others in the school, however. Mrs. Ramirez described with a tone of irony how Mrs. Cullen, the speech-language pathologist, said that she felt sorry for one of the Anglo students in Mrs. Ramirez' class on Spanish days. She thought that Faith must be very confused and have a hard time following directions when she only heard them in Spanish. No mention was made of the majority of Hispanic children and the problems they might have on English days or in the Anglo world in general. This made Mrs. Ramirez realize that she would just have to work harder to strengthen the way that they thought about themselves, making sure that it turned out to be positive.

Another way that Mrs. Ramirez worked to close the gap is to use open-ended, child-centered activities in her classroom. When she described the kinds of things she liked to do with children, she focused on the lack of worksheets in her classroom:

> I like to do a lot of hands-on types of things and I like it to be theirs. So I don't necessarily do very many ditto pages. I would much rather say, "Here's a piece of paper. Here's the glue. Here's the scissors. And I want you to make something. I don't care what you make. Let's see what your imagination will come up with." I'd much rather do that and see what they come up with. I'd much rather do that than, "Here's a piece of paper. Color it, cut it out. And then match the shape where it should be." Basically, they are doing the same thing: cutting and coloring and gluing.

This statement was backed up by what I observed in the classroom. During the period that I observed from September through December, only two worksheets were used: a shape worksheet that they colored and a Christmas wreath ditto that Mrs. Ramirez pulled out on a day that she was sick but in the classroom.

One of the most open-ended activities used in any of the classrooms was the daily High Scope period, which took up a major portion of the kindergarten afternoon. Used by both extended-day kindergartens at Rochester, Mrs. Ramirez described the program in shorthand as "plan, do, and review." In this daily activity, various areas of the classroom were made available for child play. The areas might include blocks, art, construction, housekeeping, painting, computer, the sand table, listening center, games, or gross motor equipment. Each child had a "planning book" in which s/he planned what area s/he would choose. Children would mark the area of choice, then go to an area and place a name card in the sign for that area. Most areas had a maximum of four children allowed in them at any one time. Children were to remain in the area chosen until the end of the "doing" time, when they cleaned up and returned to their planning books. They were then encouraged to review what they had done by drawing a picture of where they had played and with whom. The level of this task was modified as the year progressed from general pictures at the beginning of the year, to more emphasis on body awareness, to attempts to write stories. Both the planning and review times were supervised by adults in groups of about seven students. The High Scope activities were used to develop language, to encourage task involvement, and provide structure for social experiences. There were no right or wrong answers in these activities, allowing children positive experiences in the classroom.

Other activities that Mrs. Ramirez used in her classroom, though less open-ended, were math and literacy activities. Math was one of the most explicitly structured academic subjects in the Rochester extended-day bilingual program. Math activities were sprinkled throughout the day, starting with the opening calendar activities. After greeting each child individually with a "Good morning" or "Buenos dias" Mrs. Ramirez had the students count with her to determine the number of children at school that day. They then talked about the calendar, talking about yesterday, today, and tomorrow and finding the number of the day of the month on some kind of calendar decoration (e.g., a pumpkin or a heart, depending on the season) and placing it on the correct calendar square. The decorations were in an alternating patterns of color or shape. Mrs. Ramirez used that as an additional cue if the children had a problem finding the correct one with the number only. Periodically they counted the number of days that they had been in school, clapping on each tenth day. Other math activities included free exploration of math materials in pairs or making patterns of various materials. Mrs. Ramirez often did large group activities to practice skills. The two skills that were often practiced in large group were graphing and patterning. Mrs. Ramirez' students graphed all kinds of things: candy, pictures of different kinds of bears, pattern blocks, and leaves. Initially, the focus was primarily on sorting the materials into like groups to form a line. The groups of material were then counted and they compared which had the most and the least. Sometimes records were made on the chalkboard, other times it was done verbally only. Patterns were similarly worked out in large group, either on the board or with materials like pattern blocks.

Literacy experiences were broad based and paired with basic language activities. One of the main activities was the telling and retelling of stories from big books in both English and Spanish. After the first reading, students were encouraged to join in to read the story together. They then sometimes made a class book of a particular story in small groups, illustrating and retelling the story line. Small groups also dictated stories on a theme, like Halloween. Planning book activities moved from drawing to telling a story to writing a story. Both Spanish and English were used in literacy tasks, with children receiving exposure to both.

Public evaluation of child performance in Mrs. Ramirez' class tended to emphasize doing your best rather than a normative judgment related to some standard. When children gave what might be considered wrong answers, Mrs. Ramirez redirected conversations so that the right answer was given by someone else. No products that the children completed were marked with evaluation statements; Mrs. Ramirez tended to give positive feedback verbally at the time of the activity.

Ms. Carlin and to a lesser degree, Mrs. Sunden, talked about working with parents as part of their jobs. But neither of them involved the parents in the manner that Mrs. Ramirez did, nor did their parents change how they interacted with the school over the course of the school year. Not only did Mrs. Ramirez work to close the gap for her students, but she also worked to close the gap between the school and her parents, so that they could be involved in their children's education. Mrs. Ramirez had described her students' parents as having less than pleasant experiences with schools in the past. Simply put, they had a bad attitude about school. Mrs. Ramirez saw this as a major stumbling block to her students' progress and she worked hard to lessen its intensity.

> [I] talk to the parents and tell them, "You know, what do you want for your child?" "I want them to finish school." "Fine, your attitude is very important. You need to tell them that this is important." So I try to talk to the parents and really get to them. Or even to tell the parents who are really adamant about wanting their child in English. So I'll say, "Fine, then the bilingual [activities] will get the skills going in English for you. Do me a favor. When they have their reading skills down in English, teach them to read in Spanish. There is no reason that they cannot know both. And guess what, it's going to be of value to them as an adult."

Mrs. Ramirez felt that for her students to succeed, they needed to get positive messages about school from both home and the school. The first thing that she did was to try to communicate to parents how important it was that they get that message across to their children.

Getting that message to the parents was not always easy. These were not parents who came to the school to talk to the teacher; nor did they automatically participate in activities sent home. Part of Mrs. Ramirez' job was to draw her parents into school slowly, by showing the kinds of things that they could do with their children and by showing them that she cared. It took much effort. When I asked her how much parent education could be done in her class, this is how she replied:

Mrs. Ramirez:	Probably not very much. At the beginning of the year, we do talk to the parents and say, "This is why your child is in the extended-day program. This is what we hope to accomplish." We do send home parent activity cards. Little activities the parents can do at home with their children. And so we forewarn them saying, "This is what it's going to look like when you get it home. You don't need to have anything special. Just use materials you have available at home." So it's real limited.
Int:	How many of them use the kinds of things that you send home?
Mrs. Ramirez:	Maybe a 1/3. In my case, my incentive is that after they bring three of their homeworks they get a prize. And so it's their job to say, "Today's homework day, when can we do it?" And then the parents have to sign this little paper then the child returns it... So there are usually 1/3 of them that really get into it and they'll bring their homework EVERY week and the others are sporadic and the others you never see it. But to me, it's worth it because if five do it, even a couple, you're giving them a leg up. And maybe it even gives parents ideas.

Mrs. Ramirez took the time and made the effort to provide families with activities that they could do at home to reinforce what was going on in the class because "you're giving them a leg up." With this leg up they could slowly work to close the gap.

Another way that Mrs. Ramirez tried to get parents to make connections with the school was to go and see the ones least likely to come in to school. The children who were bussed in from Clarendon were separated from the school by more distance and were often first generation Mexican-Americans who were not sure how to go about approaching the school. While most teachers stayed at school during parent teacher conferences and had parents meet them there, Mrs. Ramirez made home visits to the "center" children from Clarendon during one of the evening conference nights. This is how she described the impact those visits had on her relationship with parents:

> Well, I think it makes a difference because I made the home visits with the center kids, and since they're not in an attendance area, for the first conference I thought, well, I'll go visit them. And I don't know what difference it would have made if I hadn't made the home visit. All I know is that they all showed and they all came to school for the second conference. Or maybe they said, "Oh, no, we don't want her to come over again. We'll go there." I don't know. Or whether it was the kids who said, "We want you to come see our school." But they *all* came.

At the first conferences in November, Mrs. Ramirez had a 50% attendance rate (including the home visits that she made). At the second set of conferences, all the parents that she had gone to visit came into school, with about 80% of the parents coming in overall.

When she went out to her students' homes she could give these parents more than feedback about how their children were doing at school and activities that they could do to reinforce concepts covered in her class. Mrs. Ramirez also used these opportunities to help socialize the parents to the school experience. For example, when she went to visit Hector's family, she helped them understand which notes that came home from school were really important to pay attention to: announcements of movies at school were not as important as announcements of inservice days when children would not attend school. Learning which messages to attend to would allow Hector's parents to focus on the things that would help him most.

Coming with minimal expectations for their child's kindergarten experience, over the year Mrs. Ramirez slowly moved the parents to the point that they can begin to invest in the academic part of the school enterprise. They started by hoping that their child would like school and by the end of the year they could begin to work with the school to help motivate learning:

> [When the year starts], it's more a feeling. "I want them to like school." It's more they want them to have a successful year. And when we talk about successful they say, "You know, I want them to like school. I want you to like my child. I want them to feel good about coming." And that's all at first. And then

it's kind of like, once they've got that established, whether it takes the first semester, first three quarters, then we can look at academics.

Mrs. Ramirez gave the example of Ernesto's mother who, at the home visit, was worried about the fact that he was not eating. That was her big concern at that point. They did not even talk about school. "He's not eating and I'm doing all these things for him and what can I do? He used to be so sweet and now that he's started school he talks back and what am I going to do?" So Mrs. Ramirez talked with her about those concerns at that meeting. In February, both of Ernesto's parents came in to talk with Mrs. Ramirez and she expressed concerns that she had about how he was progressing. When I talked to her in May, Mrs. Ramirez said that Ernesto had been making super progress since the conference: "I don't know what they do or how they've been doing it but he knows his numbers. He knows half of his letters. I mean he just really picked up and I know it's because they worked with him. It made all the difference in the world for him." At the start of the year, the parents were keying in on the social or emotional aspect of going to school. That was something that they could understand about their child and something that they could do something about (especially considering their unpleasant experiences in school). Over the course of the year, Mrs. Ramirez closed the gap for them as well by showing them the ways that they could help their child grow academically.

At Rochester, I scheduled interviews with parents during the November conferences as I did at Fulton and Norwood, with Spanish language letters sent to the Spanish speaking parents. Six conferences were scheduled during an evening, each preceding the parent teacher conference with Mrs. Ramirez. Of the six interviews scheduled, three were completed. This was on par with Mrs. Ramirez' attendance rate for conferences, so I felt that my presence did not compromise parent participation in conferences. I am aware that the parents I talked to were the most engaged at this early stage in the year and that I am missing the voices of the parents who were less involved with the school. For this reason, the topics that these parents talked about might not be representative of the Rochester bilingual kindergarten parent group.

I engaged the services of an interpreter for the interviews, providing a script of the interview protocol and having her ask the questions and pose follow-up questions. Because I do not speak Spanish, I found that I could not do the kind of subsequent questioning that hinges on the initial answers in an interview. The interpreter was highly skilled, both in terms of her grasp of the language and in interviewing techniques, therefore I feel fairly comfortable with these interactions.

The parents of two boys (Pedro and Ricardo) and one girl (Berta) were interviewed at Rochester. Two of them were Spanish dominant (Pedro and Berta) and the other an English speaker (Ricardo). When I asked them to reflect back to August, before their child started school, I received varied responses, ranging from concern about behavior to concern about language difficulties. There was really no common theme among these parents, other than they thought their children were in good shape to come to school. Both Ricardo's mother and Pedro's parents mentioned that they thought they were ready to come to school, but their talk about readiness focused more on the things that they would be doing in school rather than on child characteristics.[8] They did not have a structure that they used to make judgments about readiness before school started, they just felt confident about how their child was doing in school. In addition, they had not received school messages about their child's readiness level from Mrs. Ramirez during the school year. All three parents mentioned something about the language issue, indicating that it was a concern. Table 20 summarizes the issues that the parents in Mrs. Ramirez' class brought up when I talked to them in the fall.

Table 20
Mrs. Ramirez' Parents Talk About the Kindergarten Experience

Child Name	Anticipating Kindergarten	Readiness	Language
Berta	Berta is a very gifted person, very intelligent, and I think Berta will always do well because she pays a lot of attention to what I teach her.		I don't know English, but Spanish—I teach her what I know and she learns it very well.

Table 20 *continued*
Mrs. Ramirez' Parents Talk About the
Kindergarten Experience

Child Name	Anticipating Kindergarten	Readiness	Language
Pedro		Well, in our minds he was ready... that we had spoken to him about school, that is we had told him he would learn how to write, how to count—everything.	Maybe that he was going to have some difficulty with the language.
Ricardo	Mainly, I think I was concerned about—I know they are not going to be able to handle him, because he's a very hyper child. I just worried from the moment I woke till I went to bed—I just knew they were going to say Mrs. Baca, come and get your son—he's just too much for us.	He is real, how could I say, alert. "I'm just ready for anything that happens." He's ready... I think he'll be able to learn a lot easier, he won't have such a hard time learning because he's just ready for it—he's ready for anything. My son has always been that way.	My husband's only a Spanish-speaking person and I speak Spanish (I have to be able to speak Spanish to communicate with my husband) but I speak English. I'm from here and my husband's from Mexico. I thought that might have a lot to do with how well he was going to learn. If it doesn't confuse him.

I asked Mrs. Ramirez what she had learned from the experience of being involved in this research project. Showing how central working with parents was to the way she thought about her job and herself, she talked about how the process had worked to strengthen the way that she felt about her job, her students, and their parents:

> I think probably what it did is strengthen some of my feelings. And when I say that, I think I know what it's like for some of these parents. You know, not personally, but I can imagine what it's like. Like Juan Leon's mom, when I called and I said, "Does he have a social security number?" Obviously not. They're here illegally. And I just said, "Well, I don't know what I can do but if I can help you in any way, just let me know what

I can do so that you can get the papers that you need to get to be here." I guess I wasn't even thinking so much of the kids. But I was thinking first of the parents. If you're going to have them being involved, if you're going to have them take an interest in their child, you kind of have to make the first move. Because these parents are not going to come to you. In Glenda's room [one of the half-day teachers] they'll come to you. They'll be there. And these parents won't. And if you don't do anything you'll never see them. And that means making home visits, as much as some teachers don't like doing it.

She told me about how she asked Bea's mother about her daughter's distress at school, saying that her mother was moving or that she was gone to Mexico. Bea's mother explained that she and her husband were having problems and then asked Mrs. Ramirez if they could go out to dinner to talk about it. Dreading that moment, Mrs. Ramirez did not flinch, however:

There's that part of me that says, "I don't want to go out to dinner and let's stop talking about this." But it's also what you have to do with a lot of these parents if you're going to get them hooked into school. It's like you have to say, "I care about you." And once you have that established, then they believe you when you say, "I care about your child and we need to talk about them." I think what happens is, you can get them hooked in enough or at least get them going with their child so that it can carry them through... I think there's probably a lot of parent education that needs to take place. And that just takes time. "You can make a difference in your child's education. Here are some things that you can do."

A commitment to the families of her students, not just the students themselves was a way for Mrs. Ramirez to close the gap for both parents and children. This involved not only talking to them about school related matters but doing things to show that she cared. She hoped that this would carry over so that they would see that it was worth investing the time and energy to work with the school so that their child would succeed.

In the fall and again in February, I attempted to interview Mrs. Ramirez' students to find out what they thought about their kindergarten experience. The fall interviews were done singley, the February interviews in groups of three to five with an interpreter for the Spanish speakers. The same interview protocol was used in all three schools, but resulted in much more muddled answers at Rochester. Mrs. Ramirez' students seemed to be answering a different set of questions than I was asking; neither I nor my interpreter could make a connection between the two. The basic difficulty appeared to be language—I could not construct a situation that allowed them to discuss their kindergarten experience. Their language was very concrete, mostly in terms of physical attributes. For example, when I asked what kinds of things were hard in school, Margarite replied that "The table is hard." Easy things included taking a nap, playing, coloring. When we asked students to describe some other members of their class, the descriptions were invariably physical, even if we tried to probe to get more behavioral information. When we asked Armando to tell us about Pedro, this is how he replied:

Int:	What's Pedro like?
Armando:	He's my friend who wears a belt.
Int:	A belt?
Margarite:	She knows that. All men wear a belt. If they don't wear a belt their trousers fall down.
Int:	What else... What is Pedro like in class? What kinds of things is he good at?
Armando:	He's my friend... and we're going to get the other men... Margarite is getting them.

The discussion then moved on to a story of cops and robbers, with Margarite's hand tied and Armando saving her. One possible theme that could be taken from these interviews was that these children did not make a distinction between work and play; they enjoyed most school tasks. Because their feedback from Mrs. Ramirez was almost exclusively positive, they did not develop standards against which to measure their performance in terms of it being easy or hard. This methodological problem was something that I could not overcome in the time frame that I had available and is one of the biggest limitations of my study.

What is Readiness in This Situation?

Rochester was a school with a diverse population, with a variety of needs and expectations. In response to a trend of increasing heterogeneity, the school had developed a number of alternative programs. Their approach had been to draw their expectations with wider boundaries to maximize the possibility that children would succeed. This meant that it did not make sense for teachers to demand that children had certain skills before they moved to the next grade, as it became counterproductive for both the staff and students. When I asked Mrs. Ramirez to describe the kind of feedback she got from the first grade teachers about the skills that were necessary for children to succeed, she replied:

> There's really not much we do with that. They can say, "We want all kids to know their alphabet." And we could say, "We would *love* them all to know their alphabet." If we could do it we would, we're working on it. But pretty much their philosophy is "Take the kids where they are and go from there." We know that they have expectations. It would be wonderful if they all could do that. Just like for us to say, "It would be wonderful if all the kids came into kindergarten knowing their name." Wouldn't that be great? [laughter]

The half-day and extended-day teachers had very different expectations for their students incoming skills and progress during the year. The staff had learned to accept that and had made accommodations to make the situation work.

Within her class, Mrs. Ramirez viewed her job as bridging the gap. She had students who came in without many of the skills that were commonly assumed to be part of a kindergartners' tool chest. They spoke a different language and they did not have a grasp of the concepts that anchored the kindergarten curriculum. Their experiences were very different, though no less valuable, than those of their peers. They were seen by the school as unready to meet the demands of the regular school program so they were given an opportunity to catch up through a longer school day and more resources. Their parents were not hooked into the school system and Mrs. Ramirez found it necessary to work to draw them in so that she could elicit their co-operation in their child's school experience.

How does readiness get defined in a situation like this? At an institutional level, the children in Mrs. Ramirez' class had already been labelled as unready according to their screening test results and their dominant language. But what did that designation mean for the students? The meaning of readiness was interpreted over the course of the school year by Isabel Ramirez, first in her own mind, then for her students and parents. When

I asked her to tell me a little bit about the students she typically got in her program, Mrs. Ramirez talked about two different kinds of things: academics and maturity. Through this description, Mrs. Ramirez showed how she saw readiness as the result of environmental stimulation, which should produce maturity:

> I guess I see my kids in kind of three categories. One, the kids who come in who have had a lot of stimulation. They know their letters. They know their numbers, they know their colors, but they are lacking other areas developmentally. Maybe their language is still low. Sure they can recite the alphabet and they know all their letters, but to communicate they still need work on communication skills. Or visual skills or memory skills or whatever. Then there's the group that comes in that haven't had much stimulation. Maybe they know their colors, but they don't know letters or numbers. And they also have needs in different areas. And then the other group of kids that come in that maybe don't have the ability. And it's hard to know these kids in kindergarten... Maybe it's low ability, maybe there's a learning disability, something. You really can't tell in kindergarten.

> We had some very mature kids. What I mean by that is that they are READY for school. They come in and they are ready to listen, they are ready to do and they are excited and this is wonderful and it's fun and then we have those on the other end [laughter]... who can't sit still, can't keep their hands to themselves, want to play. That's what they want to do, they want to play. They're just real immature still. And then you've got the ones in the middle. So they either tend to be really ready or not.

The issue of environmental stimulation came up again and again in conversations with Mrs. Ramirez. When I asked her how she thought children got ready, she focused on what happened at home:

> That's always been a mystery. I think it has to do with responsibility at home. I really do. I think that makes a difference. Parents attitudes toward what their children can do. "Oh, he just can't do that, he's so little." Oh guess what, he can do that. He can have his own jobs at home. He can help you take the trash out. He can make his own bed. Granted, it's not going to be perfect but yes, he can do it. And the ones that are really mature tend to be treated that way.

One of the reasons that the Rochester staff could not use a threshold idea about readiness, in which they defined the skills that were needed to come into kindergarten, was that their students lacked school-oriented stimulation that occured at home. While at Norwood, many people would look at the skill level of the children in Mrs. Ramirez' class and say that they needed more time to develop before starting school, Mrs. Ramirez would counter that staying home is exactly what you do not want these children to do:

> For some of these kids, you might say they are not ready to be in school. What this child needs is another year at home. But then you look at home and say, "Nope! That's OK. What this child needs is to be in school. They really do need to be here." Because at home nothing is happening. Can you tell? They're five years old and look at them. There's a reason; it just doesn't happen overnight. It took five years to get this product.

For these children to grow, to become more ready, they needed to be in a situation that would reinforce their learning, that would provide them the stimulation that they needed. Because opportunities for school-related stimulation were often not available at home and because these parents could not afford sophisticated child care, her students needed to get into school as soon as possible, so that she could work with the family to get the child more ready.

Mrs. Ramirez reiterated this in October when I asked her about how various children were developing. One child whom she was concerned about was a tiny boy named Juan Leon. Compared to the rest of the children in the class, Juan Leon looked to be about three years old. He was small in stature and out of sync with everything that went on in the classroom. He stood up when everyone else was sitting down; he kept his coat on when the rest of the coats were hanging up; he shouted out to Mrs. Ramirez' in the middle of many activities. When he worked on small motor tasks he drooled and his entire body was involved in any large motor activity. According to most Gesell examiners, he was developmentally young. Should he be in kindergarten?

> I guess I could start the beginning of the year saying that I want my students to know their name and their numbers and colors. Well, that would have been out the window right away.

I'd have been upset and frustrated and nobody would have done anything. If you tell somebody like Juan Leon that they aren't ready, that they need to stay home... He needs to be here! This is exactly where he needs to be. This is the best thing for him. Of course, I'd like to have more control over what kind of things they come in with.

Because Juan Leon needed the stimulation and structure of being in school, Mrs. Ramirez had no hesitation in having him in her room. He was frustrating at times, but she did not make judgments about him based on his ability. It would not do any good. She saw him as immature, which was a combination of stimulation and biological development. I asked her if maturity was related to experiences that children have had or if she thought it was biological:

It could be both. Just think, all that you need is two of those, biology and experience and WOW, it's a double whammy. It's bad enough if it is just biological. That could be Ricardo, maybe it's just biological. Then there is Juan Leon. It could be experiential and biological. Ricardo at least... let's say that he's had the experience. If you can get him tuned in, he's going to learn and make progress. I mean you're going to have lapses where he can't control himself but then if you have Juan Leon, who doesn't have the experience and then has the immaturity on top of it, you have to do all the experience stuff to get him caught up or to at least get him to figure out where you are coming from. All you can do is keep working on the same concept but in a lot of different ways. That's kind of how I feel about shapes... Well the concept is shapes and you do it a lot of different ways... If you didn't get it, that's OK because WE'RE GOING TO DO IT AGAIN.

This maturity, which Mrs. Ramirez saw as a part of readiness, was what allowed children to learn things at different points in their lives. The mechanism for developing maturity or readiness was seen by Mrs. Ramirez as "developmental," meaning it could not be forced. It came with a critical combination of time and experience:

I went to a conference and the speaker said that in the United States, we think that there is a magic age of six. And they learn to read. He said, "You know, that's not true." He said that he would like to see everything ungraded from four to seven. Just developmental. That's your developmental time. Ungraded. So you start to read at four? How wonderful. You read at five? That's fine. You read at six? Great. Your read at seven? Wonderful. That makes so much sense. Because you can see it. And it's like anything else, it's developmental. And you can't push it. You can do everything to encourage it. Everything to bring it out and if they're not ready, they are not ready.

Mrs. Ramirez recounted how some of the children in her class got stuck on one of the auditory skills in the EPSF curriculum, following multiple part directions. She tried and tried to get them to the point where they could follow through on the directions, doing activity after activity, and she pushed them to the point that one child even cried. They were not ready, so she pulled back and did some other kinds of activities for a while. When she came back to directions, most of them did fine. That combination of time and experiences had to be in the right proportions for the children to profit.

What happened to the children who are not ready when they go on to first grade? Mrs. Ramirez acknowledged that even though the school staff had a commitment to try to widen their view of acceptable skills, especially between grades, there was still an essential structural problem. Due to the nature of the first grade objectives, there was considerable pressure for children to master them. And her students were starting out behind. Even though she had worked all year, there was still a gap:

The way the structure is, the way the set up is, it can't help but be hard. And I told one mom, I said, "You have to understand that if your child enters first grade knowing no letters, they start here. [her hand at waist height] At the bottom. Because they're going to be in a class with kids that know how to read. If they don't know how to read, the kids who know most of their letters and some sounds are ready to start reading. And then you have the kids that know a few letters, and then there's your child, who knows none. And that's where they're going to enter... Part of it's the way the curriculum is set up. When you look at what kindergarten has to teach, there's very little you're really accountable for... But the first grade I think the accountability, the pressure from that is a lot greater. Plus I think parents' expectations are a lot different. So they have the two, the district curriculum says this is what you have to do and parents are saying, well they're in first grade now and this is what we expect to see.

For the most part, her students went into the bilingual first grade, where they would have students who came from backgrounds much like their own. But there was still the overall school structure and district system that required the first grade teacher to attempt to get through a list of skills on a set of objectives or a report card. Mrs. Ramirez did not feel pressure from them, however, to develop standards so that the children going into first grade would "be ready."

In our final interview, I asked Mrs. Ramirez what she though readiness was. She had come to the conclusion that it was more socially constructed than she would have thought initially, that it depended on the people in the setting, their expectations and needs.

> Well, I think readiness is—I think there's more perception in it than I would have thought before. You know, it's a way I look at them, mainly... And so when I get them it's just really my perception of what I think readiness is. Which is, of course, influenced by my school and the school district and the world at large.

She went on to describe how her parents come in not really thinking about the kinds of things they need to do to get their child ready for school, they just bring them. The parents in the other extended-day were more involved with the school, but not to the extent that the half-day parents were. She contrasted her students' parents with herself, a middle class Hispanic woman who was a member of the education establishment: "I know what readiness is. And I know what I expect my child to learn in kindergarten. And if it doesn't happen, I will probably come and say, 'Hello, Mrs. Johnson. I would like to visit with you. No, I have some concerns here.'" Mrs. Ramirez knew what to expect about kindergarten. She knew about this thing called readiness and she knew what kinds of things were supposed to happen in a classroom to enhance it. The parents that she worked with had no idea about kindergarten or readiness and it was her job to clue them in. Readiness was something in her head and she used it to shape instruction, not to weed children out.

CHAPTER 8

8ᴥ

CONCLUSIONS

This study provided the opportunity to examine the meanings of readiness in three very different communities: a small, rural working class community, a middle class bedroom community of professionals, and a heterogeneous school community within a mid-size town. Each school and classroom had a special character, and out of that character came a story about how readiness was used in the context of the local kindergarten. Until this point the discussion has focused, for the most part, of each setting separately, without comparing extensively among the respective groups of teachers, parents, and students. In this concluding chapter, I will examine how the meaning of readiness differed in each of these contexts, how it was used to shape instruction and develop standards, and the kinds of policy implications that might be drawn as a result.

The Constructed Meaning of Readiness

Parents

More than any other grade, parents have a stake in their child's kindergarten year. Kindergarten makes an important transition in a child's life; the move from pre-school to elementary school is faced by parents eagerly or with trepidation. For this reason, I focused on how parents anticipated their child's kindergarten entrance and on the ways that they interpreted their progress as the year went on.

The way that parents discussed the kindergarten year told much about how they were thinking about readiness. At Fulton, they were excited about their child going to school, about the social and academic opportunities it would provide. At the beginning of the year, they were convinced that their children were bright and would do exceedingly well in school. They had a sense of what their children could do, which was referenced to life outside school, and they had a very general idea about what kindergarten would be about based on their own school experiences. As the year went on, they were not quite as effusive but still felt positive. Fulton parents thought that it was the school's job to educate their children; they were more than willing to support the school but would not try to advance any agenda of their own. They depended on Ms. Carlin for feedback on their child's progress and her translation of what that meant for readiness.

Norwood parents worried. They knew about a thing called readiness and they were aware that a child was supposed to have it before coming into school at Norwood. Some of them held their children out an extra year so that they would be six before entering school. They spoke about readiness in terms of age, maturity, and social behaviors necessary to do well in school. These ideas were well defined and communicated among Norwood parents and there was pressure to abide by the norm of helping your child by holding her out. They came into the school with coherent ideas about what kindergarten should be like, how their child should do and what to do if there were problems. Working as classroom helpers, these parents gathered knowledge about the school and how the teacher interacted with students. Norwood parents knew the system and how to manipulate it to get what they wanted.

At Rochester, the parents in the bilingual extended-day program were disconnected from the school by their language and their previous bad experiences with education. They presented their child to the school with the hope that the student would enjoy school and maybe even graduate. These parents were dependent on their child's teacher to translate the meaning of readiness for them; this was important because their children had already been labelled unready at the start of the school year. Rochester parents did not have a list of skills that they thought their children should have to enter school; they brought them to school when they were legally eligible to enroll and waited for education to happen. As the year went on, they were attracted slowly to the life of the school and many of them became more active in their child's education.

Table 21 summarizes how the parents in these three settings approached the school experience and how they developed a meaning of readiness:

Table 21
Parents' Interpretations of Their Role
in Kindergarten Education

Fulton	*Norwood*	*Rochester*
Anglo working class	Anglo middle class	Hispanic working class
Excited about their child going to kindergarten for social reasons & thought their child was bright. Wanted children to get a good start: to learn the fundamentals, develop social skills and good attitude for learning, prepare for later.	Apprehensive, they worried whether their child was ready (either in the past or now). They were not concerned about their child's academic readiness. Instead they worried about their child's relative age, maturity, and social readiness. They expected their child to learn basic fundamentals and to develop a good foundation for learning.	Disconnected from the school because they had had bad experiences previously, because they spoke another language, and they did not know the structure and expectations of the school. They did not have concrete expectations about what kindergarten was all about beyond wanting their child to be happy.

What was readiness for these parents?

Readiness was defined by the school for parents at Fulton. Its definition occurred through a school-dominated relationship in which the parents reacted to the requests of the school. They were dependent on Ms. Carlin to give them feedback and to interpret what their child's performance meant.	Readiness was defined in the Norwood community at large. Its definition was communicated even before the school year started, with parents talking to one another about what children needed in order to be successful at Norwood. Parents made decisions about their children based on the community meaning of readiness.	The meaning of readiness was translated to parents by Mrs. Ramirez. These children had already been judged to be unready and it was up to the school to close the gap. Parents had no investment in that meaning initially, but came to buy into it as the year went on.

According to Vygotskian theory, language is a tool that people use to understand and negotiate their way through the world. It is through the use of semiotic systems like language that people transform ideas from the social to the psychological plane; from ideas among people to ideas of one's own (Wertsch, 1985). The parents from Fulton, Norwood, and Rochester had different semiotic systems to communicate and develop the meaning of readiness (Eisenhart & Graue, 1990). The parents at Norwood were very articulate in the language of readiness: they talked about youngness, social readiness, and maturity. They built models for what a kindergarten child should look like and could compare their child to that model to decide about kindergarten enrollment. The parents at Fulton and Mrs. Ramirez' parents at Rochester thought of kindergarten in terms of the opportunities it made available and they looked forward to the year as an exciting step in their child's life. They did not have an explicit construct of readiness against which to evaluate their child. They were confident and trusting that the school would do its job; that the school was ready for their child. They did not develop a checklist of skills necessary for enrollment. To the extent that they had an implicit idea of readiness it was synonymous with normal and healthy development. Therefore, children were assumed to be ready if their ages made them eligible for school. Without a performance-based model for determining readiness, these parents did not make decisions about whether to enroll their child; they just did it. With different models for readiness, the actions available to parents varied accordingly.

How did the constructed meaning of readiness shape the interaction of these parents with the school and their child's education? At Fulton and Rochester, the parents did not enter the negotiation of the meaning of readiness; this job was entrusted to the school. The school was seen as an authority figure that made professional decisions about education with whom the parents could cooperate. Fulton parents wanted their children to get a good start and were helpful when the school tried to engage them. They came to understand their children as students through Ms. Carlin's feedback. Rochester parents had no link to the school at the beginning of the year and began to work with Mrs. Ramirez as the year progressed. She interpreted and translated the meaning of readiness with them as they became more engaged with the institution of school. They too developed a school-related view of their children throughout the year. Norwood parents were part of the power structure that defined the meaning of readiness. Parents communicated the meaning among themselves even before the school year began and they developed their own readiness intervention through the use of academic redshirting. They worked from the assumption that parents should provide their children with any advantage that they can; making sure that their children were ready was one such intervention. They approached their child's kindergarten year seeing him/her from the particular Norwood school perspective and they made decisions based on that view. The children who were held out were not necessarily the least able; in fact their parents had no concern about their academic readiness. Some would call this protection; others would call it advantage-seeking. Parents at Norwood participated in a system that resulted in escalation of expectations: while some tried to provide their child with a leg up, those left behind were seen wanting in comparison. By their individual interventions, doing what they thought was best for their child, they made important changes in the nature of the kindergarten cohort. The definition of readiness at Norwood was highly social and refined through constant communication and testing as parents made comparisons between their children and the rest of their peers.

In different ways, each set of parents was a part of the overall construction of the meaning of readiness. At Norwood, the parents explicitly advanced their ideas about how children should enter school; their actions fed the cycle of expectations that children should be ready when they came to kindergarten. At Fulton and Rochester, the influence of parents was more implicitly felt. As the parents continued to present their children to their kindergarten teachers when they were age eligible, the school responded by making a place for them. At Fulton, that place was a half-day kindergarten class; at Rochester, it was in the extended-day bilingual program.

The School

The professional network within each school provided a context for the institutionalized meaning of readiness in the setting. The relationships among teachers, the boundaries between grade levels, and the development of standards were forces that worked to construct the meaning of readiness in a particular class. The three settings varied in the degree to which teachers (both inside and outside the kindergarten) communicated ideas among themselves, the power that teachers had in terms of defining readiness and standards for their students.

At Fulton, teachers worked together to develop educational programs that bridged grade levels and specialities. When presented with children who did not fit the grade level profile, these teachers collaborated on ways to meet their needs. The school had a large number of children seen to be at risk upon kindergarten entrance and they used an interventionist approach in providing them extended-day programs to try to bring them up to expected level. The children in Ms. Carlin's class had already been judged to be ready for school. At the end of the kindergarten year, the children in all classes, regular and extended-day, would be mixed and classes made up of all first grade aged children.

Norwood was a school with explicit standards for readiness before entering kindergarten. The work of the kindergarten year was seen as getting children ready for first grade; the first grade teachers had much power in the definition of the kindergarten curriculum and judgments of performance. Adaptations had been made in the past to deal with children who did not meet the Norwood performance profile; these adaptations were extra-year programs based on a maturational view of readiness. Under pressure from parents, the programs were disbanded and unstated extra-year programs were developed. Sizable proportions of the male kindergarten population were held out so that they would be more ready when they entered kindergarten; retention was advised for a good number of first graders. For a small number of children who were not the middle class Norwood norm, K-1 programs were suggested, in which children went to first grade half-day and kindergarten the other half. The following year they went on to first grade full-time. These children were seen as unready for environmental reasons: they were not receiving the necessary stimulation at home so they needed to be in school a full day even if they were not ready. It is interesting to speculate whether they would be seen to be unready if they were not being compared to six year olds who had spent at least two years in pre-school. Extra-year programs were seen as the answer to the unready child dilemma; they came in a number of forms and participants.

Rochester was a school in transition, with an increasing number of children seen to be at risk. The most heterogeneous of the three schools, it had developed programs to meet the needs of its various constituencies. For the middle class Anglo students, many of whom had been held out the year before, the school provided half-day kindergarten with a traditional structure. For the English speaking, Hispanic, working class students, extended-day classes provided additional school experience in hopes that they could be integrated with the Anglo students in first grade. For the Spanish speaking, Hispanic, working class students, a bilingual extended-day kindergarten provided school experiences and exposure to the language they would need to progress through the school system. Because of their language needs, most of these children would remain in a bilingual classroom through grade three. The expectations for these three types of programs were clearly different and the staff worked to balance the tension between having multiple standards and integrating children from different groups. The children in the bilingual classroom were seen as different from the rest of the children in the school; different due to their language and their experiences, different due to the expectations of the school and to interaction of the school with their parents. The meaning of readiness was altered in terms of the children in Mrs. Ramirez' class; altered from the meaning that was used by the rest of the school.

Table 22 summarizes the the school characteristics related to readiness in the three settings studied:

Table 22
School Relationships Related to Readiness

Fulton	*Norwood*	*Rochester*
Staff shared responsibilities for meeting students needs by allowing performance levels to span grade levels. As the authority figure, the school took on responsibility for interpreting the meaning of readiness for parents and they developed structures to allow that interpretation to be communicated (the folders).	Staff had rigid boundaries for student performance that were used as promotional gates between grades. First grade teachers communicated their expectations in formal & informal settings so that kindergarten teachers felt that they had been judged as not doing their jobs. Getting ready for first grade was a constant worry during the kindergarten year for parents,	The staff at Rochester was working to develop alternatives to meet the needs of an increasingly heterogeneous population. This included multiple program formats (such as extended-day kindergarten) with varied expectations for child performance. The children in the bilingual program were immediately marked as different from the rest of the kindergartners at

Table 22 *continued*
School Relationships Related to Readiness

Fulton	*Norwood*	*Rochester*
	teachers, and children. The school had a history of trying various extra-year programs to keep unready children from slipping through the cracks; explicit programs were dismantled due to parental pressure and unofficial programs took their place.	Rochester due to their language and cultural experience. With the school's attempts to find a place for them they were kept separate from the rest of the five and six year olds.

What is readiness for each school?

Fulton	*Norwood*	*Rochester*
Readiness had an environmental component at Fulton with the school's commitment to the extended-day program and the belief that all kindergartners would be on equal footing at the end of the kindergarten year. In addition, it was evident in the school's attempts to develop a link with the home and the guided feedback given to parents.	A maturational model of readiness was evident at the school level at Norwood, with much talk about age and its relationship to readiness. Extra-year programs were used to provide children with more time to develop readiness.	The interventionist approach was in evidence at Rochester, with its use of extended-day programs. Because the children in the bilingual program were seen as so different from the rest of the Rochester kindergartners, a different meaning of readiness was developed for them, with a unique set of performance expectations.

Informal school structures at Fulton and Norwood were much like the low-retaining and high-retaining schools that Smith and Shepard (1988) described in their study of kindergarten teachers' beliefs and practices. Teachers in low-retaining schools tended to have more fluid relationships, with shared ownership of performance boundaries related to grade levels. They worked together to develop instructional programs and communicated concerns about individual children. That was much like the environment that existed at Fulton. The school tended to work on an interventionist model of readiness, attempting to provide students and parents with exacting feedback on performance and growth that would allow precise remediation of problems.

In contrast, high retaining schools had grade levels with rigid boundaries; teachers translated these into performance gates that children needed to get through. Similarly at Norwood, the first grade teachers continually communicated the problems they found with their students; the implicit message was that the kindergarten teachers had sent them on when they were unready. With the age-based, maturational model of readiness in place, using academic redshirting and retention seemed to be the best solution to help children fit within the school structure. When the standards were defined by older peers, children who did not have the advantages of age or middle class environment were seen to be at risk.

Rochester was different than either of the other two schools. The staff had a general commitment to avoid interventions like retention and they were trying to draw wider performance boundaries for students. The children in the bilingual program were not an integrated part of the Rochester school community; the school developed an idea about readiness that was separate for them.

As Smith & Shepard found, the ways that these teachers thought about children and readiness tended to be congruent with some overarching school philosophy and structure. There was a coherence to the beliefs of teachers who worked together and structures were developed that supported those beliefs. The data from this study however, highlight the dynamic and negotiated nature of what teachers think and do. While Smith and Shepard focused on the individual teacher working within various kinds of school structure, my focus has been on a setting in which an individual teacher works. That setting, with the many forces that shape interactions among kindergarten actors becomes the unit of analysis. This is important because teachers do not work in isolation; they are subject to requests and pressures from a variety of audiences as they make professional decisions.

At Norwood, the overall social interpretation of readiness was held and negotiated by a number of groups: the parents, the kindergarten teachers, the other staff. What Mrs. Sunden believed about readiness held pieces from all those constituencies. At Fulton and Rochester, the voice of the individual was much more salient. The other actors in the setting did not have the same power to define what happened in a classroom as the teacher. The ways that Ms. Carlin and Mrs. Ramirez played the roles that they were given (their role identity) and the individual interpretations that they held about the ways that children grow and learn were a much more potent force in the education of their students. This was true due to the nature of the setting in which they worked.

The Teachers

Each teacher worked in her classroom, using her concept of readiness to form instructional activities for her students. This particular meaning of readiness helped to guide the kindergarten experience for the children that she had in the 1989-90 school year. Whether the developing meaning of readiness was influenced by others in the setting or tended to be more individual depended on the professional atmosphere and relationships that existed in the school and community.

Ms. Carlin held a two-tiered model of readiness that combined maturational and environmental ideas. The environmental aspect of readiness was related to lack of experience with school-relevant tasks. The best way to take care of unreadiness of this type was to provide repeated exposure to activities that would enhance skills. Ms. Carlin would provide very structured practice to develop environmentally-induced readiness, doing things like erasing students' mistakes as they worked so that they would have the opportunity to do the task correctly. The maturational aspect of readiness was invoked when the environmental component could not be jump-started. This was the kind of readiness that was biological and that adults could not hasten in any way. When a variety of activities to increase environmental readiness proved futile, Ms. Carlin assumed that she needed to back off and allow children more time to mature. With time, they would be able to do the tasks.

Mrs. Sunden had two themes that structured the way that she thought about readiness. On the one hand, she interpreted much of what children did in terms of age: were they or did they act young? A birthday close to the entrance cutoff was a danger sign but could be overcome by behavior that was not seen as young. She had been a teacher for the developmental kindergarten and still thought in terms that were congruent with its philosophy. The age tag was something that structured her interpretation of children for the beginning of the year. A more pervasive context for her thoughts about readiness were the demands that she saw placed on both herself and her students by the first grade program. Its academic content privileged certain kinds of children and she calibrated her teaching and her students' performance with the first grade in mind. The question became "Will s/he be ready for first grade?" Because the first grade teachers used a maturational model of readiness, the markers of biological readiness became even more salient for Mrs. Sunden.

Mrs. Ramirez was primarily concerned with the relationship of environmental stimulation and readiness when she thought about her students. They had been labelled unready by the school and she saw their low level of readiness primarily as a result of lack of school-related activities in their lives. These children experienced lives at home that were different from the their lives at school. The judgments made by school about their readiness had very little to do with what happened to them with their families; they were based on criteria that did not have much meaning at home. Because of the disjuncture between the home and school, it was necessary for these children to get into school as soon as possible, even if a child was developmentally immature according to traditional readiness guidelines. Mrs. Ramirez worked to close the gap between the school and her students' families by providing activities that would increase levels of readiness as assessed by the school. Through school structure and increased home-school communication and co-operation the children in her class would become more ready.

Table 23 outlines how Ms. Carlin, Mrs. Sunden, and Mrs. Ramirez conceptualized readiness:

Table 23
Teachers' Conceptions of Readiness

Fulton	*Norwood*	*Rochester*
Ms. Carlin saw readiness as an instructional level which helped her know what to teach. Readiness was conceptualized as having two components: environmental (which she could affect by structured activities & feedback) and maturational (which was not amenable to adult intervention).	Readiness was constructed by Mrs. Sunden as a prerequisite to success in kindergarten. It was related to age, with younger children less likely to be ready. In addition, readiness was something that a child needed to have to go to first grade at Norwood. Kindergarten activities and judgments were framed by the demands of the first grade program, therefore readiness was inextricably bound to it.	Environmental stimulation was the primary aspect that Mrs. Ramirez thought accounted for readiness for the normal kindergarten activities. Her students lacked the kinds of experiences that the school valued so they were defined as unready. She had come to the conclusion that readiness was a matter of individual perception, but because her children had to navigate their way through the school structure, they had to develop certain skills to be ready.

With these varied conceptions of readiness, the judgments made and processes that occurred within classrooms were very different. The atmosphere for the developing kindergarten experience was framed by these conceptions of readiness, with participants coming to understand each other in ways that were connected with it. In the next section, I compare the general kindergarten experience in each setting. I begin by examining characteristics of the students that entered each classroom at the beginning of the year.

Kindergarten at Fulton, Norwood, and Rochester

The beginning of the kindergarten year was characterized by decisions. At Norwood, it was about whether to enter children into school when they were legally eligible. At Fulton and Rochester, it was about whether children were ready or whether they needed to go into an extended-day program. Note that at Norwood, these decisions were made by parents; at Fulton and Rochester, the decisions belonged to the school, for the most part.

The first decision made was about whether to enroll children in kindergarten. At Norwood, this was a popular discussion, it rarely came up at Fulton, and never arose for the parents in the bilingual program at Rochester (although it did for their Anglo peers). One way that the results of these decisions can be examined is to look at the age distributions for each classroom. Tables 24 through 26 illustrate the age distribution in each class, with bar graphs that highlight children within the traditional twelve month age range and children who are overage for kindergarten placement. The solid bars represent children within the normal age range, the striped bars represent children overage for grade (due to retention or redshirting).

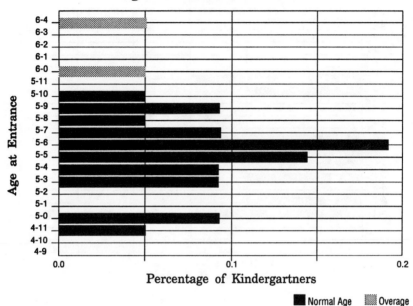

Table 24
Age Distribution at Fulton

Age at Entrance (vertical axis)
Percentage of Kindergartners (horizontal axis)

■ Normal Age   ▧ Overage

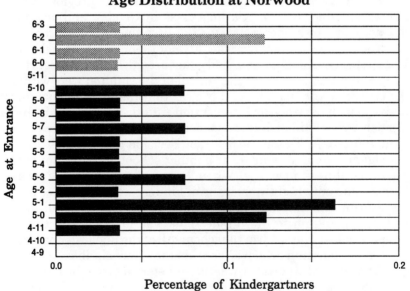

Table 25
Age Distribution at Norwood

Age at Entrance (vertical axis)
Percentage of Kindergartners (horizontal axis)

■ Normal Age   ▧ Overage

Table 26
Age Distribution at Rochester

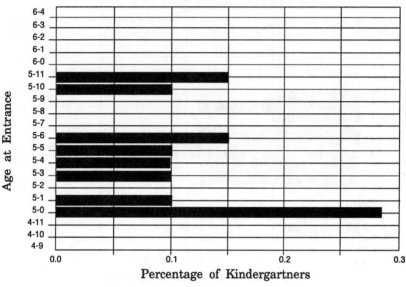

Percentage of Kindergartners

■ Normal Age   ▧ Overage

At Fulton, there were two children overage for kindergarten: one boy had been retained at another school the previous year and transferred into Ms. Carlin's class in October and one girl did not come to kindergarten for the first time until March. At Norwood, six boys were overage. Five of them had been held out by their parents and the sixth had gone through a pre-kindergarten program in the East. At Rochester, all of the children were within the twelve month age range. It is clear that the Norwood parents had taken the extra-year intervention into their own hands and almost 25% of them had chosen to delay entry into regular kindergarten. At Fulton the retention decision that made Andrew overage for grade was made at another school and was not part of the readiness ideology. When Penny was retained, it was because she only had two months of kindergarten under her belt; Ms. Carlin felt that she would be better off getting a full year in before going on to first grade. This was in keeping with the interventionist approach of the school. All of the Rochester parents put their children in school as soon as they were eligible.

At Norwood, the class was more heterogeneous in terms of age than the other two classrooms. Was this group also more heterogeneous in their incoming skills? One way to look at this is to examine kindergarten screening test results. How did the variability in age affect the skills that were addressed by the Early Prevention of School Failure screening? In Tables 27-29, the screening test results for each classroom are presented in the form of box and whisker plots for the tested areas of expressive language, auditory discrimination, visual motor, visual discrimination, fine motor, and gross motor. Children were given a score of 1 through 5 on the nationally normed screening instrument for each of the listed areas. They were also assessed in the area of receptive language but there was a problem in the scoring at Norwood, those results are not presented here. Box and whisker plots show the percentile distribution of a set of data. The ends of the whiskers represent the 10th and 90th percentiles, the ends of the box represent the 25th and 75th percentiles and the line in the middle of the box, the 50th percentile. Outliers are shown by circles. The greater the variability in a set of scores, the more elongated the box and whisker plot.

Table 27
Fulton Screening Test Results

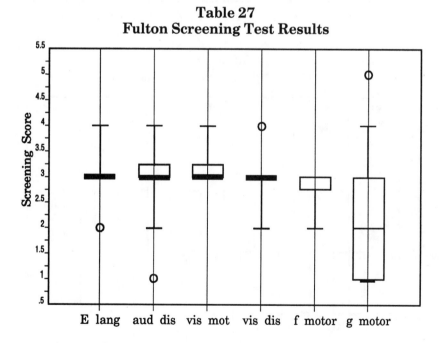

Table 28
Norwood Screening Test Results

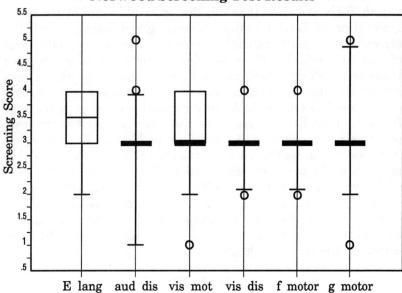

Table 29
Rochester Screening Test Results

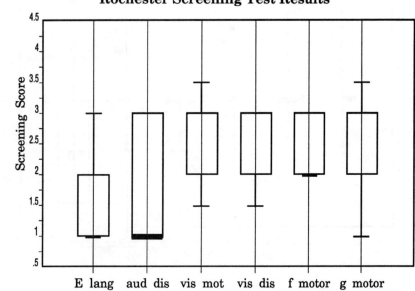

Examining the three sets of plots, there does not seem to be a great difference in the average scores at Fulton and Norwood. These two sets of children were very much the same on the skills that were assessed on the screening test. The scores of the Norwood students appeared to be slightly more variable, in keeping with the greater age range of children. Not surprisingly, the children from Rochester had lower scores than the other students; they had been chosen for placement in the extended-day program on the basis of these scores.

Putting the age ranges and screening test results together, along with what has been found out about the parental expectations and the school environment related to readiness, how was instruction defined in each classroom? How was the pace set? These are questions that can be explored by examining the instructional activities that were used in each classroom.

All three classes in this study were following the same curriculum, that of the Thomas School District. They had the same curriculum objectives. The Rochester class had the additional structure of the EPSF curriculum to guide instruction. Was there a common kindergarten experience in these three classrooms? Peering through the door of any of the classes, one would not be surprised at the activities—they had all the trappings of a kindergarten. But the experiences that these children had were very different, shaped by the expectations of the participants and the goals of kindergarten that were set forth in that setting.

Children at Fulton had a dual set of tasks presented to them in Ms. Carlin's class. They needed to follow instruction in the Doing it Right activities, completing a task just as Ms. Carlin specified it. Their performance was communicated to their parents, who took this as evidence of their progress during the kindergarten year. In addition, they had the more open-ended Writing activities, for which they presumably had complete freedom of expression. Ms. Carlin thought about children in terms of how well they did these two types of tasks and decided what to do next from their performance.

At Norwood, the curriculum was relatively preset as the kindergarten teachers used a unit or project approach. Mrs. Sunden used a "cast a wide net" technique to teaching; she presented concepts in a variety of ways but did not use a constant teach-test-teach model of instruction. Very few worksheets were used in her classroom and Mrs. Sunden tried to do general monitoring of skills acquisition. Much of her assessment was done in public or semi-public evaluations when they played games like Hangman or in small group activities when she could talk to children more interactively. Testing did occur prior to the dissemination of report cards so that Mrs. Sunden could let parents know how their children were doing. The curriculum and instruction were geared to the demands of the first grade program; Mrs. Sunden thought of children in terms of how well they would fit into next year's class. Of the three classes studied, the curriculum at Norwood was pitched at the highest level.

Rochester's kindergarten activities were primarily defined by the EPSF curriculum, which presented a very linear view of knowledge acquisition. Skills were listed hierarchically and children taught-tested-retaught until they acquired the skill. Mrs. Ramirez developed a variety of activities to address a specific skill and talked about it being OK if children did not get it the first time because they would do it again and again. Children were thought of as not having the school related experiences that they needed to succeed and Mrs. Ramirez worked to provide them at school and at home as well.

An example of the difference in instructional pacing could be seen in how the teachers covered the concept of shapes. Identification of shapes is covered by the report card, the Core Conceptual Objectives, and the EPSF curriculum. It is clearly a salient kindergarten skill. At Fulton, the class spent *one week on each shape* listed on the report card, doing worksheets, writing stories, and doing art projects on the shape of the week. When they were finished with the week, Ms. Carlin expected them to know that shape. At Norwood, they spent only *one day per shape*, doing art projects, sorting activities and going for shape walks. Shapes were talked about throughout the fall, but by the end of the week and a half of shape discussion, the Norwood students were on to letters of the alphabet. At Rochester they *discussed shapes throughout the fall,* doing activity after activity working on the language and tactile knowledge necessary to know what a shape was.

All three teachers covered the same curriculum objective of learning about shapes, but their paces were completely different. They ranged from about one week (for all shapes) to about one semester. In addition, the standards for performance in each classroom were different. Some children were expected to grasp the material after just one exposure, others only after repeated interaction. Although working from the same curricular mandates, there certainly was not a unitary kindergarten experience for these three groups of children. The interpretation of what kindergarten looked like and the end points to be achieved were locally distinct.

Again, these differences point to the dynamic nature of the school experience. I observed three thoughtful and highly professional teachers who worked to provide their students with the best kindergarten year possible. They all developed their programs from a common curricular structure, from a district vision of what kindergarten should be about. Why were the experiences so different? Each classroom was situated within a local context with a set of forces that shaped the day-to-day activities in the kindergarten room. Whether parents had tools and power to incorporate their ideas about schooling into curriculum practice or whether they waited for the school to initiate the relationship, they had some role in the way that child readiness was understood and used in everyday teaching. Whether the staff of the school dictated standards to one another or whether they shared responsibility for child performance, they influenced how the meaning of readiness was formed. Whether kindergarten teachers worked alone or in grade-level teams, they seemed to take into account the forces within and outside the school that were salient for their students: the demands of the first grade teachers, their students' language proficiency or ability to follow directions.

There have been repeated calls in the professional literature for the use of "developmentally appropriate practice" in programs for young children (NAEYC, 1988; Peck, et al. 1988). These practices have been developed from current models of child development that are accepted in the early childhood community. The focus of these guidelines is usually what happens in the classroom: the arrangement of the daily schedule, the relative allocation of time to various activities, the types of activities chosen for instruction, the discipline methods used, the choice of instructional materials and furniture. What these calls do not address, however, is the complexity that characterizes how these classroom practices came to be. What teachers do with their students does not spring from their heads to represent their isolated beliefs about how children learn. Instead, their instructional programs are the product of the social, political, and cultural forces at work in individual settings (Erickson, 1982; Smith & Shepard, 1988; Lareau, 1989; Richardson, Cassanova, Placier, & Guilfoyle, 1989).

None of the teachers who shared their classrooms with me would be rated as totally developmentally appropriate nor totally inappropriate according to professional guidelines; as with all teachers their work was a jumble of both, with a balance toward the appropriate. What I saw in the activities in these three classrooms were considered answers to the demands of a multitude of masters: personal teaching philosophies, district mandates, school requirements, parental demands, child experiences and needs, trends in community culture. The critics who frame guidelines on appropriate practice orient reform to changing a teacher's mind. It is not that easy. Understanding the forces that shape practice will be needed. One of the forces that appeared to play a role at Fulton, Norwood, and Rochester was the way that participants in the kindergarten experience constructed a meaning of readiness.

Constructing Readiness

Different meanings of readiness, different standards for performance, different kindergarten experiences. The descriptions provided of the interactions in the Fulton, Norwood, and Rochester communities indicate that the meanings of readiness were locally developed and used, that they came out of ideas about how children grow and develop, out of a local purpose for the kindergarten, out of notions for what it means to be a good parent or teacher. This work was framed from a Vygotskian perspective, which was proposed to theorize the process of social construction. How can we better understand the development of the local meaning? One way would be to discuss how the resources and ideas in a local setting helped to construct a particular social meaning of readiness, using the activity setting elements described in chapter 2. The focus is primarily on the social plane and the patterns that were shared among participants in a community.

Who was involved in constructing a meaning of readiness? Given a part to play by society, *the actors* also chose their own particular way to enact the role. Actors were clearly given different roles in these communities. For some parents (Fulton and Rochester), their job was to provide a supportive environment in the pre-school years and to present their children to the school as soon as their child was old enough to enter. Once in school, they were to assist the school's effort in response to teacher requests. In other settings, being a good parent included working to get a leg up on the competition, to find the very best pre-school, learning the expectations for performance and holding their child out if necessary. They had an active and in many ways equal role with the school in constructing their child's school experience. Teachers were given different roles as well. Ms. Carlin was supposed to provide a good start, Mrs. Sunden's job was to make sure that children were ready before they went on to first grade, and Mrs. Ramirez was to work to close the gap. Both parents and teachers had their work defined for them and given those roles, their actions were circumscribed in a particular way.

There was choice involved in acting out the socially defined role as well. Some parents resisted the social definition, as in the case of Andy's mother or Sally's parents at Norwood; they put their children into kindergarten despite the warnings of their friends. Mrs. Ramirez' role as an extended-day kindergarten teacher was shaped by her role identity as a bilingual educator; her interpretation of her students was built on that foundation. As participants in the kindergarten experience, the actors learned to carry out their roles in certain ways, which shaped patterns of interaction, allocation of responsibilities, and views of others (including children). The meaning of readiness was constructed by persons with distinctive jobs to do and views of their work.

Interpretations are the meanings given to such things as institutions and actions of a group. In the case of the construction of the meaning of readiness, they would include ideas held by the family, school, or community about how children grow and the factors that enhance or inhibit the development of readiness. Here, they have been represented in various accounts of readiness as a biological entity, as something amenable to intervention, or some combination of both. When readiness is seen as related to biology, indications of readiness problems are framed in terms of maturity. The way to solve a readiness problem is to provide time for the child to become more mature; in many cases this is done by redshirting. When readiness is seen from a more environmentalist perspective, assessment and remediation of specific skills is the key to its enhancement. Rather than waiting, it is important for the teacher to intervene by shoring up deficits. Waiting to put an unready child into school would seem foolish from this viewpoint. The mechanism proposed for the development of readiness and the characteristics that are chosen by individuals to indicate readiness both frame the way that kindergarten is perceived within a given setting and the actions that are seen as reasonable for participants. Within a context individuals react to the institutional interpretations. For example, Mrs. Sunden viewed struggling students in the context of the interpretations of the first grade teachers. Although she usually did not agree with retention for kindergartners, she also did not feel that it was justified to send them to the highly academic and stressful first grade program. Her view of children was focused in the context of the interpretations of others and it had an impact on how she did her job.

Task structure is comprised of resources available to actors, such as materials, time, and information, and the structures of interpersonal relations that allow them to participate in the experience. The *academic task structure* is represented by the curriculum, both in its stated form and in the enacted activities. In each setting, the enacted curriculum had a unique nature even though they all shared the basic district kindergarten curriculum document. For example, at Norwood, learning letters was one of the earliest tasks of the program and took up a major portion of the curriculum (important because the first grade teachers wanted readers in their classes). They started letters later in the year at Fulton but put less of an emphasis on reading than on writing. Finally, at Rochester, letters were introduced in the context of other activities, seen as less important to acquire than the more basic skills spelled out by the EPSF curriculum. In fact, after much internal conflict, Mrs. Ramirez gave up learning letters as highly prized kindergarten objective. With this diversity of academic task came corresponding variation in expectations and standards for performance in each community. Individual students and parents responded to the social demands of the local task structure as they went through the kindergarten year. The students in Ms. Carlin's class came to identify themselves as writers in a classroom that valued highly the process and products of writing.

The *participation structures* or rules for interactional etiquette in each setting formed the basis for communication and application of various kinds of standards and understandings among parents and instructional staff. The relationship between the home and school had shared characteristics within each community and served to empower certain groups and lessen the input of others about educational decision-making. At Fulton and Rochester, the school took the initiative in defining the educational process and the roles of parents within that process. Among their staff, teachers in these schools communicated across grades levels and shared information about children and teaching activities. In contrast, the interactions between parents and Norwood staff were on a more equal footing and parents came to the school with an agenda that they assumed the school would fulfill. Also different was the nature of interaction among staff. Strong grade-level boundaries for performance were enforced through a social system of expectation. The first grade teachers continually voiced their needs for the proper kind of "ready" children and disempowered the kindergarten teachers by their demands. Individuals within these systems found that they made their decisions in the context of the interactional rules; instructional decisions could be made for academic reasons at Fulton and Rochester (What does this child need next?) while frequently they were made for social reasons at Norwood (What will Mrs. Lucas say if I send Aaron on to her class?).

The final aspect of the activity setting is the idea of *motives*, which are the goals and objectives for various activities related to readiness. One of the key elements in the construction of the meaning of readiness could be seen as the goals assigned to the kindergarten year by the community. In each context, kindergarten had a different goal: at Fulton it was to give children a good start. This was accomplished by providing basic instruction, with readiness providing the guide. At Norwood, kindergarten was seen as the place to prepare for first grade. Readiness was seen as a prerequisite for success in the Norwood kindergarten and parents expended much energy checking to see if their children were ready enough to enter school. The purpose of the extended-day program at Rochester was to close the gap between children who had been identified as at-risk because they were culturally different. This label was constructed in the context of a community with a sizable proportion of families much like those at Norwood, who redshirted their children to make sure that they were ready. The reasons that individuals had for their actions were often quite variable. When parents chose to hold their children out, they often framed their decisions in the rhetoric of readiness, using words like maturity or youngness. There were interesting underlying themes in individuals motives. Some favored or rejected redshirting because of personal experience with other children, some focused on sports, some used professional knowledge as educators. The reasons underlying the actions taken related to readiness, the motives that shaped the kindergarten experience, had a profound impact on the types of interactions and the decisions made for a given group.

In examining the various aspects of the constructed meaning of readiness, it is interesting to see how overlapping the elements of the activity setting appear to be. This makes perfect sense because they represent something that is mutually constitutive—each element depends on the others for their characteristics and form. These interlocking parts, the ideas, the material and personal resources, and the institutional structures, provided a framework from which the meaning of readiness was built and a foundation for the kindergarten experience.

Readiness and the Kindergarten Experience

In each of the settings studied, people talked about how kindergarten had changed in recent years. At Fulton and Norwood, there was discussion of how the pace was now brisker; children were expected to do more. At Rochester, I heard that increasingly, some children could not meet the demands of the kindergarten program, with extended-day kindergartens a result. These are concrete examples of what has been discussed in the academic literature as "escalation of curriculum" (Shepard & Smith, 1988) or "academic trickle down" (Cunningham, 1988). More and more, the kindergarten program of today incorporates the content of the first grade of yesterday. Less time is spent on socialization activities, in play, with blocks and paints and more time on worksheets, teacher-directed activities, and writing.

What has driven this shift? All sorts of factors have been put forward as influences on the kindergarten curriculum. For example, increases in pre-school attendance and near universal kindergarten attendance have made the skills and behaviors that kindergarten and first grade children present to their teachers appear very different from the children who preceded them ten or twenty years ago. They know how to sit, they know how to get in line, many of them know their colors. Teachers come to think of these children as more ready than those who came before them; their conception of readiness changes as children's experiences change. They share this meaning of readiness with parents through conferences, instructional feedback, and informal communication. Parents interpret this meaning to each other if community structures exist for that kind of information exchange. Over time, even children begin to have an understanding of what readiness is. Rather than children changing in some absolute sense, the meaning of readiness is the thing that is changing as people interact.

How did the curriculum escalation manifest itself in the schools I studied? And how is it related to conceptions of readiness? There appeared to be two mechanisms at work shaping the kindergarten curriculum. The first was the readiness screening that pulled children with low readiness test scores out of the regular kindergarten programs. At Rochester and Fulton, this process had an impact on the range of children that were in an individual classroom. Children found to have considerable needs on the EPSF screening were typically placed in the extended-day program; these were usually children who did not know their colors or have other basic pre-school-kindergarten skills. Because these children were no longer in the regular kindergarten classroom, the rest of the class could go a little faster, even starting out with more complex material. This was shown clearly at Fulton, with Ms. Carlin cutting out coverage of colors in the fall (except in the most general presentation) and moving the introduction of letters of the alphabet from January to October. She stated that she could do this now because the children were coming into kindergarten knowing their colors. Children in the regular classes who did not have these skills were now seen to be at risk, when they might have been in the middle of the class in terms of readiness before (Ramon and Penny at Fulton, Juan and Aaron at Norwood).

In contrast, as the regular classes went faster and faster through the newly defined kindergarten curriculum, the children in the extended-day program were seen to be even farther behind, i.e, less ready. They spent the year doing what was formerly the kindergarten curriculum, using very concrete means to learn basic concepts. As their regular classroom agemates were learning to do handwriting, they were working on keeping their crayon on the paper. As the year passed, they became more ready but they did not close the gap. If the school definition of readiness was framed by the children in the regular kindergarten program, they would always be seen as different, as was the case at Rochester. If the school definition of readiness was framed by more general ideas about performance, they would be integrated into the regular school program beginning in first grade, as at Fulton.

The second force that fed the escalating curriculum related to readiness was the inclusion of older, very able children in the kindergarten as the results of academic redshirting. At Norwood and Rochester, the parents who held their children out were not concerned about academic readiness; in fact, they were quite confident about their child's cognitive skills. Their wariness about their child's readiness was related to ideas about maturity, something interpreted as a way of behaving that would ensure success in school. When they came to kindergarten the following year at age six they had a more mature demeanor. They could sit and listen for extended periods of time, they enjoyed doing fine motor tasks, and they could follow multiple part directions. Their parents wanted to see them continue to acquire skills. Particularly at Norwood where the normative expectations for performance were so intensely communicated, by so many people, the curricular demand shifted up. The pressure from parental expectations was coupled with the demands of the first grade teachers, who had come to expect a mature level of ability and behavior from their students. At the start of the year they bemoaned the fact that they had no readers. That was the kind of student they expected in their classroom. Being ready for kindergarten at Norwood meant being more like a six year old than like a five year old.

As the local meaning of readiness was constructed, it became the metric used for understanding children. In each setting, children could be measured against the meaning of readiness used by participants, with very real implications for their educational experience. At Fulton it was an instructional level that meant providing children with a good start. At Norwood, readiness became a marker related to age and a comparison to the demands of first grade. At Rochester it was a measure of difference. The kindergarten experience that developed was based on these meanings of readiness and over time, the meaning of readiness was shaped by the experience. This reciprocal relationship meant that the meaning of readiness was dynamic and changing. It was constantly rebuilt by participants, both at the social and individual levels. Readiness was more than something in a child or something used by a teacher. It was a product of the interactions of people invested in the kindergarten experience, used by them differentially depending on their roles.

Implications for Practice

Does this reconceptualization of readiness have implications for educational policy and practice? Some would argue that the social constructionist perspective is linked to a relativist view of practice in which all educational policies and practices are seen as equally valid. The coherence of belief and practice would be the legitimizing entity in judging activities with children. I suggest that this is not the most appropriate implication of the social constructionist interpretation taken here for three reasons: disjuncture in assumptions about child growth and development, criteria for resource allocation, and equality of outcomes.

First, it is important to examine the assumptions about children and education that provide the foundation for early childhood policy and practice. If there is a disjucture, as in the case of conceptualizing readiness as a child characteristic and basing practice on measuring and sorting children on measured readiness scores when in fact it is more appropriately viewed as a social meaning, then the practices themselves should be reviewed.

Second, we should consider the philosophies on which allocation of opportunities and resources are based. When we consider allocating scarce resources, such as special services, we assume that we make the decisions on the basis of unbiased criteria. For example, when we place children in special readiness programs, these placements are typically based on what is thought to be a valid and reliable measurement of a true construct. If the construct of readiness is not a stable psychological trait, if it is instead a locally generated meaning that depends on community characteristics and values, we can be less certain that our decisions are unbiased and fair. If decisions are made on what might be seen as socially negotiated meanings rather than psychological characteristics, the public rhetoric surrounding readiness practices needs to take that into account.

Finally, the outcomes for children of various policies and practices related to readiness should be taken into account when readiness is seen from a social constructionist perspective. If measures of readiness and readiness policies result in unequal educational outcomes for children, we must reconsider our strategies. This could be the case when because of others' readiness-related practices a subgroup of children is put at risk arbitrarily, for example when young five year olds are viewed as unready because an ever-growing number of six year olds appear in kindergarten.

Rather than taking a relativist approach to readiness practice, I would argue that if conceptions of readiness have such a per-vasive influence on educational practice; if they shape the way that we view children and affect their first school experience, rethinking our approach to readiness is vital if we hope to meet their needs in a more effective manner. When readiness is framed from a social rather than psychological perspective, the focus becomes broadening the views of children to enhance their experiences rather than on sorting children by readiness levels and providing services to match readiness need.

We can think of the implications inherent in this new view of readiness in terms of beliefs and services, two intertwined aspects that came up again and again in this study. The ways that people thought about children and their development were the foundation of the services provided in their educational programs. What will be required are new views of kindergarten that focus responsibility on the educational establishment to broaden the vision of children so that sorting by readiness level is not necessary. In general, there are four broad areas that should receive attention to help us reach that goal: home-school relationships, kindergarten screening, teacher education, and the structure and curriculum of the primary education program. In each of these areas the implications of readiness practice and policy will be discussed in the context of beliefs about children that these practices represent and the services that might come out of a new conceptualization.

Home-School Relationships

The home-school relationship is probably the broadest of the four and includes both services provided to children before they formally enter kindergarten and ideas about parental involvement in the educational process. In thinking about services for children, it is clear that not all children come to school with the same experience base or skills. Comparing the middle class Rochester children with at least two years of pre-school experience (many of whom had been redshirted) with the children from Rochester who were attending a structured school setting for the first time at age five, we can see that a gap existed from the first day of school. We often assume that children with special needs receive extra support and services. We rely on the early intervention programs established in the 1960s that were developed to close that gap by providing pre-school programs for children who came to school behind their peers according to white, middle class standards. It is estimated, however that only 20% of pre-schoolers eligible for Head Start receive services (Kagan, 1990).

One of the first steps in a new approach to readiness would be to assure that all children who need services in the pre-school years actually get them. To help reduce that first-day-of-school gap that justified sorting children by readiness level once they get to school, we need to provide children with the support and experiences that will maximize their chances of success in school. It could be argued that the reasons for the extended-day programs in the Thomas School district would be less urgent if the children in those classes had attended pre-school programs focussed on skills defined as essential by the school. This approach requires resources to make services available, more outreach to help families know that they are eligible for programs, and co-operation among service providers so that referrals and practice can be co-ordinated within a community. Therefore the investment in additional services comes earlier as we rethink readiness.

In much educational rhetoric, parent involvement is purported to be a key ingredient to educational reform and improvement. Finding a balance in the relationship between home and school would be the second aspect we might consider as we rethink readiness. In the communities in this study, there was interesting variation in the approaches taken by the schools and families in their interactions. In some communities, the home-school relationship was focused on school requests for parental activity. This tended to be a reactive rather than an assertive role for parents, with information residing in the school rather than the home. In contrast, in other settings parents were rabidly active in advancing an agenda for their children, working to gain an advantage by academic redshirting and garnering as much knowledge about the school program as they possibly could. But this was not all positive, in fact, it could be characterized as what Lareau (1989) has called "the dark side of parent involvement." In many ways the actions of parents at Norwood and the standards enforced by the first grade teachers worked to manufacture risk for children who came to school with just about every advantage we could list for school success. As less mature children were pulled from the group, someone was always left behind, looking even less ready in comparison to children redshirted the previous year. The community pressure to co-operate in the practice of holding out was intense and it had a significant impact on the composition of classes and the curriculum presented there. A cycle of escalation of expectations and practice seemed unbreakable; in many ways parents were less powerful because they could not resist the pressure of their peers.

A new view of readiness would involve a more co-operative relationship between home and school so that the responsibility of the school experience is shared by parents and teachers in a more equal manner. This would start in the pre-school years as community groups forge a connection between the home and the educational professionals through a variety of early childhood pre-school programs. It would continue during the kindergarten year as schools attempt to incorporate families into their programs in more than the traditional mother-helper model. Helping parents become involved through home visits, special homework activities, and school programs would make it more likely that parents could have a voice in the educational image that is constructed for their children.

At the other end of the involvement continuum, schools must work to ensure that parents do not feel pressure to protect their children from a harsh academic expectations and environment. The first step is communication that all children are welcome in school and that schooling is a process to be shared by parents and teachers. With this kind of co-operation, parents should not feel as if they need to resort to holding their child out or to coaching so that their child will be at the top of the class. This may require a closer relationship between the pre-school community and kindergarten teachers so that practices such as redshirting are not suggested before school entrance in an effort to protect children from the risk of failure. In addition, school officials should not endorse the practice implicitly or explicitly when parents suggest it as they make enrollment decisions. An example of this kind of approach is an article discussing academic redshirting in a local school parent newsletter that detailed the rhetoric and reality surrounding the practice. Prospective kindergarten parents were referred to this piece by the principal when they approached the school for advice on whether to enroll their child.

Screening

One of the time-honored activities of the kindergarten year is the annual readiness screening that occurs either prior to school entry or within the first few months of the school year. How do we approach screening as we rethink readiness? How is the screening process undertaken when readiness is conceived as a social meaning rather than a psychological trait? Examining the logic behind screening helps set the stage for a new approach. Screening has typically targeted three very different populations:

children with handicapping conditions, those with developmental lags related to socioeconomic disadvantage, and children viewed as socially immature (Shepard & Graue, in press). With the first two groups, active instructional intervention is the key, while the third requires passive allocation of time for development. All three are premised on the readiness-as-child-characteristic model and rely on instruments and teacher judgment for identification. How do we justify screening if the instruments are not valid enough to provide stand-alone judgments (and follow-up evaluation is not frequently undertaken) and if the judgment of readiness varies so much from community to community? Is it fair to sort children on the basis of such a shakey concept?

The screening process seems to reify the concept of readiness within a child in its use of instruments and potential for special treatments. Parents and teachers are set up to think of children as having a certain level of readiness when presented with a printout of a readiness assessment. To help us move away from this psychological view, a first step is to shift from what Kagan (1990) has called the conception of *readiness for school*, which relies on a gate-keeping notion of having enough readiness to succeed in school, to the idea of *readiness for learning*. This second perspective focuses on possibilities rather than deficiencies and is based on the assumption that *all* children are ready for school.

Working from this premise and assuming that more inclusive programs are in place for children during the pre-school years, two different approaches to the screening tradition could be suggested. The first would be a transformation of the screening process putting the assessment activity in a more positive light. Rather than doing screening to find deficient children, screening could be undertaken to provide information about the skills and strengths that children bring to school. This type of activity, rather than being called a screener (to catch the unready child) could be framed as a Child Development Fair (Lange, 1990) and be a first step in involving parents in the kindergarten experience. Held in conjunction with kindergarten registration and an introduction to the kindergarten program, parents could be highly involved from going through the activities with their child, participating in interviews about their child's skills at home (a sadly missed source of information in early childhood) and touring the kindergarten facility. More than a semantic shell game, this shift in perspective about early childhood assessment would not involve special treatments for the unready child and would highlight the shared nature of information about children that might come from activities and parents.

The second approach would give up readiness screening as we know it and would reallocate the resources typically provided for screening to classroom teachers to do contextualized assessments of their students in meaningful classroom tasks. This would shift the reason for assessment from what Meisels has called developmental screening which results in further assessment to readiness testing which can help teachers make instructional decisions. The focus in the contextualized assessments would be on knowing children so that better educational planning might occur. This type of assessment requires not only time to collect information in situ but also time to reflect on the implications it has for practice. Again, the practices that would be attached to such assessment would not include any of the special interventions like readiness classrooms or redshirting but would inform the teacher action rather than student placement.

At the very least the new view of readiness would suggest a transformation of the traditional screening program so that the focus shifts from the child's readiness levels to the responsibility of the school and family to facilitate development. Abandoning the screening process would not be out of the question and might help us to give up the readiness-as-child-characteristic view and all of its baggage.

Teacher Education

As teachers approach their instructional activities, their beliefs about child growth and development and their role in the educational process provide a context for decisions made (Smith & Shepard, 1988). Part of the foundation for these beliefs is laid in the process of teacher education in the courses presented and the content provided within these courses. Teacher education curriculum implicitly represents the knowledge valued in the education and helps to point teachers in certain directions as they begin their teaching careers. Because it helps provide a rationale for action, the teacher education program should be examined in the context of the implications that are inherent in a more social view of readiness.

One of the key aspects of an early childhood program is knowledge of growth and development, usually presented in Educational Psychology, Child Development, or other courses. Theories of development and ideas of developmental stages and trends are lynch pins of the ideas presented in such courses. Although such knowledge is vital to providing appropriate instruction to children, care should be taken that the ideas presented in such courses are not simplified and over-interpreted to such an extent that development is seen as a straight jacket for children and their caregivers. A typical overinterpretation is an over-reliance on stage theory in interpreting developmental regularity. This is vividly exemplified in a maturational approach to development which requires that all of a child's structures and functions to be fully developed for diagnosis as a ready child. It frames development as something that happens within a child and easily leads to an overly psychological view of child readiness.

This type of interpretation of development ignores three key aspects of the developmental process. The first is that development is not nearly as regular as that indicated in the child development textbooks (Walsh, 1991). It is much more jagged and ages are only indications of central tendency rather than rules for appropriate action. Second, it does nothing to take into account how development is socially mediated (Walsh, 1991). There is abundant evidence that the resources and constraints available in a setting are highly salient factors in developmental processes and in fact mediate the rate and nature of development. Finally, much of the information about developmental theory is itself mediated by the social and cultural context in which it was developed. The meanings that we give to various developmental events, what we attend to and what we value are highly circumscribed by our cultural heritage. It has been suggested that the reason that so many young boys are found to be unready is that their teachers are females who value certain behaviors in the classroom. Developmental theory has been criticized as being Eurocentric (Jipson, 1991) and unrepresentative of the life experiences of many children in today's schools.

A more critical presentation of developmental issues would help prospective teachers to attend to the problems of value and privilege inherent in a lockstep view of child growth. In conjunction with this more open approach to developmental theory, would be coverage of the policy issues that arise from various developmental positions. There is a growing literature on issues such as testing, grouping, promotion/retention, and entrance age but there appears to be a wide gap between the knowledge base on these topics that has been assembled by researchers and that developed by school people. Prospective teachers would be better equipped to make professional decisions on these topics if they had access to both sides of the discussion before they left their training programs.

Kindergarten Within the Primary Education Program

All of this leads to the practices in kindergarten education. There has been much focus on the nature of the kindergarten program as it has evolved from its primarily socially-oriented curriculum to an increasingly academically-based program. Discussion of the implications for the kindergarten program related to a social view of readiness can be centered on four major issues: entrance policy, curriculum, school structure and standards for performance.

Throughout this discussion of implications has been the idea that we must move to a view that all children are ready for school. Although it is clear that children develop at different rates and not all five year olds present themselves to school in the same manner, making entrance policy dependent on measures such as developmental age has proven problematic. Past work has shown the weaknesses of approaches that substitute criteria other than chronological age as a marker for school eligibility. For this reason, schools should rely on chronological age as the criterion for school entrance. The National Association for the Education of Young Children (1990) supports this stand, asserting that it is the "only legally and ethically defensible criterion for determining school entry" (p. 22). This position helps reinforce the idea that there is not a gate into the kindergarten based on child readiness and it opens services to all children who have attained the legal entrance age.

Kagan (1990) has suggested an interesting shift in the way that we think about readiness and the services that support children's learning. She proposes that we move from individualizing entry by interventions such as redshirting and special programs based on readiness assessments followed by homogenization of services after children enter school to homogenizing entry through a single entrance criterion coupled with individualized services to meet children's needs. This conception of entry and services is pivotal to the reconceptualization of readiness proposed in this study.

National professional organizations have already taken the lead in defining policies that would not reify the readiness-as-child-characteristic model so prevalent in today's schools. Developing broader curricula to meet the needs of a variety of children and eliminating the use of extra-year programs have been promoted by the National Association for the Education of Young Children (NAEYC, 1987). NAEYC, with the Association of Childhood Education International, the Association for Supervision and Curriculum Development, the International Reading Association, and the National Council of Teachers of English have issued a joint policy statement that voices concern about current curriculum trends in schools related to readiness and provides directions for future educational practice (International Reading Association, 1986). As indicated previously, these recommendations should take into account the contextual nature of classroom practice, incorporating all participants as forces that shape what happens with children.

At the classroom level, for example, the work of a kindergarten teacher does not happen in isolation, affecting only her classroom. It happens within a set of collegial relationships among staff, within a school-community relationship, and within a larger national education context that frames how we look at children and schools. The development of structures that would allow communication and shared responsibility across grade level boundaries would be one step that could be taken to help teachers diffuse the need to make sure that only certain types of children came into or left their classrooms based on judgments of readiness. Primary level units, including teachers in grades kindergarten through two or three, might be one way to broaden the view of children. Teachers could plan curriculum that spanned a variety of age levels rather than seeing education from the grade level, incremental approach. Variations on this theme include both ungraded primary classes, with children of a variety of ages and self-contained, traditional graded classrooms whose curriculum is planned by a team of teachers (Katz, Evangelou, & Hartman, 1990). With a focus on activities that are available to children of a variety of developmental levels, programs of this type would not need to have readiness as a foundation for instruction. Including pre-school teachers in this unit would broaden the view of children even further and provide a bridge between structured school experiences before formal schooling and the kindergarten year. One of the most fundamental aspects of this kind of co-operative effort is the provision of time for teachers to work together. Collaboration of this sort does not occur on the fly, with teachers meeting before or after school as they manage to fit their schedules together. A commitment must be made by school administration to provide time within the teacher's professional day to do both intra- and inter-grade curricular planning.

Related to the curriculum planning for kindergarten education is the institutional and classroom standard-setting process that portrays children as ready or unready to enter kindergarten or to move on to first grade. Within the collaborative model suggested for curriculum would be a broadened view of end-of-grade standards. Supportive learning settings would allow children to move from grade to grade with individualized help if there were concerns about progress (as suggested in Leinhardt's work). In opening the grade expectations, communication of standards could also become less grade-level bound through multi-grade report cards. For example, the kindergarten through second grade could share a common report card so that teachers and parents could more clearly see the continuum of development that is targeted in the primary unit. More narrative reports would provide teachers the opportunity to focus on strengths and potentials rather than deficits.

Such adaptations should not be seen as weakening the standards or system of accountability in early education. In fact, quite the opposite is true. A more social view of readiness makes the school much more accountable by requiring it to meet the needs of individual children rather than relying on readiness assessment, sorting, and special interventions that pull children out of the regular school program. It focuses attention on making each classroom responsive to all kinds of students, not just those seen as ready.

Explicit extra-year programs (like developmental kindergartens or transitional first grades), unstated extra-year programs (like academic redshirting), the shifting kindergarten entrance age, and readiness screening programs are legacies of the child characteristic orientation to readiness. They are all aimed at making school easier for teachers and children by making students more ready. None of them appear to work, however, because they are based on incorrect assumptions about what readiness is. If readiness is viewed from outside the child, as something that is shared by people in a kindergarten setting and used to understand children, some reworking of practice is necessary. It moves us to re-evaluate the assumptions on which policies related to readiness are based. Assessing readiness and sorting children on the basis of that assessment becomes problematic. It encourages us to think in broader, more inclusive terms. It charges us with more responsibility in developing educational programs for all young children.

Notes

1. Taking this orientation excluded work on specific content area readiness such as reading or math readiness (although many of the skills based tests currently in use are only a slight modification of traditional reading readiness tests).

2. This dimension describes the degree to which teachers believed that development was a function of biology or environment.

3. This is in contrast to the traditional focus of the kindergarten curriculum, which stresses getting children ready during the kindergarten year.

4. As a reminder, redshirting is originally a term that comes from athletics. When teams (usually college) redshirt their players, they have them sit the year out to allow an additional year of growth and development, increasing their power on the playing field. The year that they sit out is not counted against their eligibility; their last year playing, they are older than most of their teammates.

5. Teacher grade level is indicated in parentheses.

6. If these words seem familiar, it is because they were used earlier in the vignette about the mothers' discussions of readiness at the nursery school.

7. In fact, Mrs. Ramirez told me that she had given up her struggle to decide whether her students knew their letter names. In the past, she worried about whether they picked up on them and spent much time trying to structure things so that they would. She had recently decided that it is not so important, that in real life people do not spend much time with individual letter names, so she did what she could to introduce them but did not lose sleep trying to figure out ways to make sure they had the names down.

8. In none of the interviews did the interviewer bring up the word *readiness*, in every case it came up spontaneously from the parents. If they mentioned readiness, they were then asked to explain how they were thinking about it.

APPENDIX 1

ॐ

STUDY DESIGN AND ELEMENTS

The Study

Research took place from the month preceding the start of school to the end of the academic year. To understand the developing meaning of readiness, it was necessary to talk to the participants in the kindergarten experience and to observe the instructional applications of readiness ideas in classrooms. This required three main data collection types: interviews with parents, teachers, and children; participant observations in kindergarten classes, and analysis of documents.

Sampling

Schools within a single school district were chosen that represented different orientations to readiness and a range of demographic characteristics. Because entrances policies (explicit and unstated) and promotion practices have been connected in the public conceptualization of readiness, the use of academic redshirting and retention were used as measures of local views of readiness. To estimate the degree of academic redshirting in a setting, data on age ranges of the 1988-89 kindergarten cohort were analyzed. The proportion of children redshirted, estimated from the percent of children missing from the youngest six months of the twelve month age distribution (calculated separately for males and females), was the starting point. In addition, a simple calculation of the proportion of children overage-for-grade placement provided information on children who may be been redshirted or retained the previous year. Because the estimator for percent redshirted is very unstable (because the total number of children is small at the school level), information was solicited for potential sites on past entrance patterns, curricular expectations and school culture.

In addition to age range, socioeconomic status of the school was a sampling consideration. Socioeconomic status was examined at the school rather than the individual level using the proportion of students eligible to receive federal Free and Reduced lunch.

Data Collection

PARTICIPANT OBSERVATIONS

Classroom visits were made one day per week during the fall with a January and May visit in the second half of the year. A total of thirteen visits were made per classroom. In my role as teacher aide, I arrived in each school at least one half hour before the start of the kindergarten session to help the teachers prepare materials. I typically cut paper, mixed paint, or filed forms. I worked at whatever tasks the teacher asked me to do while the students were in attendance and then stayed after to help with clean-up. During class time I played games with groups of children, ran centers, supervised library trips, did cooking activities, read stories, zipped coats, and searched for headphones. At Norwood and Rochester, I worked on the kindergarten screening program, using the Early Prevention of School Failure screening packet. At Rochester, the staff tested children who did not pre-register for kindergarten during the first week of school to determine placements in the extended day programs (a bilingual classroom and regular classroom). At Norwood, screening took place during the third week of school, with Mrs. Sunden working with her students and the testers pulling children out of class as needed.

After each classroom visit, fieldnotes were written recalling the day's events. The fieldnotes were a running account of classroom activity, including descriptions of activities that were not observed by me but were recounted by teachers or students. Questions for the teachers were marked as comments and were included in the text of the notes. Fieldnotes were given to teachers on the following visit and they were asked to read the notes and make any comments that they felt were appropriate. This technique was used to get direct teacher feedback on my observations and to allow questions to be posed in the context of the observation. Teacher comments were then included as data along with the notes themselves.

INTERVIEWS

A small group of parents was interviewed before the start of school to examine parental expectations for the upcoming kindergarten year. To try to capture the variability in belief related to chid age at enrollment, the sample from each school was comprised of the five oldest and the five youngest children registered for kindergarten. Because students were not at this point assigned to classes, this sample represented how parents in the school thought about kindergarten entrance. Parents were sent postcards describing the study and were then contacted by phone to set up an interview. The interview was semi-structured, focusing on the positive and negative aspects the parents could foresee as they approached their child's kindergarten experience. Interviews were done by telephone, ran from five to thirty-five minutes in length, and were taped and transcribed for analysis.

A sample of classroom parents was interviewed during parent-teacher conferences in November . Appointments were scheduled for the twenty minutes before each parent-teacher conference. In most cases, parents were interviewed, then I sat in on the parent teacher conference. At Fulton, all parents contacted came in; at Norwood I talked with five of seven parents contacted; and at Rochester I saw four of eight. These percentages were equivalent to the overall conference attendance patterns in each classroom. In these interviews, parents were asked to reflect on their expectations for the kindergarten year and to discuss their impressions of their child's progress in the first quarter of school.

Before school started in the fall, I contacted teachers to ask them for time to do an initial interview and to offer to help them set up their classroom. I met with Mrs. Sunden and Mrs. Ramirez in their homes and then spent half a day with each of them in their classrooms, unpacking materials, putting up bulletin boards, and assembling packets for parents for the beginning of the year. I met Ms. Carlin at school, helped around the classroom, then completed the interview. These interviews focused on the general characteristics of the school (its staff, parents, and students), her goals and expectations for her students, and the place of the kindergarten program within the structure of the school. Subsequent interviews occurred in October, December, and May at the end of a classroom visit day. The foci of those interviews were feedback about last year's class and the current class characteristics, developing a curriculum map, reaction to the vignettes, and review of the year's events and discussion of the meaning of readiness. All interviews were audiotaped and the tapes transcribed for analysis.

Children were interviewed in groups of three or four during January. The interview focused on the ways that children viewed the things that they did in kindergarten as relatively easy or hard and whether they had ideas about the relative ranking of the other students' abilities on those tasks. Initially interviews were done singly, but after having great difficulty, group interviews were used to help children prime the pump for each other. That strategy was not without problems either in that children tended to give the same types of response when they were grouped together. Children were also asked to draw pictures for me about things that they did in kindergarten and then tell me about the picture. This strategy worked relatively well at Norwood, because that was a format used frequently in classroom activities. At Fulton it was only used with one group because the children got so involved in the drawing task that they found it hard to talk to me. At Rochester, this task was abandoned to concentrate on the interview to maximize the interaction among children.

DOCUMENT COLLECTION

Documents were collected throughout the year. District curriculum materials, such as content area goals were collected. Worksheets, school and classroom communications, and project samples were given to me by the teachers. In addition, student screening results and report cards were recorded.

Data Analysis

Data analysis was an ongoing process, which began with my first interactions with teachers and parents and continued into the preparation of the final document. The conceptual framework shaped and guided data collection and first pass data analysis. Transcripts and fieldnotes were read and reread to attach salient codes, then synthesized into themes and patterns related to readiness. The theme codes represented ideas that came out of interviews or observations. Some were anticipated by the structure of the data collection; for example, specific questions were asked about parental expectations for their child's kindergarten experience. Other codes emerged after repeated reading of the data, such as the repeated references to parental experiences with older siblings that had an effect on their orientation to readiness. Coded text was sorted and printed using the Ethnograph (Seidel, Kjolseth, & Seymour, 1988) and these examples were again read and reread for site-specific themes. These themes emerged as patterns in the talk of participants and their actions were noticed and verified in the data, using analytic induction (Goetz & LeCompte, p. 180). Impressions about themes were checked through the use of frequency counts and narrative data displays that contained portions of text. Vignettes, a data reduction and low inference representation technique (Erickson, 1986), were developed from the coded data to illustrate themes that were beginning to emerge that related to the site-specific construction of the meaning of readiness. In developing these vignettes, quotes were pulled from interviews and fieldnotes and woven into a story. Teachers were asked to read each vignette and verify both the typicality of the event described and the tenor of the description as evoking the "spirit" of their settings. With their feedback, the vignettes were fine-tuned and thematic narrative developed to illustrate the specific themes that emerged in analysis. The coding, vignette and the thematic narrative were joined to create a case describing the construction of the meaning of readiness for each setting.

The final stage of data analysis involved feedback from teachers about individual case descriptions. The teachers were given copies of the text and their comments requested. In fact, in each case another informant from the setting read the text of the social dimension for each setting to confirm the teacher's reaction (this was done by each teacher on her own, without my prompting). Errors in data were corrected and politically sensitive information was deleted at the teachers' request. The substance of the final text was negotiated with each teacher; however, very little was changed in the text itself.

APPENDIX 2

&

CORE CONCEPTUAL OBJECTIVES
FOR KINDERGARTEN

Art

The student will select the appropriate elements of art to use when accomplishing an assigned task.

The student will select & manipulate various materials in order to express him/herself.

The student will expand his/her visual awareness by collecting and organizing various works of art.

The student will study a variety of primitive, folk & realistic art to gain an understanding that art can be categorized according to style.

Computers

The student will demonstrate an understanding, to a steadily increasing level of sophistication, that the computer is a non-judgmental interactive tool which can be used to augment & enhance learning.

Health

The student will compare the body parts & the associated five senses.

The student will practice the proper care of teeth & classify teeth as to type & function.

The student will investigate the unsafe practices that occur at home & school resulting in disease & injury.

The student will demonstrate ways of sharing, expressing feelings & behaving toward each other.

273

The student will practice safety rules at home & at school.

The student will compare the type of foods & personal practices beneficial to good health.

The student will distinguish between good & harmful substances.

Language Arts/Reading

The student will use speaking & listening skills to interact with others in classroom situations.

The student will expand his/her language base through various experiences & utilize written symbols to record thoughts.

The student will demonstrate an awareness of the functions of the instructional media center.

The student demonstrates an understanding of the concept of "reading" as a communications process.

The student will use story structure (beginning, middle, end) to demonstrate his emerging understanding of "story."

The student demonstrates an understanding that reading is an activity that can bring pleasure to both the reader and the listener.

Map/Globe Skills

Students will be able to recognize & use terms that express relative shape & size.

Students will be able to use general terms relative to location, direction & distance.

Students will be able to use small items to represent real life objects.

Students will be able to recognize a globe as a model of the earth.

Students will be able to use globes, relief maps or pictures to identify land & water representations.

Students will be able to identify & use geographic terms (mountain, ocean,...)

Students will be able to locate North & South Poles on a globe.

Students will be able to make simple observations & describe characteristics of weather & season, & impact on self.

Students will be able to identify physical features in his/her personal environment.

Students will be able to identify school & local community by name.

Students will be able to understand that maps are pictures representing real places & things.

Students will be able to identify his/her personal space and space occupied by other people & objects.

Students will be able to describe ways in which he/she interacts with the physical environment.

Math

The student will verbalize, compare, and extend patterns with concrete objects.

The student will understand simple number values.

Demonstrates an understanding of one to one correspondence, invariance and conservation of number.

The student will form graphs using real objects to compare sets.

Combine & separate collections of objects (0-10) & verbally describe the result.

Demonstrate an understanding of flat & non-flat figures.

Measures time by comparison.

Act out or solve oral problems as a class or in small groups.

Science

Observe & describe likenesses & differences between simple objects using all senses.

Classify objects using one characteristic.

Measure things using direct comparison.

Use correct terms for locations of objects. Be able to represent some of their thoughts on paper.

Begin to make simple predictions about short term events.

Do one thing at a time and complete one activity before going on to something else.

Social Studies

The student will demonstrate acceptable behavior in the classroom.
    The student will:
        Identify and talk about positive and negative feelings.
        Demonstrate acceptable ways of acting in various situations.

Choose an appropriate behavior when placed in a confronting situation with other people.

Accept the consequences of inappropriate behavior.

The student will demonstrate his/her sense of identity & self worth by coping with experiences & change in an appropriate way.

The student will:

Identify the uniqueness of each individual.

Describe similarities and differences between individuals.

Recognize his/her successes and failures.

Measure/monitor one personal change during the year.

Describe his/her participation in holidays.

Recognize and develop relationships with community helpers.

The student will demonstrate responsibility of self in a classroom setting.

The student will:

Identify tasks or expectations that are a part of functioning in a class.

Evaluate the effect of his actions upon others in positive and negative terms.

Begin to develop independence from constant supervision.

The student will plan, practice & adopt basic rules of classroom/ community.

The student will:

Identify the purpose of following rules.

Describe their feelings, values, and beliefs regarding co-operating/sharing.

Participate in setting classroom rules.

The student will identify the individual need to plan, and utilize a resource.

The student will:

Demonstrate a basic need.

Differentiate between wants and needs.

Demonstrate ways to meet his/her basic and material needs in a small group.

The student will demonstrate his/her ability to exist in the physical environment.

The student will:

Identify physical features in his/her personal environment.

Make simple observations about weather and describe the impact on him/her.

Demonstrate his/her respect for the space of others.

Assemble simple models or maps of his/her personal environment.

APPENDIX 3

ટે.

EXAMPLE OF
MATHEMATICS OBJECTIVE

KINDERGARTEN
MATH
CONCEPTUAL OBJECTIVES

NUMBERS AND THEIR RELATIONSHIPS

CONCEPTUAL OBJECTIVE

MAK.1 THE STUDENT WILL VERBALIZE, COMPARE, AND EXTEND PATTERNS WITH CONCRETE OBJECTS

Enabling Processes:

1. The students recognizes which ones does not belong.
2. The student recognizes which object is like the rest.
3. The student classifies objects by attributes such as size, shape color, use.
4. The student describes a patterns.
5. The student continues a pattern.
6. The student creates a pattern.

Primary Trait

Demonstrates an understanding that a pattern is a predictable repetition.

Application Level Assessment Activity:

DESCRIPTION OF THE ACTIVITY

The teacher will create a sample linear pattern with pencils. An example of a pattern that the teacher might select is long, short, long, short, or fat, fat, thin, thin, or eraser, no eraser, eraser, no eraser.

The teacher gives the following instructions:
Look at what I made.
Tell me what you see.
Use these pencils and make a new pattern, one that is not like the one I made.
(Make the entire set of pencils available.)
Tell me about your pattern.

MANAGEMENT

This activity should be done with the children alone in small groups. Each child is assessed individually. This is a process oriented activity that will have to be assessed during class.

Preparation time is needed to collect the pencils. The activity will take each group about fifteen minutes.

When students explain their pattern, they may translate it into a general form or simply name the elements and identify the repetitions.

Rating Criteria:

    3. Proficiency
        a. The student explains the given pattern, without examples or prompting by the teacher, showing an understanding of the elements that are repeated and how they are repeated.
        b. The student extends the pattern quickly and without hesitation.
        c. The student creates a new pattern that is different from the original but maybe only in a very simple way.

    2. Minimally Attained (After questioning by the teacher)
        a. The student describes the given pattern showing that the elements are repeated.
        b. The student extends the pattern correctly but needs some prompting or suggestions from the teacher.
        c. The student creates a new pattern that is different from the original only in a trivial way, like changing the orientation of the pencils.

1. Unattained (Any of the following is unacceptable)
    a. The student cannot extend the given pattern or cannot verbalize the pattern rule.
    b. The student creates a configuration which does not follow a predictable repetition or reconstructs the original pattern.

0. No Responses

APPENDIX 4

૨৯

THOMAS KINDERGARTEN PROGRESS REPORT

EXPLANATION OF MARKS

O - Child is doing very well
S - Child is making satisfactory progress
N - Child needs time and help to develop
I - Not graded at this time

PERSONAL INFORMATION (can give)

First & last name
Address
Phone number
Birthday

BEHAVIORAL SKILLS
Has good attention span
Listens attentively without
interrupting
Follows directions
Works & plays well independently
Works & plays well in a group
Respects the rights & property of
others
Takes pride in best work
Displays self control

INTEGRATED ACTIVITIES (participates in)
ART   COMPUTER   HEALTH
MUSIC   SCIENCE   SOCIAL
                               STUDIES
PHYSICAL EDUCATION

MOTOR DEVELOPMENT

Draws basic shapes (circle, square, tri-
angle, rectangle)
Prints first name
Prints letters
Prints numerals
Controls large muscles — demon-
strates movements
BALANCES   JUMPS   HOPS
GALLOPS   SKIPS
BOUNCES/CATCHES BALL
Controls small muscles — uses mate-
rials properly
SCISSORS   PENCILS   CRAYONS
GLUE

MATH READINESS
Distinguishes likenesses & differences
of objects
Sorts & compares objects
Measures time by comparison
Recognizes & completes patterns
Matches numerals to sets of objects
Combines & separates sets of objects

281

APPENDIX 4 *continued*
THOMAS KINDERGARTEN PROGRESS REPORT

ATTENDANCE
Date of Late Entry:
Date of Early Withdrawal:
Conferences attended:

Fall	Yes	No
Spring	Yes	No

Days Absent:
Days Tardy:
Days Present:
School work was affected by frequent:

Absences	Yes
	No

RECOGNIZES COLORS & SHAPES

RED	PINK	GREEN
BLUE	PURPLE	YELLOW
WHITE	BROWN	BLACK
ORANGE	CIRCLE	OVAL
SQUARE	RECTANGLE	
TRIANGLE	DIAMOND	

LANGUAGE ARTS/READING READINESS
Speaks in complete sentences
Expresses thoughts & ideas clearly
Uses drawings & written symbols to record thoughts
Tells stories in sequences
Enjoys listening to & telling stories
Can identify sounds at the beginning of words
Identifies rhyming words
Is establishing left to right movement

RECOGNIZES LETTERS & SOUNDS (circle items attained)
(Out of sequence)
Capitals: A B C D E F G H I J K L M N O P Q R S T U V W X Y Z
Small: a b c d e f g h i j k l m n o p q r s t u v w x y z
Consonant Sounds: b c d f g h j k l m n p q r s t v w x y z

RECOGNIZES NUMERALS
(out of sequences)

0	1	2	3	4	5
6	7	8	9	10	11
12	13	14	15	16	17
18	19	20	21	—	—

APPENDIX 5

❧

COMPARISON OF CORE CONCEPTUAL OBJECTIVES & THE KINDERGARTEN REPORT CARD

The following table maps Core Conceptual Objectives to the Thomas Kindergarten Report Card. It is organized by subject matter content, as are the objectives. The objectives are listed in mixed upper and lower case and report card objectives are noted in upper case letters. Report card objectives have been paired with each Core Conceptual Objective that matches, therefore report card objectives may occur more than once.

Math

The student will verbalize, compare, and extend patterns with concrete objects.
RECOGNIZES & COMPLETES PATTERNS

The student will understand simple number values.
Demonstrates an understanding of one to one correspondence, invariance and conservation of number.
MATCHES NUMERALS TO SETS OF OBJECTS

The student will form graphs using real objects to compare sets.
SORTS & COMPARES OBJECTS

Combine & separate collections of objects (0-10) & verbally describe the result.
COMBINES & SEPARATES SETS OF OBJECTS

Demonstrate an understanding of flat & non-flat figures
> SORTS & COMPARES OBJECTS
> DISTINGUISHES LIKENESS & DIFFERENCE OF OBJECTS
> RECOGNIZES SHAPES: CIRCLE, RECTANGLE, TRIANGLE, SQUARE, OVAL, DIAMOND

Measures time by comparison
> MEASURES TIME BY COMPARISON
> TELLS STORIES IN A SEQUENCE (LA/RDG READINESS)

Act out or solve oral problems as a class or in small groups.

Language Arts/Reading

The student will use speaking & listening skills to interact with others in classroom situations
> HAS GOOD ATTENTION SPAN
> EXPRESSES THOUGHTS & IDEAS CLEARLY
> SPEAKS IN COMPLETE SENTENCES
> LISTENS ATTENTIVELY WITHOUT INTERRUPTING (BEHAVIORAL)
> TELLS STORIES IN SEQUENCE (LA/RR)
> ENJOYS LISTENING TO & TELLING STORIES (LA/RR)
> FOLLOWS DIRECTIONS (BEHAVIORAL)

The student will expand his/her language base through various experiences & utilize written symbols to record thoughts.
> USES DRAWINGS & WRITTEN SYMBOLS TO RECORD THOUGHTS

The student will demonstrate an awareness of the functions of the instructional media center

The student demonstrates an understanding of the concept of "reading" as a communications process.
> IS ESTABLISHING LEFT TO RIGHT MOVEMENT

The student will use story structure (beginning, middle, end) to demonstrate his emerging understanding of "story."
> TELLS STORIES IN A SEQUENCE (LA/RR)

The student demonstrates an understanding that reading is an activity that can bring pleasure to both the reader and the listener.
> LISTENS ATTENTIVELY WITHOUT INTERRUPTING (BEHAVIORAL)
> ENJOYS LISTENING TO AND TELLING STORIES (LA/RR)

Health

The student will compare the body parts & the associated five senses.

The student will practice the proper care of teeth & classify teeth as to type & function.

The student will investigate the unsafe practices that occur at home & school resulting in disease & injury.

The student will demonstrate ways of sharing, expressing feelings & behaving toward each other.
TAKES PRIDE IN BEST WORK
RESPECTS THE RIGHTS & PROPERTY OF OTHERS
DISPLAYS SELF CONTROL

The student will practice safety rules at home & at school.

The student will compare the type of foods & personal practices beneficial to good health.

The student will distinguish between good & harmful substances.
PARTICIPATES IN HEALTH

Computers

The student will demonstrate an understanding, to a steadily increasing level of sophistication, that the computer is a non-judgmental interactive tool which can be used to augment & enhance learning.
PARTICIPATES IN COMPUTER

Art

The student will select the appropriate elements of art to use when accomplishing an assigned task.

The student will select & manipulate various materials in order to express him/herself.

The student will expand his/her visual awareness by collecting and organizing various works of art.

The student will study a variety of primitive, folk & realistic art to gain an understanding that art can be categorized according to style.
PARTICIPATES IN ART

Map Globe Skills

Recognize & use terms that express relative shape & size.

Use general terms relative to location, direction & distance.

Use small items to represent real life objects.

Recognize a globe as a model of the earth.

Use globes, relief maps or pictures to identify land & water representations.

Identify & use geographic terms (mountain, ocean,…).

Locate North & South Poles on a globe.

Make simple observations & describe characteristics of weather & season, & impact on self.

Identify physical features in his/her personal environment.

Identify school & local community by name.

Understand that maps are pictures representing real places & things.

Identify his/her personal space and space occupied by other people & objects.

Describe ways in which he/she interacts with the physical environment.

Social Studies

The student will demonstrate his/her ability to exist in the physical environment.

The student will identify the individual need to plan and utilize a resource.

The student will plan, practice & adopt basic rules of classroom/ community.

The student will demonstrate responsibility of self in a classroom setting.
WORK & PLAY WELL INDEPENDENTLY

The student will demonstrate his/her sense of identity & self worth by coping with experiences & change in an appropriate way.

The student will demonstrate acceptable behavior in the classroom.
WORKS & PLAYS WELL IN A GROUP
PARTICIPATES IN SOCIAL STUDIES

Science

Observe & describe likenesses & differences between simple objects using all senses.
> DISTINGUISHES LIKENESS & DIFFERENCES OF OBJECTS (MATH)

Classify objects using one characteristic.
> SORTS & COMPARES OBJECTS (MATH)

Measure things using direct comparison.

Use correct terms for locations of objects. Be able to represent some of their thoughts on paper.
> USE DRAWING & WRITTEN SYMBOLS TO RECORD THOUGHTS (LA/RR)

Begin to make simple predictions about short term events.

Do one thing at a time and complete one activity before going on to something else.
> PARTICIPATES IN SCIENCE

Report Card Items Not Keyed To Objectives

CAN GIVE FIRST & LAST NAME

CAN GIVE ADDRESS

CAN GIVE PHONE NUMBER

CAN GIVE BIRTHDAY

PARTICIPATES IN PHYSICAL EDUCATION

DRAWS BASIC SHAPES

PRINTS FIRST NAME

PRINTS NUMERALS

CONTROLS LARGE MUSCLES (BALANCES, JUMPS, HOPS, GALLOPS, SKIPS, BOUNCES/CATCHES BALL)

CONTROLS SMALL MUSCLES (SCISSORS, PENCILS, CRAYONS, GLUE)

CAN IDENTIFY SOUNDS AT THE BEGINNING OF WORDS

IDENTIFIES RHYMING WORDS

RECOGNIZES CAPITAL LETTERS

RECOGNIZES SMALL LETTERS
RECOGNIZES CONSONANT SOUNDS
RECOGNIZES COLORS
RECOGNIZES NUMERALS 0-21

APPENDIX 6

ネ♪

EARLY PREVENTION OF
SCHOOL FAILURE CURRICULUM

Language

Identify and name common objects and pictures.

Use singular and plural forms of common words.

Communicate thoughts and needs in complete sentences of four to six words.

Recognize and name basic colors, shapes, and sizes.

Dictate simple sentences about objects and illustrations.

Tell stories in sequence with and without the aid of pictures.

Understand the meaning of basic concepts.

Recognize and name letters and some words.

Interpret story situations and predicts story outcomes.

Auditory

Listen without interrupting while maintaining eye contact.

Follow one or easy two step directions.

Recall familiar nursery rhymes, poems, alliterative phrases.

Identify and recognizes difference in volume, tone, quality, and type of sound.

Listen to and retell a story in sequence.

Follow instructions in sequence (2-3 parts).

Repeat a pattern or series of sounds, words, or numbers.

Finish an incomplete sentence with an appropriate word.

Match and identify like and different letter sounds.

Match and identify beginning, ending and middle sounds (placement).

Visual

Follow fixed and moving objects with eyes without moving head.

Identify likenesses and differences of objects and pictures.

Match color, shape, and size.

Identify likenesses and differences and recall basic colors, shapes, and sizes.

Put simple puzzles together (6-8 pieces).

Identify and name missing items from memory.

Identify and locate objects from a complex background (figure-ground).

Classify and sort pictures and objects into sets.

Place 2-4 items in sequence by memory.

Repeat patterning of 3 or 4 items.

Arrange pictures in sequence of events.

Identify, name, match, and sequence letters.

Match upper and lower case letters.

Match and name quantitative concepts with numerals, numerals with numerals, and arrange numerals in order.

Fine Motor Coordination

Manipulate small objects (with both hands).

Hold crayons and pencils appropriately (scribbles).

Hold scissors appropriately and cut.

Trace, copy, and draw basic shapes.

Draw a man with six body parts.

Lace shoes, tie knots, fold triangles from square.

Finish incomplete designs.

Write letters.

Write numerals 1-10 (uneven).

Gross Motor Coordination

Walk forward, backward and sideways on tape/footprints.

Imitate body movements.

Descend steps with alternating feet.

Identify and use body parts.

Run, jump, and hop.

Throw and catch ball with limited control.

Manipulate body in space in both directionality and laterality.

Walk forward, backward, and sideways on balance beam and balance on balance board.

Gallop, skip, and jump rope.

BIBLIOGRAPHY

A Gift of Time. (1985). New Haven, CN: The Gesell Institute.

Applebee, A. N. & Langer, J. A. (1983). Instructional scaffolding: Reading and writing as natural language activities. *Language Arts,* 60(2), 168-175.

Au, K. J. & Kawakami, A. J. (1984). Vygotskian perspectives on discussion processes in small group reading lessons. In L. C. Wilkinson, P. L. Peterson, & M. Hallinan (Eds). *Student diversity and the organization, processes, and use of instructional groups in the classroom.* New York: Academic Press.

Ausubel, D. P. (1963). *The psychology of meaningful verbal learning.* New York: Grune & Stratton.

Beattie, C. (1970). Entrance age to kindergarten and first grade: Its effects on cognitive and affective development of students. ED133050.

Bell, M. (1972). *A study of the readiness room program in a small school district in suburban Detroit, Michigan.* Unpublished doctoral dissertation, Wayne State University,

Berger, P. & Luckmann, T. (1966). *The social construction of reality.* Garden City, NY: Doubleday.

Bigelow, E. B. (1934). School progress of under-age children. *The Elementary School Journal,* 25, 186-192.

Bjorklund, D. & Bjorklund, B. (June 1988). Is your child ready for school? *Parents,* 110-116.

Bossing, L., & Brien, P. (1979). A review of the elementary school promotion/retention dilemma. ED 212362.

Bredekamp, S., & Shepard, L. (March 1989). How best to protect children from inappropriate school expectations, practices, and policies. *Young Children, 44*(3), 14-24.

Brown, A. L. & Campione, J. C. (1984). Three faces of transfer: Implications for early competence, individual differences, and instruction. In M. E. Lamb, A. L. Brown, & B. Rogoff (Eds.) *Advances in developmental psychology (Vol. 3).* Hillsdale, NJ: Erlbaum.

Bruffee, K. A. (1986). Social construction, language, and the authority of knowledge: A bibliographic essay. *College English, 48*(8), 773-790.

Byrnes, D., & Yamamoto, K. (1984). Grade repetition: Views of parents, teachers and principals. Unpublished paper, Utah State University.

Cameron, M. B. & Wilson, B. J. (1990). The effects of chronological age, gender and delay of entry on academic achievement and retention: Implications for academic redshirting. *Psychology in the Schools, 27,* 260-263.

Campione, J. C., Brown, A. L., Ferrara, R. A., Bryant, N. R. (1984). The zone of proximal development: Implications for individual differences and learning. In B. Rogoff & J. W. Wertsch (Eds) *Children's learning in the zone of proximal development.* San Francisco: Jossey-Bass.

Carroll, M. L. (1963). Academic achievement and adjustment of underage and overage third graders. *Journal of Educational Research, 56,* 415-419.

Charlesworth, R. (1989). "Behind" before they start? Deciding how to deal with risk of kindergarten failure. *Young Children, 44,* 5-13.

Connell, D. R. (1987). The first 30 years were the fairest: Notes from the kindergarten and ungraded primary (K-1-2). *Young Children, 42*(5), 30-39.

Cook-Gumperz, J. (1986). Introduction: the social construction of literacy. In J. Cook-Gumperz (ed.) *The social construction of literacy.* New York: Cambridge University Press.

Cunningham, A. E. (1988). Eeny, meeny, miny, moe: Testing policy and practice in early childhood.

Dalton, S. (1989). Teachers as assessors and assisters. Paper presented at the symposium *Extending Vygotskian theory: Interpersonal relationships and the teaching-learning process.* At the annual meeting of the American Educational Research Association, San Francisco.

Davies, B. (1983). The role pupils play in the social construction of classroom order. *British Journal of Sociology of Education, 4*(1), 55-69.

Davis, B. G., Trimble, C. S., & Vincent, D. R. (1980). Does age of entrance affect school achievement? *The Elementary School Journal, 80*, 133-143.

Diamond, G. H. (1983). The birthdate effect—a maturational effect. *Journal of Learning Disabilities, 16*, 161-164.

DiPasquale, G. W., Moule, A. D., & Flewelling, R. W. (1980). The birthdate effect. *Journal of Learning Disabilities, 13*, 234-238.

Donofrio, A. F. (1977). Grade repetition: Therapy of choice. *Journal of Learning Disabilities, 10*, 349-351.

Education Commission of the States. (1985, November). *State characteristics: Kindergartens.* Denver, CO: Education Commission of the States.

Educational Research Service. (1958). *Administration policies for kindergarten and first grade, circular no. 3.* Arlington, Virginia: Educational Research Service.

Eisenhart, M. A., & Graue, M. E. (1990). Socially constructed readiness for school. *International Journal for Qualitative Studies in Education, 3*(3) 253-269.

Ellwein, M. C., Walsh, D. J., Eads, G. M. & Miller, A. K. (1991). Using readiness tests to route kindergarten students: The snarled intersection of psychometrics, policy, and practice. *Educational Evaluation and Policy Analysis, 13*(2), 159-175.

Engel, P. (1989). Assessment of kindergarten readiness for first grade: Policies and practices of industrialized nations. Paper presented at the 1989 Annual Assessment Conference, Education Commission of the States. Boulder, CO.

Erickson, F. (1982). Taught cognitive learning in its immediate environments: A neglected topic in the anthropology of education. *Anthropology & Education Quarterly, 13*(2), 149-180.

Erickson, F. (1986). Qualitative methods in research on teaching. In M. Whitlock (Ed.), *Handbook of research on teaching.* New York: Macmillan Publishers.

Ferguson, P. M. (1987). The social construction of mental retardation. *Social Policy, 18*(1), 51-56.

Freeman, E. B. (May 1990). Issues in kindergarten policy and practice. *Young Children, 45*(4), 29-34.

Freeman, E. B., & Hatch, J. A. (1989). What schools expect young children to know and do: An analysis of kindergarten report cards. *The Elementary School Journal, 89*(5), 595-605.

Gallimore, R., Dalton, S. & Tharp, R. G. (1986). Self-regulation and interactive teaching: The effects of teaching conditions on teachers' cognitive activity. *The Elementary School Journal, 86*(5), 613-631.

Gallimore, R. & Goldenberg, C. (in press) Activity setting of early literacy development: Home and school factors in children's emergent literacy. To appear in E. Forman, N. Minick, & C. A. Stone (Eds.). *Education and mind: The integration of institutional, social, and developmental processes.* Oxford: Oxford University Press.

Gallimore, R., Weisner, T. S., Kaufman, S. Z. & Bernheimer, L. P. (1989). The social construction of ecocultural niches: Family accommodation of developmentally delayed children. *American Journal of Mental Retardation, 94* (3), 216-230.

Geertz, C. (1973). *The interpretation of cultures.* New York: Basic Books.

Geertz, C. (1987). Interpretive anthropology. In H. Applebaum (Ed.) *Perspectives in cultural anthropology.* Albany: State University of New York Press.

Gergen, K. J. (1985) The social constructionist movement in modern psychology. *American Psychologist, 40*(3) 266-275.

Gergen, K. J., Gloger-Tippelt, G. & Berkowitz, P. (1990). The cultural construction of the developing child. In G. R. Semin & K. J. Gergen (Eds) *Everyday understanding.* London: Sage.

Goetz, J. P., & LeCompte, M. D. (1984). *Ethnography and qualitative design in educational research.* Orlando, FL: Academic Press.

Graue, M. E., & Shepard, L. A. (1989). Predictive validity of the Gesell School Readiness Tests. *Early Childhood Research Quarterly, 4*(3), 303-316.

Graue, M. E., & Shepard, L. A. (in press). School entrance age. In L. R. Williams & D. P. Fromberg (Eds.) *Encyclopedia of Early Childhood Education.* New York: Garland Publishing.

Gredler, G. (1975). *Ethical and legal dilemmas in the assessment of readiness of children for school. In G.R. Gredler (Ed.) Ethical and legal factors in the practice of school psychology,* 196-221. Harrisburg, PA: State Department of education.

Gredler, G. R. (1980). The birthdate effect: Fact or artifact? *Journal of Learning Disabilities, 13,* 239-242.

Gredler, G. R. (1984). Transition classes: A viable alternative for the at-risk child? *Psychology in the Schools, 21,* 463-470.

Green, D. R., & Simmons, S. V. (1962). Chronological age and school. *The Elementary School Journal, 63,* 41-47.

Greenfield, P. M. (1984). A theory of the teacher in the learning activities of everyday life. In. B. Rogoff & J. Lave (Eds.) *Everyday cognition.* Cambridge, Mass: Harvard University Press.

Haddad, W. D. (1979). Educational and economic effects of promotion and repetition practices. ED 195 003.

Hall, R. V. (1963). Does entrance age affect achievement? *The Elementary School Journal, 63,* 391-396.

Halliwell, J. W., & Stein, B. W. (1964). A comparison of the achievement of early and late starters in reading related and non-reading related areas in fourth and fifth graders. *Elementary English, 41,* 631-639.

Hammond, C. H. (1986). Not ready! Don't push me! *Childhood Education, 62*(4), 276-280.

Hart, S. (1982). Analyzing the social organization for reading in one elementary school. In George D. and Louise Spindler (Eds.) *Doing the ethnography of schooling: Educational anthropology in action,* 410-438. New York: Holt, Rinehart, and Winston.

Heath, S. B. (1983). *Ways with words.* Cambridge: Cambridge University Press.

Holmes, C. T., & Matthews, K. M. (1984). The effects of nonpromotion on elementary and junior high school pupils: A meta-analysis. *Review of Educational Research, 54,* 225-236.

Ilg, F. L., Ames, L. B., Haines, J., & Gillespie, C. (1978). *School readiness: Behavior tests used at the Gesell Institute.* New York: Harper & Row.

Jinks, P. C. (1964). An investigation into the effect of date of birth on subsequent school performance. *Educational Research, 6,* 220-225.

Jipson, J. (1991). Developmentally appropriate practice: Culture, curriculum, connections. *Early Education and Development, 2* (2), 120-136.

Kagan, S. L. (1990). Readiness 2000: Rethinking rhetoric and responsibility. *Phi Delta Kappan,* 272-279.

Kalk, J. M., Langer, P., & Searls, D. (December 1981). *Trends in achievement as a function of age of admission.* Denver, CO: National Assessment of Educational Progress, Education Commission of the States.

Karweit, N. (1988). Quality and quantity of learning time in preprimary programs. *The Elementary School Journal, 89,* 119-133.

Katz, L. G., Evangelou, D. & Hartman, J. A. (1990). *The case for mixed-age grouping in early education.* Washington, DC: National Association for the Education of Young Children.

Katz, L., Raths, J., & Torres, R. (1987). A place called kindergarten. Urbana, IL: University of Illinois. ED 280595.

Kessen, W. (1979). The American child and other cultural inventions. *American Psychologist, 34*(10), 815-820.

Kinard, E. M., & Reinherz, H. (1986). Birthdate effects on school performance and adjustment: A longitudinal study. *Journal of Educational Research, 79,* 366-372.

King, I. B. (1955). Effect of age of entrance into Grade 1 upon achievement in the elementary school. *The Elementary School Journal, 55,* 331-336.

Kitzinger, C. (1987). *The social construction of lesbianism.* London: Sage.

Kuhn, T. S. (1970). *The structure of scientific revolutions (2nd ed.).* Chicago: University of Chicago Press.

Lange, J. (1990). Ridding the schools of the readiness round-up. Unpublished paper.

Langer, P., & Kalk, J. M. , & Searls, D. T. (1984). Age of admission and trends in achievement: A comparison of blacks and caucasians. *American Educational Research Journal, 21,* 61-78.

Lareau, A. (1989). *Home advantage: Social class and parental intervention in elementary education.* London: The Falmer Press.

Lave, J. (1988). *The culture of acquisition and the practice of understanding* (Report No. IRL 88-0007). Palo Alto, CA: Institute for Research on Learning.

Lave, J., Murtaugh, M. & de la Roche, O. (1984). The dialectic of arithmetic in grocery shopping. In B. Rogoff & J. Lave (Eds.) *Everyday cognition.* Cambridge, Mass: Harvard University Press.

Leinhardt, G. (1980). Transition rooms: Promoting maturation or reducing education? *Journal of Educational Psychology, 72,* 55-61.

Lubeck, S. & Garrett, P. (1990). The social construction of the "at-risk" child. *British Journal of Sociology of Education, 11*(3), 327-340.

Maddux, C. D. (1980). First-grade entry age in a sample of children labeled learning disabled. *Learning Disability Quarterly, 3,* 79-83.

May, D. C., & Welch, E. L. (1984). The effects of developmental placement and early retention on children's later scores on standardized tests. *Psychology in the Schools, 21,* 381-385.

Mehan, H. (1980). The competent student. *Anthropology and Education Quarterly, 11*(3), 131-152.

Mehan, H. (1981). Social constructivism in psychology and sociology. *The Quarterly Newletter of the Laboratory of Comparative Human Cognition, 3*(4), 71-77.

Mehan, H., Hertwick , A. & Meils, J. L.(1986). *Handicapping the handicapped.* Stanford, CA: Stanford University Press.

Meisels, S. J. (1985). *Developmental screening in early childhood: A guide.* Washington, D.C.: National Association for the Education of Young Children.

Meisels, S. J. (1987). Uses and abuses of developmental screening and school readiness testing. *Young Children, 42*(2), 4-9.

Meyers, G. (1985). The social construction of two biologists' proposals. *Written Communication, 2*(3) 219-245.

Miller, W., & Norris, R. C. (1967). Entrance age and school success. *Journal of School Psychology, 6,* 47-60.

Minick, N. J. (1989). Mind and activity in Vygotsky's work: An expanded frame of reference. *Cultural Dynamics, II*(2), 162-187.

Moll, L. C. & Diaz, S. *Towards an interactional pedagogical psychology: A bilingual case study.* San Diego: Center for Human Information Processing, University of California, San Diego, 1983.

Napier, S. F. (1976). Grading and young children. S. B. Simon & J. A. Bellanca (Eds.), *Degrading the grading myths: A primer of alternatives to grades and marks.* Washington, D.C.: Association for Supervision and Curriculum Development.

National Association for the Education of Young Children. (1988). NAEYC position statement on developmentally appropriate practice in the primary grades, serving 5- through 8-year-olds. *Young Children, 43,* 64-84.

National Association for the Education of Young Children. (1990). Position statement on school readiness. *Young Children, 46* (1), 21-23.

National Association of Elementary School Principals (1990). *Early childhood education. Standards for quality programs for young children.* Alexandria, VA: Author.

Newman, D., Griffin, P. & Cole, M. (1989). *The construction zone: Working for cognitive change in school.* Cambridge: Cambridge University Press.

Nurss, J. R. (1987). Readiness for kindergarten. ED PS-87-2.

Peck, J. T., McCaig, G. & Sapp, M. E. (1988). Kindergarten policies: *What is best for children?* Washington, D.C.: National Association for the Education of Young Children.

Pestello, F. P. (1987). The social construction of grades. *Teaching Sociology, 15,* 414-417.

Polakow, V. (1989). Deconstructing development. *Journal of Education, 171*(2), 75-87.

Proctor, T. B., Black, K. N., & Feldhusen, J. F. (1986). Early admission of selected children to elementary school: A review of research literature. *Journal of Educational Research, 80*(2), 70-76.

Raygor, B. (1972). *A five-year follow-up study comparing the school achievement and school adjustment of children retained in kindergarten and children placed in a transition class.* Unpublished doctoral dissertation, University of Minnesota.

Reese, L., Goldenberg, C., Loucky, J. & Gallimore, R. (1989). Ecocultural context, cultural activity, and emergent literacy: Sources of variation in home literacy experiences of Spanish-speaking children. Paper presented at the annual meeting of the American Anthropological Association, Washington, D.C.

Richardson, V., Casanova, U., Placier, P., & Guilfoyle, K. (1989). *School children at-risk* London: The Falmer Press.

Rogoff, B. (1990). *Apprenticeship in thinking.* London: Oxford University Press.

Rogoff, B., Malkin, C., Gilbride, K. (1984). Interaction with babies as guidance in development. In B. Rogoff & J. W. Wertsch (Eds) *Children's learning in the zone of proximal development.* San Francisco: Jossey-Bass.

Rogoff, B. & Wertsch, J. V. (1984). *Children's learning in the zone of proximal development.* San Francisco: Jossey-Bass.

Rorty, R. (1979). *Philosophy and the mirror of nature.* Princeton, NJ: Princeton University Press.

Rose, J. S., Medway, F. J., Cantrell, V. L., & Marus, S. H. (1983). A fresh look at the retention-promotion controversy. *Journal of School Psychology, 21,* 201-211.

Rueda, R. & Goldenberg, C. (1991). When is an instructional conversation? Paper presented at the annual meeting of the American Educational Research Association, Chicago.

Saracho, O. N. (1986). Play and young children's learning. In B. Spodek (Ed.) *Today's kindergarten: Exploring the knowledge base, expanding the curriculum.* New York: Teachers' College Press.

Saxe, G. B., Gearhart, M. & Guberman, S. R. (1984). The social organization of early number development. In B. Rogoff & J. W. Wertsch (Eds.) *Children's learning in the zone of proximal development.* San Francisco: Jossey-Bass.

Schickedanz, J., Schickedanz, D., & Forsyth, P. (1982). *Toward understanding children.* Boston: Little, Brown.

Seidel, J. V., Kjolseth, R., & Seymour, E. (1988). *Ethnograph.* Littleton, CO: Qualis Research Associates.

Shepard, L. A. (1989). A review of research on kindergarten retention. In L. A. Shepard & M. L. Smith (Eds.). *Flunking grades: Research and policies on retention.* London: The Falmer Press.

Shepard, L. A. (1990). Readiness testing in local school districts: An analysis of backdoor policies. *Journal of Educational Policy, 5,* 159-179.

Shepard, L. A. & Graue, M. E. (in press). The morass of school readiness screening: Research on test use and test validity. In B. Spodek (Ed.). *Handbook of research on the education of young children,* 2nd ed. New York: Macmillan.

Shepard, L. A., Graue, M. E., & Catto, S. F. (1989). Delayed entry into kindergarten and escalation of academic demands. Paper presented at the annual meeting of the American Educational Research Association. San Francisco.

Shepard, L. A., & Smith, M. L. (March, 1985). *Boulder Valley kindergarten study: Retention practices and retention effects.* Boulder, Colorado: Boulder Valley Public Schools.

Shepard, L. A., & Smith, M. L. (1986). Synthesis of research of school readiness and kindergarten retention. *Educational Leadership, 44,* 78-86.

Shepard, L. A., & Smith, M. L. (1988). Escalating academic demand in kindergarten: Counterproductive policies. *The Elementary School Journal, 89*(2), 135-145.

Sleeter, C. E. (1986). Learning disabilities: The social construction of a special education category. *Exceptional Children, 53*(1), 46-54.

Smith, M. L. (1982). *How educators decide who is learning disabled. Challenge to psychology and public policy in the schools.* Springfield, IL: Charles C. Thomas Publisher.

Smith, M. L., & Shepard, L. A. (1988). Kindergarten readiness and retention: a qualitative study of teachers beliefs and practices. *American Educational Research Journal, 25*(3), 307-333.

Spodek, B. (1973). What are the sources of early childhood curriculum? In B. Spodek (Ed.) *Early childhood education.* Englewood Cliffs, NJ: Prentice-Hall, Inc.

Spodek, B. (1986). Development, values, and knowledge in the kindergarten curriculum. In B. Spodek (Ed.) *Today's kindergarten: Exploring the knowledge base, expanding the curriculum.* New York: Teachers' College Press.

Tharp, R. G., & Gallimore, R. (1988). *Rousing minds to life: Teaching, learning, and schooling in social context.* New York: Cambridge University Press.

Turiel, E. (1989). The social construction of social construction. In W. Damon (ed.) *Child development today and tomorrow.* San Francisco: Jossey-Bass Publishers.

Uphoff, J. K. (1985). Pupil chronological age as a factor in school failure. Paper presented at the annual conference of the Association for Supervision and Curriculum Development. Chicago.

Uphoff, J. K., & Gilmore, J. E. (1986). *Summer children: Ready or not for school.* Middletown, OH: J & J Publishing.

Valsiner, J. (1984). Construction of the zone of proximal development in adult-child joint action: The socialization of meals. In B. Rogoff & J. W. Wertsch (Eds.) *Children's learning in the zone of proximal development.* San Francisco: Jossey-Bass.

Vygotsky, L. S. (1978). *Mind in society.* Cambridge: Harvard University Press.

Walsh, D. J. (1991). Extending the discourse on developmental appropriateness: A developmental perspective. *Early Education and Development, 2* (2), 109-119.

Weinstein, L. (1968-69). School entrance age and adjustment. *Journal of School Psychology, 7,* 20-28.

Weisner, T. S., Gallimore, R., & Jordan, C. (1988). Unpackaging cultural effects on classroom learning: Hawaiian peer assistance and child-generated activity. *Anthropology and Education Quarterly, 19,* 327-353.

Wertsch, J. V. (1979). Introduction. In J. V. Wertsch (Ed.) *Culture, communication, and cognition.* New York: Cambridge University Press.

Wertsch, J. V. (1985). *Vygotsky and the social formation of mind.* Cambridge, Mass.: Harvard University Press.

Wertsch, J. V., Minick, N. J., & Arns, F. (1984). The creation of context in joint problem-solving. In B. Rogoff & J. Lave (Eds.), *Everyday cognition: Its development in social contexts.* Cambridge, MA: Harvard University Press.

Wertsch, J. V., & Toma, C. (March 1990). *Discourse and learning in the classroom: A sociocultural approach.* [Presentation made at the University of Georgia Visiting Lecturer Series on "Constructivism in Education"].

Willer, B. & Bredekamp, S. (1990). Redefining readiness: An essential requisite for educational reform. *Young Children, 45*(5), 22-24.

Wood, D., Bruner, J. L., & Ross, G. (1976). The role of tutoring in problem-solving. *Journal of Child Psychology and Psychiatry, 17,* 89-100.

INDEX

305

Constructivism, 8.
See also Piaget.
Core Conceptual Objectives, 51, 53, 54-57, 273-279, 283-88
Curriculum, kindergarten
academic focus of, 55-56, 137-138, 144
child-oriented approaches to, 52
and Early Prevention of School Failure program, 204-205
escalation of, 144, 253-254
evaluation of students in, 57-61
first grade effect on, 152-157, 184, 227-228, 234, 252
and Gesellian theory, 52
influences on, 247, 252-253
international debate about, 17
pacing of, 111-114, 179-180, 246-247
parental expectations of, 68-70, 78-81, 136-140, 146-149, 194-195, 201-202
and Piagetian-based programs, 52-53
planning, 144-146, 209-210, 263-264
and play, 60
policy, school district, 51-62
reform of, 262-263
social tasks in, 96-97
and standards of accountability, 170, 264
subject matter organization of, 53-57
teacher decision-making power in, 233-235
and testing, 11, 53.
See also Activities, curricular; Bilingual kindergarten.

Daberon Screening for School Readiness, 11
Data generation, 44, 48, 51.
See also Study design.
Developmental Indicators for the Assessment of Learning-Revised, 11
Developmental kindergarten, 4, 159
Donofrio, 12

Early Prevention of School Failure Program:
and bilingual education, 209

description of, 51-52, 289-291
and the environmental approach to readiness, 7
and instruction, 206-209, 227
screening for, 202-205, 243-245
teacher planning for, 209-210
Early intervention programs, 256
Eisenhart and Graue, 33
Ellwein, Walsh, Eads, and Miller, 11
Engel, 16-17
Entrance, kindergarten:
and age, 262
parental attitudes toward, 85, 151-152, 191-196, 240
and student services, 262
Environmental view of readiness:
and the Early Prevention of School Failure Curriculum, 205
and home experiences, 224-225, 234
and extra-year programs, 234
and instruction, 109-110, 224-227, 238-239
and psychological theory, 6-7
Erickson, 19
Eurocentrism, 261
Extended day kindergarten:
and at-risk students, 204
and bilingual students, 196, 235
curriculum of, 253
and Early Prevention of School Failure screening, 253
and escalation of the kindergarten curriculum, 253
and heterogeneous student populations, 198
motives for, 251
parental beliefs about, 77-78
parental involvement in, 202-203
and preschool programs, 257
and readiness, 189
screening process for, 204
Extra year programs:
and at-risk students, 185
backdoor policies in, 4
benefits of, 5, 15-16
elimination of, 263
policy-explicit programs, 4
policy regarding, 3-4
and views of readiness, 234
reasons for, 4
studies of, 12-14

Transitional first grade, 4, 12-13, 16, 159

Vignettes:
bilingual kindergarten, features of, 203-204
construction of, 270
Ellen and Hilary, 67-68
learning tasks at Fulton, 88-94
learning tasks, Mrs. Sunden, 163-165
modality groups, 206-207
readiness at Rochester, 196
parental expectations of Norwood kindergarten, 122-123
in study design, 270
Mrs. Sunden, 140-141
Vygotsky:
and activity theory, 28, 31-36
and adult-child interaction, 30
as compared to American psychological tradition, 29
and cognition, 26-27
and consciousness, 27
and constructivist theory of development, 8
educational implications of, 29-31

and the genetic method, 26-27
and interactive instruction, 31
and language theory, 28, 232
and learning theory, 29-30
and the study of readiness, 36, 248-252
and teacher education, 31
and Marxism, 27
and semiotics, 28
and the socio-historic approach, 25
and the Zone of Proximal Development, 29

Weinstein, 9
Weisner, Gallimore and Jordan, 33
Wertsch, 26, 28, 31
Wertsch, Minick and Arns, 32
Wertsch and Toma, 26-28
Willer and Bredekamp, 18
West Germany, 16-17

Youngness, 9-10, 16.
See also Age, Child Development.

Zone of Proximal Development, 29-30.
See also Vygotsky.